A CRITIC'S CHOICE

Of 300 key performances
for your record shelf by
Conrad Wilson, music
critic of "The Scotsman"

CONRAD WILSON

A CRITIC'S CHOICE

CORGI BOOKS
A DIVISION OF TRANSWORLD PUBLISHERS

A CRITIC'S CHOICE

A CORGI BOOK

First publication in Great Britain

PRINTING HISTORY
Corgi Edition published 1966

This book is set in 10 pt. Times

Corgi Books are published by Transworld Publishers Ltd.,
Bashley Road, London, N.W.10.
Made and printed in Great Britain by
Hunt Barnard & Co., Ltd., Aylesbury, Bucks.

CONTENTS

INTRODUCTION

Since the birth of LP in 1952, the output of records has increased enormously and the gramophone has become a major force in our lives. For more than a decade, as many as a hundred new classical records have been issued each month. Where the collector at one time had two or three performances of a popular classic to choose between, he now has twenty or thirty. Composers who, in 1950, were little more than text-book names have gained a new lease of life via the gramophone. Every year our musical horizons widen still farther; and every year the record scene becomes increasingly complicated, what with the advent of stereo, the release of bargain records at prices as low as ten shillings, the importing of more and more records from other countries, the rise of record clubs, and the sale of records in shops that formerly specialised in quite different commodities.

This book maintains what I hope will be deemed a "sensible" attitude to all the changes that have been taking place in the record world. A survey made a few years ago by the consumer magazine, *Which*, implied that bargain records were a risky buy; but the careful shopper will find some pearls among them, and, where appropriate, bargain records are recommended in these pages. The stereo addict tends to proclaim the supremacy of stereo over mono, but it is foolish to be too narrow-minded about this and to dismiss as "antique" all records (stereo included) made before, say, 1965. The wise collector, who possesses the fine Boult recording of Vaughan Williams's fifth symphony, made as far back as the early nineteen-fifties and available in mono only, knows how misleading is the argument that only the latest records provide the best quality of sound. Some LPs made in the nineteen-fifties do sound feeble (so do some LPs made today); others still sound remarkably fresh, and records made even earlier, especially those included in the H.M.V. *Great Recordings of the Century* series, have often been transferred to LP with great success.

Perhaps I should say whom I have in mind in preparing this book. It is written for the music-lover who already owns a few records, wants more, but is not quite sure where to turn

7

next. I hope this book will help him, and that its suggestions will stimulate in him a sense of musical adventure. Inevitably, there are gaps. For a start, it is a "selective" guide. Some important works—*La Traviata*, for instance—have had to be omitted because they seem for ever to defy a really good recording. Some important works—despite the number of new issues each month—never seem to be recorded at all. And some works — Rimsky-Korsakov's *Scheherazade*, Franck's symphony in D minor, pieces by Martinu and Honegger—are omitted simply because the author has no place for them in his collection and has no intention of acting as propagandist for music he dislikes.

Most record guides devote a large part of their space to comparisons between one performance and another. For this guide, however, most of the comparing has been done "behind the scenes", and as far as possible a straight recommendation is given for each of the works included. Of course, the chosen record should not necessarily be regarded as "the best"—tastes differ, and when comparing the Bruno Walter recording of Mahler's ninth symphony with the Barbirolli, how can we possibly say that one is "better" than the other? Ideally, the collector ought to possess both, because in this way he will learn more about the music and not become too tied to a single performance of it—always a risk where records are concerned. But few people can afford more than a single recording of a work; and since most of the inquiries I receive as music and record critic of *The Scotsman* are for a direct recommendation—"Whose performance of the *Emperor* concerto should I buy?"—I have tried not to complicate matters with too many alternatives. The records described in these pages are ones which have given me special pleasure as a reviewer, and which I still play for friends, and for private enjoyment, whenever I have a spare hour away from the current month's supply. They are records that could be called "evergreens"—though in the record world even evergreens are sometimes deleted by the companies if they fail to sell the required number of copies (in which event, second-hand shops are always worth exploring).

In layout the book is divided into four more or less chronological sections: (1) orchestral music; (2) chamber and instrumental music; (3) choral and song; and (4) opera. Of these the orchestral section is the largest, partly because more orchestral records are issued than anything else, partly because the orchestral repertoire forms the basis of most collections. Yet it is chamber music perhaps that suits the gramophone best of all, and whose weight and character are best in tune with home listening; and anyone who does not yet have any chamber records is strongly advised to start now, perhaps with some Haydn quartets, Mozart's clarinet quintet, or Schubert's *Trout* quintet.

Opera, since it requires the largest and most varied forces, is naturally the most expensive and difficult form of music to record. Some opera recordings are *ad hoc* affairs, with routine casts assembled around a "star" name; others are live recordings made during actual opera-house performances, complete with the thud of the singers' feet and coughs from the audience; but the ideal opera recording is usually one made in the studio with a cast who have sung the work together in an opera house, and who can devote themselves to obtaining a more perfect performance than could be achieved in ordinary theatre conditions. Since the advent of stereo, it has been possible to give opera recordings more atmosphere, although this sometimes results in irritating gimmicks, like the click of the dancers' heels in the Decca *Carmen* and the cavernous sound effects for the dungeon scene in the Decca *Fidelio*. But to give honour where it is due, Decca has also been responsible for the greatest advances in opera recording, with special "productions" supervised by John Culshaw, in which recorded opera emerges as a valid and imaginative medium in its own right.

Finally, my thanks must go to the companies that have been of help to me in the preparation of this book—especially the E.M.I. group, Philips, D.G.G., Argo, and, among the bargain labels, Supraphon, Saga, and Delta Fidelio.

As this book goes to press, E.M.I. have announced the deletion of some of their most cherishable recordings—part of the Beecham series of Haydn's *Salomon* symphonies, the Beecham recording of Brahms's second symphony, the Kempe recording of *Die Meistersinger*. The Wagner is soon to be reissued in the bargain-price *Everyman Opera* series. It will be tantamount to an act of vandalism if the Beecham performances are not also reissued. Readers who do not already possess them are meanwhile urged to explore the shelves of second-hand dealers. Ideal alternatives are hard to find, but in the case of the Brahms the Philharmonia/Klemperer recording (Columbia mono 33CX 1515) and the Berlin Philharmonic/Karajan (D.G.G. stereo SLPM 138930, mono LPM 18925) are recommended, though both lack the sunniness of the Beecham performance; the old Decca *Meistersinger*, nobly conducted by Knappertsbusch but rather congestedly recorded, will serve until the reissue of the Kempe (mono LXT 2659–64); but the Beecham Haydns are irreplaceable, and all we can do is to wait for E.M.I. to regain their senses.

C. W.

A CRITIC'S CHOICE

The English translation of the Choral portion is by Natalia Macfarren, published by Novello & Co. London, by whose kind permission that translation is used in this edition 9th July 1941)

VIVALDI (1675-1741): The Four Seasons, Op. 8.
Felix Ayo/I Musici. Philips mono ABL 3128.

Ten years older than Bach, upon whom he exerted a considerable influence, Vivaldi spent most of his life as music teacher at a conservatory for orphan girls in Venice, a post that left him time to travel widely and to compose more than 40 operas and 400 concertos (including about 200 for violin and 38 for bassoon). In Britain the boom in his music did not really begin until the birth of long-playing records. In 1950 none of his concertos was to be found in the British record catalogues; today more than a hundred recordings are listed. Those works, as we have discovered, are by no means consistent in interest, and an evening of Vivaldi can be a torpid experience. It can also be an enchanting one if the programme happens to contain *The Four Seasons*, the first four of a set of twelve concertos saddled with the unprepossessing title of *Il Cimento dell' Armonia e dell-Invenzione*, or *The Trial between Harmony and Invention*. In fact, the music, which dates from 1725 and is scored for solo violin and strings, is delightfully varied, melodious, and picturesque. Each concerto, prefaced in the score by a sonnet, describes one of the seasons—the gentle breezes and bird songs of springtime, the sunshine and storms of summer, the peasant celebrations that follow the gathering of the autumn harvest, the chittering cold of winter. The scenery, nearly a century before Beethoven's *Pastoral* symphony, is depicted with remarkable vividness and atmosphere, beautifully caught in this delicate performance by the twelve superb players who form I Musici.

VIVALDI: Violin concerto in E minor (Il Favorito); Flute concerto in D (Il Cardellino). CORELLI (1653-1713): Concerto Grosso for strings in D, Op. 6, No. 4. ALBINONI (1671-1750): Oboe concerto in D minor, Op. 9, No. 2. MANFREDINI (1688-1748): Concerto for strings in A minor, Op. 3, No. 2.
I Musici. Philips mono GBL 5621.

Anyone whose appetite for Vivaldi is not assuaged by *The Four Seasons* may safely proceed to this baroque concert in which two more of his concertos (the flute one, with its

15

delicate bird-calls, is a particular charmer) are joined by works by three other Italian composers of the period. Corelli, often called the father of the concerto grosso, was perhaps not the inventor of the form; but he brought it to a high state of perfection, as the concentrated, lithe, and beautiful work on this record testifies. Albinoni and Manfredini were lesser figures, but each had his own personality; and the slow movement of the oboe concerto by Albinoni, who styled himself a "Venetian dilettante," has great tenderness. The performances by I Musici have all the intimacy and refinement of tone that the music calls for, without lacking anything in vigour.

TELEMANN (1681-1767): Suite in C major; Two concertos. *Moscow Chamber Orchestra conducted by Rudolf Barshai.* H.M.V. stereo ASD 631, mono ALP 2084.

Few composers have written more music than Telemann; and the record companies, having lavished their attention on a few hundred of Vivaldi's works, now seem set to do the same for the self-taught North German composer who was once considered superior to Bach. Already there are signs that the Telemann boom has begun. The American magazine *High Fidelity* hailed him in 1966 as the "in" composer. In France, it is said, "Telemania" refers not to television but to Telemann. Like Vivaldi, he wrote many works which today sound inconsequential—which explains why they serve so well as background music. But amid the mass of trim, well-tailored suites and concertos—so many of which seem as alike as pins—there are nevertheless some pearls, such as the airy little concerto in B flat on this record, with its unusual combination of three oboes, three violins, and continuo. This and the entertaining ten-movement "water music" suite, picturesquely entitled *Hamburg Ebb and Flow*, are, as the cover of the record suggests, ideal music to eat by; and any banquet that is graced by a background of these genial scores will be a feast indeed. The third work, an oboe concerto in the darker key of F minor, is in a more serious vein. The performances are deft and spirited, and the recording finely balanced. Readers who find themselves sympathetic to Telemann are advised to sample D.G.G.'s extensive survey of his *Musique de Table*, intimate and imaginative pieces for delightfully contrasted instrumental forces, performed with appropriate period atmosphere by the Schola Cantorum Basiliensis under August Wenzinger.

BACH (1685-1750): The Brandenburg Concertos.
Bath Festival Chamber Players conducted by Yehudi Menuhin.   H.M.V. stereo ASD 327-8, mono ALP 1755-6.

"I have taken the liberty of fulfilling my very humble duty to Your Royal Highness with these concerti which I have scored for several instruments. Humbly I pray you not to judge their imperfections by the fine and delicate taste for music which everyone knows you possess . . ." Thus Bach, in his middle thirties, inscribed to Christian Ludwig, Margrave of Brandenburg, his first large-scale experiment in composing instrumental music. It is not known if the Margrave so much as glanced at the manuscript, for it was found in a job lot of pieces by various composers after his death. Since then the six concertos for various groups on instruments—scored, according to Schweitzer, with the "audacity of genius"—have become Bach's most popular works, and several recordings of them are obtainable. They are not concertos in the popular sense: they do not pit a soloist against the rest of the orchestra, but instead tend to contrast a small group of instruments with a larger one, on the principle of the *concerto grosso*. The second concerto, with its passages for high trumpet, is dazzling; the fourth explores the exquisitely cool sonorities of solo violin, two flutes, and strings; the fifth is a triple concerto of great splendour, with impressive parts for flute, violin, and harpsichord, which makes a shimmeringly lovely contribution to the first movement.

Yehudi Menuhin is sometimes accused of romanticising Bach, but here he directs performances of wonderful lightness and freshness, capturing with a happy style the buoyant rhythms and youthful adventurousness of the writing. The records, available separately, contain three concertos apiece—Nos. 1-3 on the first record, and 4-6 on the second. A bargain issue, by the Stuttgart Chamber Orchestra under Karl Münchinger, is included in the Decca Ace of Clubs series (mono ACL 68-9). Although the recording is not of the newest, and the performance more burgomasterly than masterly, the discs have many virtues and can be recommended to those who prefer a more soberly Germanic approach to Bach than Menuhin provides.

BACH: Suite No. 2 in B minor; Suite No. 3 in D.
Munich Bach Orchestra conducted by Karl Richter.
D.G.G. Archive stereo SAPM 198272, mono APM 14272.

Around the same time as the Brandenburgs, Bach composed four orchestral suites, into the second and third of which he poured some of his most magical ideas. Each has an elaborate opening movement, solemn and fugal, succeeded by a chain of deelctable dances of a kind played by French orchestras of the seventeenth century. The B minor, deftly scored for flute and strings, includes a wistful, fluttering *rondeau*, a sturdy, staccato polonaise (a sensational new dance in Bach's time, with a sharp rhythm in which he here takes obvious delight), and a fast final *badinerie* with a sparkling part for the flute. The D major, more grandly written, opens with high trumpets and drums and closes with a splendidly rolling gigue. In between is the sustained beauty and tranquillity of the slow *air*, a movement that has won universal fame, out of context, as the so-called "Air on the G string." The Munich Bach Orchestra, as its name implies, has this sort of music in its bones. The playing, intimate yet with ample vitality, underlines with a clear pulse the dancing rhythms and well-defined cadences of each work.

BACH: Violin concertos in A minor and E major.
David Oistrakh/Vienna Symphony Orchestra.
Two-violin concerto in D minor. *David and Igor Ostrakh/Royal Philharmonic Orchestra conducted by Sir Eugene Goossens.* D.G.G. stereo SLPM 138820, mono LPM 18820.

These three concertos, like the Brandenburgs and the orchestral suites, date from the six years Bach spent as Kapellmeister to Prince Leopold of Cothen. His heavy concentration on instrumental music at this time was not fortuitous.

Because Cothen was a Calvinist stronghold, where only the most austere hymns were permitted in chapel, Bach had temporarily to renounce his vow to devote all his music to the service of God. Instead he devoted it to the service of Prince Leopold, a keen amateur musician who played the violin, viola da gamba, and harpsichord with a hand-picked group of resident musicians. Bach called him "a gracious Prince, who loved and understood music," and the happy atmosphere of the court is reflected in the violin concertos, alternately bracing and serene in mood. The slow movement of the D minor is particularly lovely—tender, exquisitely poised, with the two soloists flowing and intertwining above a simple, chordal accompaniment from the rest of the orchestra. The impression is one of heavenly length; in fact the movement is a mere 50 bars long. On this record the two Oistrakhs, father and son, pour out the long-breathed phrases with the utmost beauty and purity of tone. The solo concertos are both played by the elder Oistrakh, who dispenses with a conductor and directs the performances himself, with satisfyingly clear-cut results.

BACH: Clavier concertos in D minor, A major, and F major.
Edwin Fischer (piano)/Chamber Orchestra conducted by Edwin Fischer.   H.M.V. mono COLH 15.
BACH: Clavier concertos in D minor and E major.
Ralph Kirkpatrick (harpsichord)/Lucerne Festival Strings conducted by Rudolf Baumgartner.   D.G.G. Archive stereo SAPM 198013, mono APM 14122.

Bach's seven keyboard concertos are nowadays played on either the harpsichord or the piano. Although, in general, the older instrument brings out the character of the music more vividly than the newer, much depends on the artistry of the player; and a sensitive, sparkling rhythmic performance on a piano is preferable to a pedantic, plodding one on the instrument for which Bach conceived his music. In the performances of Edwin Fischer and Ralph Kirkpatrick, to say that one instrument is more "correct" than the other seems mere pettifogging. Fischer's piano performances, issued in H.M.V.'s valuable *Great Recordings of the Century* series, date back to the nineteen-thirties. The quality of the recording, by today's standards, is far from perfect; but the quality of the playing would be hard to surpass, and is an object-lesson in how to breathe life into every note of these fine-spun essays in instrumental polyphony. Conducting from the keyboard, just as Bach would have done in his Cöthen days, Fischer performs the three most popular of the concertos with a shining, natural eloquence and ease. Kirkpatrick's 1959 performances, too, are object-lessons, shedding a different but equally fascinating light on the music; and although one of the concertos he plays is included also on the Fischer disc, the contrast between their performances is so fascinating that the overlap is more a virtue than an extravagance.

BACH: The Art of Fugue. *Philomusica of London conducted by George Malcolm.* Argo stereo ZRG 5421-2, mono RG 421-2.

Listening to the whole of the *Art of Fugue* at one sitting can be a daunting experience—like working one's way non-stop through a book of chess problems. At the end, after the eight fugues, one double fugue, two triple fugues, two mirror fugues, and four canons have run their unhurried contrapuntal course, one understands why Parry believed the work was never actually intended for performance. It was Bach's last major achievement, a grand summing-up of his mastery of counterpoint. His rapidly failing health prevented him from finishing it: the music stops in the course of a quadruple fugue based partly on the letters of his own name in German notation. And because he left the work in open score, with no instruments specified, nobody has ever been sure what his intentions were for it. Tovey, who performed a spectacular feat of scholarship by completing the unfinished fugue and composing a final quadruple mirror fugue to round the work off, thought it was all intended for a single keyboard. Other authorities, fearing such a medium to be too dry and restricted, have preferred to think it a work for more than one player, and have accordingly prepared a variety of instrumentations: for two pianos, for two harpsichords, for string quartet, for orchestra.

In this performance by members of the Philomusica of London, directed from the harpsichord by George Malcolm, the solution employed is by Leonard Isaacs; and it is an eminently sensible, painless, and beautiful one, involving a string sextet (two violins, viola, two cellos, double bass) and woodwind (flute doubling bass flute, oboe d'amore, oboe doubling cor anglais, two bassoons). Such an instrumentation, as Isaacs claims in a lucid sleeve-note, enables the contrapuntal lines to be clearly heard by means of interplay of tone colours. The performance ends with the last completed fugue and does not include the Tovey conjectures. The result is music and not, as so often happens in performances of this intricate masterpiece, merely mathematics. But varied and fascinating though it is, it is better savoured in small doses than taken in a 90-minute gulp; and for the savouring of so large a work, a gramophone recording is the ideal answer. This one is adequately banded, cleanly recorded.

HANDEL (1685-1759): Water Music (complete Gesellschaft edition); *Concertgebouw Orchestra conducted by Eduard van Beinum.* Philips stereo SABL 125, mono ABL 3249.

People usually tend to bracket Handel with Bach, Haydn with Mozart, Mahler with Bruckner, and Sibelius with Nielsen. The pairing is convenient, so long as we remember that each couple were in many ways musical and temperamental opposites, not twins. Handel and Bach were born within a month of each other in Saxony, but thereafter each went very different ways—Handel to settle in London at the age of 25, becoming a great public figure, the most celebrated musician of his day, whose ultimate honour was a grave in Westminster Abbey; Bach to remain in Germany as a far more private composer, not widely appreciated until long after his death. It would be hard to imagine Bach composing a work for performance on a Thames barge, but Handel revelled in "occasional" music of this kind, as the gusto of the *Water Music* bears witness.

Like some of his other works, the *Water Music* has collected legends the way a ship collects barnacles, and in recent years there has been a move to put it in dry dock and give it a good scrape. Although its history now seems less romantic than was once thought—no evidence has been found to support the theory that it was composed to patch up a dispute between Handel and King George I—

21

the music sounds just a fresh and buoyant today as it must have done originally. Composed five years after Handel's arrival in London, its robust themes and rhythms show his music to have already acquired more than a hint of an English accent. Perhaps because of this, some British conductors fall into the trap of treating it in a broad, majestic style. In this admirable Dutch performance, Eduard van Beinum never forgets that the music is by a lively young composer of thirty. He preserves the dancing nature of each movement—even the famous *Air*, which he takes at a brisk clip and not at the dirge-like pace favoured by conductors intent on drawing the last ounce of expressiveness from the music. Furthermore, he bases his performance not on the familiar truncated version of the score prepared by Sir Hamilton Harty, but on the Chrysander edition, which boasts twenty movements, including a splendidly festive final *Coro*.

HANDEL: Six Concerti Grossi, Op. 3. *Academy of St Martin-in-the-Fields conducted by Neville Marriner.* Argo stereo ZRG 5400, mono RG 400.

Handel's two sets of concerti grossi—six for wind and strings, Op. 3, and twelve for strings only, Op. 6—belie their low opus numbers, for they were not published until he was in his middle forties. The Op. 6 concertos are the better known, and are staple fare of string orchestras, both professional and amateur, all over the world. But the Op. 3 works, though less often performed, are quite as delightful; and in their effects, which explore various combinations of wind instruments and strings, they are even more varied and captivating. This marvellously clean and lissom performance, in which some of Britain's most polished wind and string players come under the direction of the violinist Neville Marriner, is good value, for it crams about an hour of music on to one record with no deterioration in quality.

HANDEL: Twelve organ concertos. *Karl Richter/ Chamber Orchestra.* Decca stereo SXL 2115, mono LXT 5578 **(Op. 4, Nos. 1-4);** stereo SXL 2187, mono LXT 5579 **(Op. 4, Nos. 5-6; Op. 7, Nos. 1-2);** stereo SXL 2201, mono LXT 5580 **(Op. 7, Nos. 3-6).**

In Britain it is traditional to deliver Handel's two sets of organ concertos in big, booming Albert Hall versions, with heavy reliance on pedals. But this is not at all how Handel conceived the music; and in these records, which are available separately, Karl Richter strips away the layers of fat that have gathered on the concertos, so that Handel's thoughts emerge, fresh, light and springy. The result is a revelation. The playing of the chamber orchestra is beautifully scaled to suit the clear, silvery sounds that Richter obtains from the organ of St Mark's Church, Munich. Each record contains its delights; and anyone wishing to sample the set can do no better than try Op. 4, No. 5, in which a sprightly opening allegro gives way to a brief larghetto, gentle and subdued, and a gracefully swinging finale.

HANDEL: Music for the Royal Fireworks. *Wind Ensemble conducted by Charles Mackerras.* **Concerto a due cori in F major.** *Pro Arte Orchestra conducted by Mackerras.* Pye Golden Guinea stereo GSGC 14003, mono GGC 4003.

Thirty-three years separate Handel's *Water Music* from his *Fireworks Music*, composed in 1749 in celebration of the Peace of Aix-la-Chapelle. Both works were intended for outdoor performance; but whereas the *Water Music* includes strings in its scoring, the *Fireworks* was written exclusively for wind. Arrangements of it, such as Sir Hamilton Harty's, for full symphony orchestra thus give a false impression of Handel's sensitive and striking scoring. The great advantage of this performance is that it as near as possible restores the original instrumentation; it is played by 26 oboes, 14 bassoons, 4 double-bassoons, 2 serpents, 9 trumpets, 9 horns, 3 timpanists, and 6 side drums, and the sound, far from being elephantine, is wonderfully crisp and alive. Charles Mackerras conducts with a careful regard for

23

Handelian ornamentation, and throws in, on side two, a handsome echo concerto for two wind bands and strings, among whose seven movements are an instrumental adaptation of *Lift up your heads* from *Messiah* and extracts from a lesser-known oratorio, *Esther*. In the stereo recording, the call-and-response patterns of the music are effectively divided between the two speakers.

HAYDN (1732-1809): Symphonies Nos. 44-49. *Symphony Orchestra of Radio Zagreb conducted by Antonio Janigro.* Philips stereo SGL 5784, mono GL 5784 **(Nos. 44 and 45)**; stereo SGL 5785, mono GL 5785 **(Nos. 46 and 47)**; stereo SGL 5786, mono GL 5786 **(Nos. 48 and 49).**

In spite of the vast number of Haydn recordings issued since the arrival of LP, and of the efforts of the Haydn Society of Boston and of enthusiasts like Robbins Landon, our knowledge of this great, humane, and prolific composer is still far from complete. Only a handful of his 104 symphonies are regularly heard in the concert hall, and many music-lovers—not to say programme-planners—still suffer from the delusion that the first eighty or so symphonies are devoid of interest.

The refutation of this theory is to be found in these three records, offering six of Haydn's pioneer symphonies. The writing may be cruder than that of his later works, but it has a jabbing and stormy intensity which Haydn to a large extent lost in his mellower old age. When he composed these symphonies he was about forty years old and seemed to be going through a phase of protest similar to that of the young angries of English literature in recent years. Even the *Farewell* symphony, No. 45, in which the players drop out one by one during the finale, is far from being a Haydn "joke" of the kind he liked to perpetrate in his later works: the first movement is a highly dramatic allegro in F sharp minor, the minuet is plaintive, and the first part of the finale is a waspish presto, again in the minor. The *Mourning* symphony, No. 44, which Haydn wanted to be played at his own funeral service, has a dark, abrupt energy that must have seemed startling in 1771. The 46th symphony has no title but has been scored, with what seems a touch of

These you have loved

1 Canto Gregoriano, Benedictine Monks of Silos
2 Fauré: Requiem, King's College Cambridge Choir
3 Allegri: Miserere, King's College Cambridge Choir
4 Hildegard of Bingen: A Feather On The Breath Of God, Emma Kirkby and Gothic Voices

5 Mozart: Requiem, cond. J E Gardiner
6 Bach: St Matthew Passion, cond. J E Gardiner
7 Bach: Mass in B minor, cond. J E Gardiner
8 Monteverdi: Vespro della Beata Vergine, cond. J E Gardiner
9 Bach: St John Passion, cond. J E Gardiner
10 Handel's Messiah, cond. Trevor Pinnock

The 10 best-selling sacred music CDs at HMV, Oxford Street, last week, compiled by Grania Brenells

● *Free CD offer, The Culture, page 28*

Sunday Times — 4 Sep 94

Ortega.

For him, Hannah's Grecian-go-
dess looks and light-headed char
were compulsively attractive. It w
said that he agreed with the fil
critic Pauline Kael's description
her as "a perfect combination
carnality and moonglow". In re
ality, the relationship was fraug
One minute the couple appear
love-struck, the next would fir
them in public slanging matche
quickly followed by passiona
reunions.

None the less, the break-up w
unexpected. It had been widely b
lieved that Jackie Onassis's dea
from lymphatic cancer would ha

al all-American Gap kids: Catholic, athletic and not too smart'

rebelliousness, in the outlandish key of B major; the 47th boasts a reversible minuet; the 48th, *Maria Theresa*, is a festive, well-chiselled work in C major, with features anticipating Mozart's *Jupiter* of twenty years later; and the 49th, *La Passione*, believed to have been written for Holy Week, is fierce, sombre, and disturbing, full of what seem to be deliberate archaisms, employed with agitating effect.

Antonio Janigro draws neatly-scaled, energetic, rather brusque performances from his Yugoslav players. At times the approach may seem too masculine; yet it is entirely suited to the music on hand. The records are available separately, but all three are eminently desirable—especially as they have been released by Philips at bargain price.

HAYDN: Cello concerto in D. BOCCHERINI (1743-1805): Cello concerto in B flat. *Maurice Gendron/ Lamoureux Orchestra conducted by Pablo Casals.* Philips stereo SABL 188, mono ABL 3355.

The two most familiar cello concertos of the eighteenth century have often been coupled on records, but never in such endearing performances as these. Haydn composed far fewer concertos than Mozart; and indeed, compared with his symphonies, they are a fairly unimportant part of his output and not always typical of him. The D major cello concerto (1783) was long believed to be by Anton Kraft, a cellist in Haydn's orchestra at Esterházy, and not by Haydn at all. Certainly, the serenely melodious score contains fewer than usual Haydnish flashes of surprise; but the tender adagio reveals the master's hand so clearly that one wonders how it could ever be mistaken for the work of another.

Boccherini, Haydn's Italian contemporary, held a similar musical outlook and was nearly as prolific in output. It is sad that this great and lovable composer, with 125 string quintets and much else to his credit, should be so poorly represented in record catalogues—the number of works available can be counted almost on one's fingers. For eighteen years Boccherini was court cellist in Madrid, and his B flat concerto reveals his affection for, and deep understanding of, that instrument. In this recording, Maurice Gendron, one of today's most gifted cellists, is accompanied by an orchestra conducted by the greatest cellist of a previous generation. The result is an inspired and warm-hearted piece of music-making, enhanced by the use of trimly classical versions of each work and not the inflated nineteenth-century editions, by Grutzmacher, etc., favoured by too many performers.

HAYDN: Symphony No. 57 in D major; Symphony No. 86 in D major. *Cincinnati Symphony Orchestra conducted by Max Rudolf.* Brunswick stereo SXA 4540, mono AXA 4540.

The famous Haydn scholar, Karl Geiringer, has divided the composer's career into five distinct periods. Although the 57th symphony (like the Symphonies Nos. 44–49) dates from the third, or "Storm and Stress", period, its mood is far sunnier than most of the earlier works. It is one of Haydn's most exuberant and inventive scores, full of humorous touches, with a slow movement and minuet that rank among his best. Yet it is practically never performed in the concert hall. How casually we treat Haydn's masterpieces! The other symphony belongs to his fourth period, when he was in his middle fifties and his fame was spreading far beyond Esterházy and Vienna. It comes from a series of six works commissioned by the Concerts de la Loge Olympique in Paris—to which they owe their blanket nickname, the *Paris* symphonies—and they mark a new and still more potent phase in Haydn's symphonic inspiration. More serious in character than the 57th symphony, the 86th here makes a sublimely lovely companion piece. Max Rudolf's is not a name we see frequently in the record catalogues; but he clearly has the music at his finger tips, and draws from his American players a lively and warm-hearted account of each work. Another magnificent and little-known product of Haydn's middle years, the 60th symphony, full of sonorous trumpet and drum effects and containing far more surprises than the later *Surprise* symphony, has been recorded by the Esterházy Orchestra under David Blum, with the grimmer 52nd symphony as coupling (Philips stereo SGL 5854, mono GL 5854).

HAYDN: Symphony No. 88 in G major. *Vienna Philharmonic Orchestra conducted by Karl Münchinger.* Decca mono LW 5280.

With its noble largo, so admired by Brahms, this work was composed between the great *Paris* and *Salomon* series of symphonies and has the same depth of inspiration. The first movement, after a solemn introduction, is vigorous and sharply chiselled; the minuet uses horns and drums with new imagination; and the finale is a rustic rondo, launched by bassoon and violins in unison. Karl Münchinger, whom we know best for his performances of Bach, shows himself to be also very much at ease in Haydn. The speeds are unhurried yet alive; the slow movement is eloquently sustained; and in the trio of the minuet, the hurdy-gurdy effect is made to sound deliciously lazy. The performance has been conveniently issued on a ten-inch cheap-price LP.

HAYDN: The Salomon symphonies. *Royal Philharmonic Orchestra conducted by Sir Thomas Beecham.* H.M.V. mono ALP 1624 (Symphonies Nos. 93 and 94); mono ALP 1625 (Nos. 95 and 96); mono ALP 1626 (Nos. 97 and 98); stereo ASD 339, mono ALP 1693 ★★★(Nos. 99 and 100); stereo ASD 340, mono ALP 1694 (Nos. 101 and 102); stereo ASD 341, mono ALP 1695 (Nos. 103 and 104).

Towards the end of his life, Haydn made two important visits to Britain and was commissioned by the impresario J. P. Salomon to write twelve symphonies and a number of other works for performance in London. The occasion, the warmth with which he was greeted, the presence in London of a finer orchestra than any with which he had previously worked, and the fact that his inspiration had reached its full rich maturity all served to make these symphonies his supreme, and most subtle, contribution to the form which he had done more than any other composer to perfect.

The writing has a depth of feeling, a clarity of thought, an imagination and an orchestral mastery unequalled in any of his earlier works. The slow movements are more varied and profound, the minuets and finales wittier than their predecessors. Each of the twelve has its own special character, its own particular endearing features. The slow movement of No. 93, another Brahms favourite, is Haydn at his most serenely magical; that of No. 94 contains the famous "surprise" intended to make the ladies jump. No. 95 opens with the tensest and most dramatic C minor movement written before Beethoven; the broad, tender adagio of No. 97 contains a Haydnish echo of *God Save the Queen*; No. 101 has a sublime contrapuntal strength and vigour, and an endearing, ticking slow movement to which it owes its nickname, the *Clock*; No. 102, structurally one of the finest of the series, contains an inimitable mingling of gravity and humour.

No conductor has caught the essential spirit of Haydn with more elegance, point, and understanding than Sir Thomas Beecham; and no orchestra has taken more delight in the vitality of the music than the Royal Philharmonic in its heyday. Although, in the light of modern scholarship, the editions of the music used by Beecham were "corrupt" ones, and his approach grew rather mannered towards the end of his life, correctness for once seems of small consequence in the face of performances in which Haydn's genius is so vividly and memorably captured. As a sample of the riches of these records, readers are recommended first to the coupling of Nos. 101 and 102, perhaps the most endlessly fascinating of the set; but the others are scarcely, if at all, less desirable. The last three records, slightly more recent than the others, are available in excellent stereo pressings as well as in mono.

MOZART (1756-1791): Symphony No. 28 in C major, K.200; Symphony No. 38 in D major, K.504 (Prague); Four minuets, K.601. *English Chamber Orchestra conducted by Colin Davis.* Oiseau-Lyre stereo SOL 266, mono OL 266.

No composer is better suited to the gramophone than Mozart. The intimacy of style, the clarity of texture and argument, these make his music ideal for reproduction in home surroundings; and the record companies and public have not been slow to recognise this. The master edition of the *Gramophone* catalogue reflects Mozart's greatness, as well as his fecundity and popularity, in the 26 columns required to list the recordings of his music—as against 24 devoted to Bach, 19 to Beethoven, 12½ to Schubert, 12 to Verdi, 10½ to Brahms, 9 to Handel, 9 to Tchaikovsky, 7 to Wagner, and 7 to Haydn (this last figure is a disgrace, considering that Haydn was in many respects Mozart's equal, was almost as prolific, and is just as well suited to the gramophone).

The great Mozart scholar, Alfred Einstein, called the headlong finale of the 28th symphony a "milestone in Mozart's development". And indeed this witty presto—more audacious, more assured than anything he had previously written—gives an exuberant hint of what the seventeen-year-old composer would later produce. The rest of the work, including a graceful slow movement amazingly mature in its beauty, is on a scarcely lower level of achievement. The extent of Mozart's development is shown in the great *Prague* symphony composed twelve years later, a work of profound animation, radiance, and tension, written in such white heat and with such drive that he dispensed with including a minuet. It was first performed in Prague (hence its title), one of the few cities to treat Mozart with the admiration he deserved.

Of all the conductors of the younger generation, none has revealed a more instinctive ability that Colin Davis to get right inside a Mozart work and make it pulse. Here he brings every phrase meaningfully to life and draws wonderfully pointed performances from his small, alert band of players. To complete the record are four dances from the last year of Mozart's short life—charming examples of the multitude of pieces he composed throughout his career for court balls and other festivities. Today we may think it sad that the composer of the *Prague* symphony had to waste his time on trivia, but it is only in fairly recent years that symphonic music and dance music have come from different sources; in Mozart's day they were ground in the same mill, and even his least important pieces tended to be written with love and reveal the authentic stamp of his genius. These four minuets, exquisitely turned and full of surprises, are no exception.

MOZART: Symphony No. 25 in G minor, K.183; Symphony No. 29 in A, K.201; Symphony No. 32 in G, K.318. *London Symphony Orchestra conducted by Colin Davis.* Philips stereo SAL 3502, mono AL 3502.

Mozart's 25th and 29th symphonies were two of a group of three he wrote at the age of seventeen (the other, No. 28, is referred to above; in spite of its number, it is the earliest of the three). In them the child prodigy turns practically overnight into a great composer. The 25th was the first symphony he composed in a minor key; and in its mixture of melancholy and sweetness, its panting syncopations and sighing chromaticisms, it looks forward to the greater and more famous symphony in the same key that he produced towards the end of his life. The 29th symphony, in contrast, is radiant and tender, written with the lightest of touch and with the transparency of chamber music. It is a honey of a work. The 32nd dates from six years later and is not really a symphony at all, but a brilliant and festive concert overture with a quick-slow-quick pattern similar to that of the *Seraglio* overture. Colin Davis here conducts typically sensitive performances, beautifully fashioned and alive to the mood and colours of these three very different pieces.

MOZART: Violin concerto in G major, K.216; Violin concerto in A major, K.219. *Arthur Grumiaux/London Symphony Orchestra conducted by Colin Davis.* Philips stereo AY 835112, mono AL 02224.

At the age of twenty, Mozart poured out five violin concertos in quick succession—and thereafter more or less turned his back on the form, preferring instead to use the piano concerto as a vehicle for his inspiration. Nevertheless the violin works, especially the two on this record, have their own particular appeal and beauty. Einstein has drawn attention to the new depth and richness of Mozart's whole language that arrives in the adagio of the G major work, a movement which, he says, "seems to have fallen straight from heaven"; and the A major, he adds, is "unsurpassed for brilliance, tenderness, and wit." In Arthur Grumiaux's hands, the music sounds as light as air; and his performance, along with the orchestral accompaniment, is a model of classical poise and feeling.

30

MOZART: Symphony No. 31 in D, K.297 (Paris);
Symphony No. 34 in C, K.338 *Philharmonia Orchestra
conducted by Otto Klemperer.* Columbia stereo SAX
2546, mono 33CX 1906.

The intimacy of Mozart's adolescent symphonies here gives
way to music that is more ceremonial, and more elaborately
orchestrated. The *Paris* symphony of 1778 was the first in
which he included—if only in a subsidiary role—what was to
become one of his favourite instruments, the clarinet. It is
a glittering work, composed at short notice during a visit
to Paris, intended to please the supporters of the famous
Concerts Spirituels (whom, in fact, he despised), yet making
a virtue out of French musical conventions of the period.
Many authorities dismiss it as cold and superficial in its
inspiration, but Klemperer's performance proves otherwise.
Perhaps it lacks something of the swagger that Beecham
could bring to Mozart, but it has a magisterial splendour
that is immensely compelling, a strength and sweep that look
forward to Beethoven. Beecham could make it sound witty;
Klemperer makes it sound great.

The 34th symphony opens, like the *Paris*, with a martial
call to attention, but thereafter pursues a moodier and more
subtle course, with that mingling of sunshine and shadow
that characterises all Mozart's mature and most human
masterpieces. Yet, when he composed it, he was only 24;
and, as with the *Paris* symphony, he composed it for an
audience he scorned (in this case the court of the Archbishop of Salzburg, who, far from recognising his genius,
treated him like dirt). Klemperer unfolds its beauties with
great care and with an utter refusal to hurry; and the result,
far from sounding sluggish, has much more vitality than
many a faster performance.

MOZART: Sinfonia concertante in E flat major for
violin and viola, K.364; Violin concerto in D major, K.211.
*Arthur Grumiaux/Arrigo Pelliccia/London Symphony
Orchestra conducted by Colin Davis.* Philips stereo
SAL 3492, mono AL 3492.

The sinfonia concertante is the greatest of Mozart's string
concertos, and one of the last important works he wrote

31

before quitting, at the age of 25, the services of the ungrateful Archbishop of Salzburg and moving on to Vienna to become a freelance composer. Eric Blom was enamoured of the beautiful dark colouring of the music—"not at all suited," as he put it, "to archiepiscopal court, and perhaps disclosing active revolt against it." The first movement is a passionate allegro maestoso in Mozart's broadest vein, the slow movement an eloquent, troubled conversation piece in C minor, and the finale a racy rondo in which the cares of the previous movements are at last banished.

It seems likely that, at the first performance of the sinfonia, Mozart himself played the viola part, for he was an accomplished performer on that instrument. Today the soloists should be, ideally, section leaders of the orchestra, who are likelier than famous star performers to achieve the proper rapport and blend of tone. But not all section leaders are equipped to extract the full beauty from the music, or to probe the passion that simmers beneath its elegant surface. The advantage of the Grumiaux/Pelliccia performance is that both soloists have carefully matched their individual personalities in order to obtain a corporate, balanced sound (something that is not so happily achieved in the rival Menuhin/Barshai recording on H.M.V.). The result, complete with one of Colin Davis's most alert and sensitively-paced accompaniments, is entrancing.

The filler on side two is a generous one—a performance of the second of Mozart's five 1775 violin concertos, not so well known or so richly characteristic of him as its three successors, but with some delightful moments nevertheless; and with Grumiaux and Davis to champion it, it is heard at its very best.

MOZART: Symphony No. 33 in B flat major, K.319; Symphony No. 36 in C major, K.425 (Linz). *English Chamber Orchestra conducted by Colin Davis*. Oiseau-Lyre stereo SOL 60049, mono OL 50218.

The 33rd symphony, another of Mozart's Salzburg works, is written in his most intimate vein and scored with chamber-music delicacy for oboes, bassoons, horns, and strings; the 36th is a much grander affair, composed at high speed during a visit to Linz for a fete organised by a local count, whose daughter-in-law was one of Mozart's pupils and whose orchestra included trumpets and drums (which Mozart here employs with evident relish). Only three years separated the two works; but during that period Mozart had met Haydn, and the influence of the older composer reveals itself in the new depth and richness of Mozart's symphonic thinking, in the grave introduction to the first movement of the *Linz* (the first time he had ever opened a symphony in this way) and in the veiled, swaying beauty of the adagio. Colin Davis, with some of Britain's finest players at his disposal, obtains performances that are models of Mozartian style—tingling with life yet never overpressed, and with due attention paid to the wind parts so that they are never swamped by the strings. The recording is outstandingly clear and warm-toned.

No 6

No 22

MOZART: Piano concerto in B flat major, K.238; Piano concerto in E flat major, K.482. *Geza Anda/Salzburg Mozarteum Camerata Academica.* D.G.G. stereo SLPM 138824, mono LPM 18824.

Mozart's are the greatest piano concertos ever written. Beethoven, Brahms, and Tchaikovsky may have enlarged the form, and provided a more powerful cut and thrust between soloist and orchestra; but Mozart's concertos, for all their surface elegance and sparkle, strike deeper and sharper to the heart. Einstein considered them the most characteristic of all his works; and at least a dozen of them can be counted among the supreme and most cherishable experiences that music has to offer, provided they are in the hands of performers who fully understand their style and who are able to convey, without over-romanticising it, the wealth of feeling that lies below the surface.

The B flat concerto, written at the age of twenty, is among the best of the early works, with a peaceful slow movement that is disrupted from time to time by what Eric Blom expressively called "curious little gusts of agitation, like an affectionate woman who is quick to be hurt but remains loyal." The E flat concerto, on the other hand, is one of the twelve mature masterpieces dating from that miraculous burst of inspiration between 1784 and 1786, when Mozart poured out not only those works but also *The Marriage of*

Figaro, the *Prague* symphony, and some of his finest pieces of chamber music. The deep emotion of *Figaro*, indeed, seems to be not far away from parts of this concerto, especially the disturbing C minor passages of the slow movement; elsewhere, the golden woodwind tone and general gentleness of line give the music considerable claim to be the most meltingly lovely of all Mozart's concertos.

As recently as 1948, in his absorbing book on Mozart's piano concertos, Arthur Hutchings felt impelled to write that this series of works was "rarely and badly played, rarely and erroneously considered." Since then, things have improved—but not, perhaps, so much as the music deserves, and the record collector who wishes to possess all the main concertos will find that he sometimes has to make do with second-rate performances. It is good news that the gifted young Austrian pianist, Ingrid Haebler, has embarked on what promises to be a comprehensive survey of the concertos and sonatas. But for fine performances of K.238 and K.482, and for some of the other concertos, one need look no further than Geza Anda, who, dispensing with a conductor, directs the music from the keyboard; and he achieves a rapport and a wonderful luminosity of detail (the woodwind sing exquisitely through the delicate string tone) which he matches with piano playing of unfailing sensitivity and rightness.

MOZART: Piano concerto in C major, K.246; Piano concerto in B flat major, K.595. *Wilhelm Kempff/Berlin Philharmonic Orchestra conducted by Ferdinand Leitner.* D.G.G. stereo SLPM 138812, mono LPM 18812.

The C major concerto is an early Salzburg work of no great moment—except that it is by Mozart, and thus contains, within its very formal design, countless miraculous little touches. The B flat major is the last of his concertos, dating from only a few months before his death—"a truly valedictory work," says Blom, "with a kind of chastened mood occasionally verging on a feeling of oppressive foreboding." The style, like that of the C major, is kept as simple and as restrained as can be; but between the youthful Salzburg work and the mature Vienna one, much water went under the bridge; and the simplicity of the latter is of a kind that breaks the heart. It is one of Mozart's most concentrated utterances. Shadows are forever darkening its flashes of sunshine; and even in the swinging finale, there is an aching air of resignation behind the Mozartian gestures of good humour. The veteran German pianist Wilhelm Kempff is—like Geza Anda—one of those rare musicians capable of conveying intensity of feeling while retaining a classical poise and evenness of execution. Here he is as at home in the charm of the C major as in the deeper reaches of the B flat; and Ferdinand Leitner and the Berlin Philharmonic give him the alert, devoted accompaniment he deserves.

No 12

MOZART: Piano concerto in A major, K.414. *Benjamin Britten/Aldeburgh Festival Orchestra.* Decca mono LW 5294.

Usually known as the "little" A major in order to differentiate it from its more famous successor, this was one of the first concertos Mozart wrote after leaving Salzburg and moving to Vienna to work as a freelance. It is a work of mingled wit and tenderness, "little" only in that its range of emotion is narrower than that of the later Vienna concertos. None of his works, early or late, has a more limpid flow of melody or is more exquisitely balanced. This performance by a great pianist-composer of the present century was recorded live at a concert given during the 1956 Aldeburgh Festival. The sound, inevitably, is not perfectly focussed; but the performance has a spontaneity and subtlety that override any deficiencies in the recording. The music has been accommodated on a ten-inch record—a size ideally suited to Mozart's concertos, and nowadays much too rarely used.

15

MOZART: Piano concerto in B flat major, K.450; Piano concerto in D major, K.451. *Ingrid Haebler/London Symphony Orchestra conducted by Colin Davis.* Philips stereo SAL 3545, mono AL 3545.

Mozart wrote these concertos as a pair. They are in his most brilliant vein, with solo parts which, he said, were "bound to make the performer sweat." Perhaps because they are

35

more open-hearted than most of his other mature concertos, and untroubled by dark thoughts, they have come to be regarded by some commentators as "secondary" Mozart. But if they are secondary, it is by the most exalted standards. The B flat major is witty and beautifully turned, full of enchanting dialogue between soloist, strings, and woodwind. The first movement of the D major has a noble, symphonic strength, with the solo part so tightly woven into the orchestral texture that the work has sometimes been described as a symphony with piano obbligato. The andante and finale, though to some ears rather light-weight, are delicious foils to the big opening movement. Many pianists are happy just to skate over the highly-polished surface of these two works. No so Ingrid Haebler, who—as does Colin Davis in his accompaniment—treats them with a relaxed, warm humanity that is perfectly in keeping with their mood.

MOZART: Piano concerto in G major, K.453; Piano concerto in C major, K.467. *Geza Anda/Salzburg Mozarteum Camerata Academica.* D.G.G. stereo SLPM 138783, mono LPM 18783.

The gentle G major is perhaps the most consistently happy and relaxed of Mozart's mature Viennese concertos. "No words," says Einstein, "can describe the continuous iridescence of feeling of the first movement, or the passionate tenderness of the second." The finale, a witty theme and variations, seems to look forward to the enchanting childlike songs that Mozart was to write, seven years later, for Papageno in *The Magic Flute.* The C major, too, is a happy work—in its outer movements at least. It opens with a prancing symphonic march, complete with trumpets and drums, and ends with a vivaciously pattering rondo; but the nocturnal slow movement, with its softly throbbing strings, its pure, songlike main theme, and its sudden stabbing discords, inhabits a different and more disturbing world, in which the eighteenth-century elegance of style enhances rather than detracts from the passionate melancholy of feeling. Geza Anda and his players here catch to perfection the veiled, questioning beauty of the music; and their handling of the rest of the record, with the important and delectable woodwind detail always given its full value, is equally exemplary.

MOZART: Piano concerto in B flat major, K.456; Piano concerto in D minor, K.466. *Geza Anda/Salzburg Mozarteum Camerata Academica.* D.G.G. stereo SLPM 138917, mono LPM 18917.

Hutchings calls K456 a "toy" concerto; Blom sees it as a "fairy" one with Oberon, Puck, and Titania never far away. Certainly the themes, the orchestration, and the keyboard writing are Mozart at his lightest and freshest; but sorrow is always just around the corner, and the plaintive G minor slow movement, with its drooping main theme and its sudden fierce cries of loneliness, has a black despair about it that not even the frolics of the finale can dispel from the memory. In K.466, scored in the same dark key as the Commendatore's and Donna Anna's music in *Don Giovanni*, the emotion is even more tense and agitated. The first movement, with its syncopations and shooting scales, has more than a touch of hellfire and brimstone; the peacefulness of the opening of the slow movement is soon disrupted by swirling arpeggios; and the grim, excitable intensity of the finale is not alleviated until the closing pages, where the sun is briefly but magically allowed to break through. Geza Anda superbly sets the mood, and weight, of each work. K.456 is made to sound delicate but never fussy; and so the opening movement, which, in the wrong hands, can seem merely decorative, beautifully paves the way for the deeper feeling of the andante. K.466 sounds powerful, as it should; but Anda always remembers that its power is of the eighteenth century, and that the whole work loses its point if its Beethovenian features are treated as if they are *by* Beethoven, instead of being prophetic of him.

MOZART: Piano concerto in F major, K.459; Piano concerto in D major, K.537. *Ingrid Haebler/London Symphony Orchestra conducted by Colin Davis.* Philips stereo SGL 5813, mono GL 5813.

For smiling beauty, the F major concerto rivals the more famous G major, completed eight months earlier. The first movement is a joyful march, full of enchanting detail; the swaying slow movement is untroubled by the darker thoughts that often overcame Mozart at this point in his

37

concertos, and its atmosphere is that of a warm summer night, with Susanna, singing *Deh vieni* in the last act of *Figaro*, not far away; the finale is one of Mozart's most spirited and sparkling rondos, with a contrapuntal and formal mastery on the same sublime level as that of the *Jupiter* symphony. The D major concerto, sometimes known as the *Coronation* because Mozart played it (along with its companion-piece on this record) at the coronation of Leopold II in 1790, is an altogether cooler work, plainer and more archaic in its material, and providing fewer of the *frissons* we expect to experience on listening to one of Mozart's mature concertos. Perhaps because of this, it is often cited as an example of Homer nodding; but when played with love, as it is here, it can sound magical nevertheless. Ingrid Haebler shares with Kempff and Anda the ability to perform Mozart with a touch that is gentle but always firm and alive, so that the music never becomes mannered or emasculated; and she receives from Colin Davis the most radiant of accompaniments, shaped with delightful grace and purity of line.

MOZART: Piano concerto in A major, K.488; Piano concerto in C minor, K.491. *Wilhelm Kempff/Bamberg Symphony Orchestra conducted by Ferdinand Leitner.* D.G.G. stereo SLPM 138645, mono LPM 18645.

Like K.482, these concertos were written during the winter of 1785/6, when Mozart was also at work on *Figaro*. The first movement of the A major, says Hutchings, begins like someone resuming a pleasant tale, not like a speaker making a dramatic announcement; and the whole work is informed with a warm confidential quality, softly poignant in the slow movement—one of Mozart's most intimate inspirations —and with the wittiest of rapid repartee between soloist and orchestra in the finale. The C minor is a very different affair. As with the D minor concerto—the only other that Mozart wrote in a minor key—the colour and mood are predominantly sombre; but whereas in the D minor the sun breaks though in the end, the C minor has no such respite in the veiled, brooding theme and variations that form its finale. Here, even more than in his coupling of K.246 and K.595, Wilhelm Kempff shows himself to be as adept at conveying Mozartian tenderness as at uncovering

38

Mozartian despair; and once again, Ferdinand Leitner supports him admirably.

MOZART: Piano concerto in C major. K.503; Rondo in D major, K.382. *Alfred Brendel/Vienna Pro Musica Orchestra conducted by Paul Angerer.* Vox stereo STGBY 512110, mono GBY 12110.

Tovey and Robbins Landon have both singled out the first movement of this work as perhaps the most sublime example of the spirit and structure of the classical concerto. Hutchings has called it Mozart's *Emperor*—though it might be more apt to call the *Emperor* concerto Beethoven's K.503. Yet, curiously, this has never been a popular masterpiece; it is seldom heard in the concert hall, and seldom recorded; and Eric Blom, in one of his rare moments of aberration where Mozart was concerned, described it as "rather frigid and comparatively unoriginal." Alfred Brendel here treats it as the masterpiece it is. The first movement is played with breadth, but never ceases to sound Mozartian; the wonderfully poised andante is given the hint of mystery it needs if it is to make its due impact after the symphonic grandeur of the opening movement; and the finale, which in insensitive hands can sound merely skittish, is taken at an unhurried pace that enables the pianist to bring out the character of the music and to enjoy the decorative passage-work. The rondo, K.382, was composed as an alternative finale for the early D major piano concerto K.175. Although not top-flight Mozart, it has a square-cut vigour and humour that make it an attractive occasional piece, especially when played as charmingly as here.

MOZART: Four horn concertos—in D major, K.412; in E flat major, K.417; in E flat major, K.447; in E flat major, K.495. *Dennis Brain/Philharmonia Orchestra conducted by Herbert von Karajan.* Columbia mono 33CX 1140.

Mozart's four horn concertos (of which the first is really a conflation of two works) are among his wittiest and most charming scores. The invention is exquisite: the music abounds in the most light-heartedly felicitous ideas, to which the particular timbre of the solo instrument gives an additional fillip. Yet for all the wonderful ease of the writing, the solo part is wickedly difficult to put over. No one has done so with more zestful brilliance than Dennis Brain, whose recording, dating from 1953, is surely still the delight and despair of all would-be hornists. Karajan's accompaniment is splendidly deft, and the recording, though it now sounds a little woolly in quality, is easily bearable for the sake of what is surely an unsurpassable performance.

MOZART: Symphony No. 39 in E flat major, K.543; ✻ ✻ ✻
Symphony No. 40 in G minor, K.550. *London Symphony Orchestra conducted by Colin Davis.* Philips stereo AY 835113, mono AL 02225.

Mozart's last three symphonies—the 39th, 40th, and 41st—are the most perfectly balanced and contrasted trilogy of masterpieces ever written. They were poured out in a miraculous six-week burst of inspiration during the summer of 1788, when Mozart was within three years of his death, and so weighed down by family and financial problems that one wonders how he had the energy to compose anything at all, let alone three such peerless works as these. Of the three, only the G minor reveals his troubled frame of mind: in the restless, plaintive beauty of its opening movement, and in the sombre, disturbing passion of its finale. In contrast, the E flat major symphony is mainly sunny and relaxed—though no less great, and no less moving, for being so. Colin Davis catches the spirit of each work with great understanding, realising to perfection the smiling beauty of the E flat and conveying the heart-breaking intensity of the G minor without ever over-romanticising its character.

MOZART: Symphony No. 41 in C major, K.551 (Jupiter); ✻ ✻
Symphony No. 35 in D major, K.385 (Haffner). *Columbia Symphony Orchestra conducted by Bruno Walter.* C.B.S. stereo SBRG 72005, mono BRG 72005.

After the passion of the G minor, Mozart produced in his final symphony a cool, lucid, perfectly-chiselled summing up of his symphonic mastery, a work fully deserving the Olympian splendour of its nickname. Bruno Walter, who could sometimes be a little over-romantic in Mozart, is here heard at his finest in a strong, athletic performance of a strong athletic work. The coupling is a lesser symphony, but a very likeable one, which Mozart originally conceived as a serenade for the Haffner family of Salzburg (he had already written one serenade for them, and they wanted another). Although part of the score has been lost, the four remaining movements form a symphony in Mozart's most genial vein, the serenade-like character of the music being specially noticeable in the slow movement and minuet, sandwiched between a vigorous, concentrated opening movement and a whizzing, comic finale. Another of Bruno Walter's Mozart recordings—of the *Linz* symphony—is specially fascinating since it includes a rehearsal of each movement and gives us memorable insight into how he approached this composer. This two-record set, originally issued by Philips but withdrawn after a change of contract, is at present hard to obtain but is well worth searching for.

MOZART: Eine kleine Nachtmusik, K.525; Serenata notturna, K.239; German Dances, K.605; Minuet, K.409; Minuet from Divertimento in D major, K.334.
Philharmonia Orchestra conducted by Colin Davis.
H.M.V. stereo SXLP 20019, mono XLP 20019.

No one knows why Mozart wrote his *Little Night Music*, or whether it was ever performed in his lifetime; but melodiously and beautifully fashioned for a small string orchestra, it has become the most popular instrumental serenade in the world. The *Serenata notturna* for two orchestras is scarcely less delectable, especially when played, as here, with the utmost affection and artistry. The rest of this enchanting late-night concert includes the flamboyant minuet which Mozart wrote as an afterthought for his 34th symphony, and one of the many sets of dances he turned out at the end of his life when he held the post of Court Chamber Musician.

MOZART: Clarinet concerto in A major, K.622; Flute and harp concerto in C major, K.299. *Jack Brymer (clarinet)/Hubert Barwahser (flute)/Osian Ellis (harp)/ London Symphony Orchestra conducted by Colin Davis.* Philips stereo SAL 3535, mono AL 3535.

Mozart's clarinet concerto is the greatest of his works for solo wind instrument and orchestra. Dating from only a few weeks before his death, and inspired (like the clarinet quintet and trio) by his clarinettist friend Anton Stadler, it is the last instrumental piece he completed. "No other work," says Robbins Landon, "is more imbued with that final, quiet resignation; but no other concerto has such a deep-seated satisfaction in pure orchestral sound." Jack Brymer performed it many times with Sir Thomas Beecham, and a recording by them is still obtainable; but in liveliness and beauty of tone, it is surpassed by this more recent recording, in which Colin Davis shows himself to be no less eloquent in his shaping of the sublime orchestral part and in establishing a partnership with the soloist; and in place of the very bland account of the bassoon concerto with which the Beecham performance is coupled, there is an exquisitely-turned performance of the little concerto for flute and harp which Mozart wrote at the age of 22 for the Duc de Guines and his daughter—not a major Mozart masterpiece, to be sure, but one that has never sounded more intimate and enchanting than here, with the harp part treated with a gentle delicacy of touch which brings to mind something of the tone quality of the old *fortepiano* of Mozart's day.

BEETHOVEN (1770–1827): Symphony No. 1 in C; Symphony No. 2 in D. *Berlin Philharmonic Orchestra conducted by Herbert von Karajan.* D.G.G. stereo SLPM 138801, mono LPM 18801.

Beethoven's nine symphonies are the bread and butter of the orchestral repertoire. It is an unusual concert season indeed that does not include at least a few of them; and Beethoven "cycles," when all the symphonies are performed in close formation, have become a frequent feature of the concert scene. Many of the greatest conductors—Weingartner, Furtwängler, Toscanini, Walter, Klemperer,

Kleiber, Karajan—have to a considerable extent built their reputations on these well-known, well-loved masterpieces; and via the gramophone, we have been able to study and compare and be enthralled by their often very different approaches to this seemingly bottomless music. There is, happily, no "correct" way of playing Beethoven's symphonies. Furtwängler's performances, flexible in shape and metaphysical in nature, inhabited a different world from the fierce, bracing, hard-driven performances of Toscanini. Today we turn to Klemperer for masterly structural control, to Karajan for brilliance and excitement. The person who says that Klemperer is right and Karajan wrong has allowed himself to become too set in his ways (or has listened so often to the Klemperer recordings of the symphonies that he cannot bear any other performance). The person who listens with open mind to both conductors will learn more about Beethoven than the person who does not.

A good performance of a Beethoven symphony should heighten one's perceptions of the music, revealing aspects of it unnoticed or not fully appreciated before. Thus there is a case for having more than one recording of each symphony in one's collection. There are certainly plenty to choose from: the catalogues list around thirty each of the fifth symphony, the *Eroica*, and the *Pastoral*. Some of these performances do no more than scratch the surface of the music; others are evergreens which, although they may not reveal the whole truth about Beethoven, nevertheless carry immense conviction and capture the particular, essential Beethovenian inspiration. The records mentioned on this and the following pages have been chosen to show how a variety of conductors, and orchestras, approach Beethoven; and to show each at the top of his form.

The two early symphonies, conveniently coupled, receive typically alert, streamlined performances under Herbert von Karajan. Even in his first symphony, which he finished when he was thirty, Beethoven proved himself to be a *force majeur* in the world of symphonic music. In scheme and in weight, the music is of the eighteenth century; but it contains many passing features—a discordant opening, a soft drum passage in the slow movement, a minuet so fast it is really a scherzo—that must have surprised its early audiences. That it was composed in 1800, on the threshold of a new century, seems particularly apt. The second symphony, dating from two years later, is written with still more panache and on a slightly larger scale than its predecessor. Karajan treats both works with the vigour they deserve, and, in the second symphony especially, he produces a rhythmic impulse that is superbly exhilarating. The string tone is clean and vital; the woodwind playing, though it lacks the pure colours of the best British instrumentalists, is airy and always audible (as it should be, but by no means always is, in performances of the classics); the brass and percussion are wonderfully crisp. The slight resonance of the recording, made in a Berlin church, enhances the warmth of the playing.

BEETHOVEN: Piano concerto No. 3 in C minor.
Wilhelm Kempff/Berlin Philharmonic Orchestra conducted by Ferdinand Leitner. D.G.G. stereo SLPM 138776, mono LPM 18776.

In some of his concertos, Mozart labelled the slow movements "romances"; Beethoven carried this romantic feeling a stage further. His first two concertos kept their feet firmly planted in the eighteenth century, though they contained some characteristic Beethovenian touches of pugnacity and rough-and-tumble. With the third concerto, dating appropriately from 1800, he entered the new century with a vengeance. The writing is bolder, the range of feeling wider, than anything he had hitherto produced. "Conventional elements are still retained," says Marion Scott, "but the imperious stride of the first subject, the impassioned quietude of the largo, the biting brilliance of the rondo and the subtle key scheme underlying the whole work are pure Beethoven."

The five piano concertos, like the symphonies, have been recorded so often that the collector has now a bewildering variety of performances to choose from. But no recordings are more convincing, or stand up better to repeated performance, than those of Wilhelm Kempff. He has recorded all five concertos twice on LP, first with the Berlin Philharmonic under Paul van Kempen and more recently (1962) with the same orchestra under Ferdinand Leitner. The second series is the better. The records can be bought singly, and are also available as a set in a presentation box.

BEETHOVEN: Symphony No. 3 in E flat (Eroica).
Philharmonia Orchestra conducted by Otto Klemperer.
Columbia mono 33CX 1346.

In his third symphony, Beethoven reinforced the orchestra of his second symphony by the addition of one more horn; but the difference between the two works is much greater than that. In the few months that separated them, he was increasingly tortured by his growing deafness, and his battle with his affliction is waged throughout the *Eroica.* Its proportions are nearly twice as vast as those of its predecessors, its energy and its emotions more violent than anything previously unleashed in a symphony. Beethoven has been called the poet of heroism, and this symphony, which was his own favourite, clearly shows why. One can hear it a thousand times and still be swept up by the power and intensity and drama of a good performance. Its shock effect on those who attended its premiere in 1804 can well be imagined.

Bernard Shaw said the first movement of the *Eroica* should be played by giants led by a demigod, and this is exactly the impression conveyed by Klemperer's monumental and justly-famous performance, which has a spontaneity and an unhurried steadiness of impulse that reveal the music's greatness uncluttered by any of the spurious effects employed in performances under lesser conductors. For a more impetuous, but no less valid, conception of the symphony, there is a brilliantly incisive account of it by Karajan and the Berlin Philharmonic on D.G.G., which, being a more recent recording, is also available in stereo (stereo SLPM 138802, mono LPM 18802).

BEETHOVEN: Triple concerto in C major for violin, cello, piano, and orchestra. *Jaime Laredo/Leslie Parnas/ Rudolf Serkin/Marlboro Festival Orchestra conducted by Alexander Schneider.* C.B.S. stereo SBRG 72202, mono BRG 72202.

Beethoven's Triple is the Cinderella of his concertos. Its comparative neglect is due not only to the expensiveness of performing it (three soloists instead of one) and the amount of rehearsal time it needs, but also to the widespread belief that it is a dull work, in which Beethoven says three times what is hardly worth saying once. Not even Marion Scott, that most devoted of Beethoven scholars, could find a good word for it, and in her book on the composer she dismissed it curtly in four lines ("rouses expectations of great music it never fulfils, deals out platitudinous craftsmanship, and is, in fact, Beethoven animated by duty, not inspiration."). All this seems a pity, for it is not such a bad work at all; there are only bad performances of it. Too often are the delicate balance and continuity of the music upset by the unequal merits of the soloists. An ideal violinist may be undermined by a heavy-handed pianist, a feeble cellist, and a conductor who considers his only responsibility to the score is to keep it going.

In this recording a world-famous pianist is joined by a violinist and cellist who are far from being household names; but any fears that the piano will be spotlighted at the expense of the other instruments are soon dismissed by the radiance and rapport of the performance, which is so persuasive, so full of understanding, that one loses one's heart to the music completely. The first movement grows compellingly out of a gently climbing theme on the cellos and basses. After the orchestral exposition the solo cello enters with its own version of the theme; then the violin; then the piano. Each instrument throws its own particular light on the music, and so deeply do the three soloists submerge their personalities that the sounds seem to come from one person with three different voices. Schneider's conducting, as was noticeable when he appeared at the 1964 Edinburgh Festival, tends to be a little reticent—a defect not helped in this recording by the placing of the microphones in favour of the soloists. But the flaw is a small one in a performance so sensitive to the beauty of this leisurely score.

BEETHOVEN: Fidelio overture; Leonora overtures Nos. 1, 2, and 3. *Philharmonia Orchestra conducted by Otto Klemperer.* Columbia stereo SAX 2542, mono 33CX 1902.

Beethoven made four attempts at an overture for his only opera. Happily for posterity, he decided not to destroy the three rejected versions (as Brahms would surely have done), so that today, in addition to the official *Fidelio* overture, we have the trio of *Leonoras*, the second and third of which are magnificent dramatic paraphrases of the opera. "The trouble with *Leonora No. 3*," wrote Tovey in one of his rare blinkered moments, "is that, like all great instrumental music from Haydn onwards, it is about ten times as dramatic as anything that could possibly be put on the stage." The trouble with *Leonora No. 3*, in fact, is that it is out of keeping with the genial opening scene of the opera, as Beethoven sensibly recognised; but of the drama Beethoven unfolded later in the opera, *Leonora* gives only a taste, albeit a sublime one.

Having all four overtures on one record enables us conveniently to weigh up the merits of each; and the second and third *Leonoras*, so similar in layout and material, and yet with so many subtle differences, make a particularly fascinating and rewarding comparison—*Leonora No. 2* a masterpiece with some of the rough workshop edges still on it, *Leonora No. 3* a later, more exalted and purified version of the same. Klemperer's performances have all the nobility we expect of him. They move unhurriedly, yet have a splendid feeling of controlled energy. Every detail of tone and texture, of line and rhythm, is immaculately balanced and placed. Rarely do the soft semibreves of the strings after the trumpet calls in *Leonora No. 3* flow so simply, naturally, and eloquently; rarely does the start of the presto coda leap upwards with such steady, exultant vitality. These are great performances.

BEETHOVEN: Overtures—Coriolan; Prometheus; Egmont; King Stephen; The Consecration of the House.
Philharmonia Orchestra conducted by Otto Klemperer.
Columbia stereo SAX 2570, mono 33CX 1930.

Here are the rest of Beethoven's most famous overtures in performances of similar authority and splendour. The earliest of them, *Prometheus*, was written in 1800 for a ballet about a kind of classical Lord Reith, who "drove ignorance from the people of his time, and gave them manners, customs, and morals." *Coriolan* (1807) and *Egmont* (1810), terse and dramatic, were both written for

47

Viennese productions of plays, King Stephen (1811) for the opening of a theatre in what is now Budapest, and *The Consecration of the House* (1822) for the reopening of one in Vienna. *King Stephen* begins with "Hungarian" music—and an anticipation of Bartók. *The Consecration* was composed in a few days in order to meet a deadline, but sounds in no way a rush job: it is one of Beethoven's most spacious overtures, written in a solemn, contrapuntal, rather Handelian vein. An under-valued work, it needs to be played with great breadth, mellowness, and rhythmic strength, and with perfectly judged tempi, in order to sound well. All this Klemperer achieves in one of his most outstanding performances, full of humanity, sober grandeur, and beauty of line.

BEETHOVEN: Symphony No. 4 in B flat major; Symphony No. 5 in C minor. *Columbia Symphony Orchestra conducted by Bruno Walter.* C.B.S. stereo SBRG 72058, mono BRG 72058.

The popular rule-of-thumb about Beethoven's symphonies is that the odd-numbered ones are masculine, assertive, dramatic, noble, full of cosmic gestures and wrestlings with fate; the even-numbered ones lyrical, relaxed, good-tempered, more personal and less universal in their utterances. Although the latter did not always stem from happy periods in his life, they nevertheless manage to sound like the products of a happy man. Their composition seems to have been Beethoven's method of loosening up between, and in the case of the fourth symphony during, the formulating of the more powerful works. This does not imply that the even numbers are on a lower level of achievement. Anyone who dismisses them as "too light" has a sadly incomplete understanding of Beethoven's music and personality.

The fourth and fifth symphonies were both begun in 1806; but whereas the former was completed the same year, the composition of the latter dragged on until 1808. The first movement of the fourth symphony grows sunnily out of a long, slow, mysteriously veiled introduction, whose apparent inactivity caused Weber's famous jeer about a few notes spread over five minutes; the slow movement, which deeply moved the more sensitive Berlioz, is one of Beet-
48

hoven's most tender inspirations. The fifth symphony is a progress from darkness to light, a symphony of victory whose countless descendants include the first symphony of Brahms and the fourth and fifth of Tchaikovsky. Terser and even more dramatic than the *Eroica*, it shows Beethoven's genius at its sharpest and has become the most famous symphony in the world, an obligatory inclusion in any record collection. So incisive is it, so carefully weighed and so right in its every note, that one understands why Beethoven spent so long over it. The result is a work of extraordinary strength and clarity: of idea, of gesture, of rhythm, of texture. As Tovey remarked, it shares with the seventh symphony the distinction of being not only among the most popular but also among the least misunderstood of musical classics.

Some conductors—Klemperer, for instance—are thought to be better at conveying the grandeur of the odd-numbered symphonies than the geniality of the even numbers, in which they tend to sound too gruff and heavy. Other conductors— and here Beecham is perhaps the best example—are happier among the even numbers than pitting themselves against the odds. Bruno Walter was able to make the best of both worlds. He could bring out all the warmth and felicity of the fourth symphony, yet give the music a vitality, too; and he could convey the sweep and intensity of the fifth symphony without lapsing into the mechanical squareness that undermines so many performances. This recording, made shortly before his death in 1962 at the age of 86, is a moving and exhilarating tribute to his insight.

BEETHOVEN: Piano concerto No. 4 in G major; Piano concerto No. 2 in B flat major. *Wilhelm Kempff/Berlin Philharmonic Orchestra conducted by Ferdinand Leitner.* D.G.G. stereo SLPM 138775, mono LPM 18775.

Beethoven is usually said to have made musical history by opening his fourth piano concerto with a statement of the main theme by the soloist, instead of—as tradition demanded—by the orchestra. In fact he was beaten to the draw by Mozart's piano concerto, K.271, which did the same thing 28 years earlier. But this in no way diminishes Beethoven's achievement, for it is hard to think of may concerto, either before or since, which begins quite so magically and intimately as the G major. One of Beethoven's most humane and tenderly conversational utterances—written throughout with a calmness not always characteristic of its composer—it is also one of his most elusive. In performance, its delicate hues can be dulled by an insufficiently poetic pianist, and the long opening movement can sound depressingly uneventful. In Wilhelm Kempff, however, it finds its ideal interpreter, and every note of his performance (including, as in his recording of the third concerto, his beautifully conceived cadenzas, which grow naturally and graciously from the music, instead of being passages of gratuitous thumping display) is instinct with sensibility and a sense of wonder at the sublimity of the music. In the slow movement, which Liszt compared with Orpheus taming the wild beasts, he draws from his instrument the most comforting sounds on earth; and the sunny finale is treated with generous warmth of feeling by soloist and orchestra.

The inclusion of the B flat major concerto on side two is a delightful bonus. Although the slightest of Beethoven's concertos, wrongly numbered (it was in fact the first of the set to be written, not the second) and sneered at by its composer ("I value it at only ten ducats," he wrote candidly to his publisher, "because I do not give it out as one of my best"), it can become an object of beauty in the hands of a pianist prepared to open his heart to its limpid charms. Kempff does so; and the result is enchanting.

BEETHOVEN: Violin concerto in D major. *Henryk Szeryng/London Symphony Orchestra conducted by Hans Schmidt-Isserstedt.* Philips stereo SAL 3538, mono AL 3538.

Dismissed as insignificant when first performed in 1806, Beethoven's violin concerto is today recognised as the most serenely lovely of all his works. "Its beauty," says one commentator, "lies deep, and for many performers is not get-at-able; tone, not display, is its secret." Although it has not lacked recordings, few have caught and held its atmosphere of sublime serenity. Perhaps the clinical conditions of the studio are against it. But the Polish violinist, Henryk

Szeryng, has come nearer than most to the ideal performance of one's imagination. When he played this work, with
the same conductor, at the 1965 Edinburgh Festival, his
approach seemed a little too sweet; but here he strikes just
the right intimate note, and his softly sustained radiance of
tone and unhurried pensiveness of expression reach to the
heart of the music.

BEETHOVEN: Symphony No. 6 in F major (Pastoral).
*Vienna Philharmonic Orchestra conducted by Pierre
Monteux.* R.C.A. Victrola stereo VICS 1006, mono
VIC 1006.

Berlioz, who claimed to be more profoundly affected by the
Pastoral than by any of Beethoven's other symphonies, called
it "an astounding landscape that seems to have been composed by Poussin and painted by Michelangelo." Beethoven
himself preferred to think of it as "more an expression of
sentiment than a painting." Either way, it is one of his
sunniest and most serene inspirations—although (the composer, after all, being Beethoven) room is found along the
way for a vigorous thunderstorm, which recedes, with the
arrival of the last movement, into a peaceful "song of
thanksgiving."

Conductors able to cope confidently with the hurdles of
Beethoven's "deeper" symphonies sometimes trip over the
straws of the simple, open-hearted *Pastoral*. Not so Pierre
Monteux, who, although more famous for his performances
of music of later generations, turned increasingly in his last
years to the German classics, bringing to them the same
clarity of thought and vitality of rhythm and phrasing that
he gave to Debussy, Ravel, and Stravinsky. His *Pastoral*
sounds wonderfully fresh and springy, with the speed of
each movement crisply chosen, so that the music is neither
overpressed nor dragged (two major pitfalls in performances of this work). The first movement repeat, vital to the
balance of the symphony, is included; the playing of the
Vienna Philharmonic glows handsomely, without sounding
too cushioned; and, added inducement, the record costs
little more than half the price of all other recommended
versions.

51

BEETHOVEN: Piano concerto No. 5 in E flat major (Emperor). *Wilhelm Kempff/Berlin Philharmonic Orchestra conducted by Ferdinand Leitner.* D.G.G. stereo SLPM 138777, mono LPM 18777.

The last, longest, and most splendid of Beethoven's piano concertos was written in an atmosphere of tumult, with Vienna occupied by Napoleon's troops and the composer working in his cellar with pillows tied over his ears. But its nickname, the *Emperor*, had nothing to do with Napoleon, who, six years earlier, had lost Beethoven's admiration; it refers to the grandeur of the music, which continues, more flamboyantly, the innovations in concerto-form explored in the two preceding concertos. The work is one step further away from the piano concerto as Mozart knew it, more aggressive in outlook, more free in layout. With Mozart, passion was rarely allowed to upset the surface good manners of his concertos, no matter what might be brewing underneath. With Beethoven, passion does indeed sometimes upset those surface good manners. Much of the work seems to anticipate the contention, later to be made by Tchaikovsky, that a concerto should be a duel rather than a duet.

Ideal performances, maintaining the right balance of power between soloist and orchestra, and conveying not only the grandeur but also the vitality of the music, are hard to come by. The first movement is very long; it can be made to seem even longer when performers adopt a square, mechanical approach to its main theme. Again, out of the thirty-odd recordings available of this work, Kempff's is especially endearing, for his crisply rhythmic and finely phrased performance always ensures that the music sparkles where necessary (he is particularly happy at shaping the main theme of the finale, whose rhythm and phrasing few pianists get exactly right); and in the adagio he turns the dreamily descending series of triplets, with which he makes his entry, into a miracle of simplicity. Here, as in the earlier concertos, Ferdinand Leitner provides a luminous, expressive, beautifully gauged accompaniment.

BEETHOVEN: Symphony No. 7 in A major.
Philharmonia Orchestra conducted by Otto Klemperer.
Columbia mono 33CX 1379.

Wagner, in tribute to its rhythmic vitality, called this symphony the "apotheosis of the dance." Although slightly longer than the fifth symphony, it is even more concentrated, and more relentless, in its writing. Because of this, many conductors like to treat it as a showpiece for their ability to generate not merely rhythmic vitality, but rhythmic ferocity. The distinction of Klemperer's performance is that he makes the music sound lively without for a moment overdriving it. Many performances of the seventh can be judged by their opening chord. If it cuts like a guillotine, one has a right to feel suspicious. Klemperer's is round and beautifully weighted—like the rest of his performance, which has a sense of line and proportion that is deeply satisfying. The recording, which dates from 1956, is not by today's standards a model of hi-fi; but the performance speaks more eloquently than many that are more brilliantly presented.

BEETHOVEN: Symphony No. 8 in F major; Symphony No. 9 in D minor (Choral). *Soloists/Berlin Philharmonic Orchestra conducted by Herbert von Karajan.* D.G.G. stereo SLPM 138807-8, mono LPM 18807-8.

Beethoven's eighth symphony is short, lithe, and epigrammatic; the ninth is vast, questing, and cataclysmic. Between them they give us the essence of the composer's style and character. And although the *Choral* remains one of his most controversial works—is its finale, a roof-raising and elaborate setting of Schiller's *Ode to Joy,* a climax or anti-climax?—there is no questioning the feeling of profound exhilaration that can be created by a well-rehearsed and vital performance. From Karajan and his Berlin forces (with Gundula Janowitz outstandingly lovely in the solo quartet) it receives just such a reading, and one is swept up by the whirlwind intensity of the result. The playing of the eighth symphony is equally fine; it is elegantly phrased and has an intoxicating rhythmic propulsion.

SCHUBERT (1797-1828): Symphony No. 5 in B flat major, D.485; Symphony No. 8 in B minor, D.759 (Unfinished). *Philharmonia Orchestra conducted by Otto Klemperer*. Columbia stereo SAX 2514, mono 33CX 1870.

In his fourth symphony, Schubert tried—and failed—to write a "significant" work à la Beethoven in the key of C minor, with the unconvincing subtitle of *Tragic*. In his fifth symphony, he went back to Mozart, pouring some of his most delectable airy melodies into a clear, classical mould. And this time he succeeded. The symphony, from start to finish, is a gem; and the fact that it was consciously modelled on earlier music is excusable when one remembers that its composer was only nineteen years old at the time. The *Unfinished* dates from six years later, by which time Schubert's personality had flowered. Its two movements—the one dramatic and genuinely tragic, the other gentle and consoling—complement each other so beautifully that one does not regret the absence of a scherzo and finale. Klemperer conducts it with characteristic perception, giving the first movement a dark, unhurried intensity that is extremely convincing. And if his account of the earlier symphony lacks something of the bewitching elegance that Beecham used to bring to this score, it has other and equally valuable features: a benign graciousness coupled with an alert feeling for the pulse and pace of the music.

SCHUBERT: Symphony No. 6 in C major, D.589. GRIEG (1843-1907): In Autumn, concert overture; Old Norwegian Romance with variations. *Royal Philharmonic Orchestra conducted by Sir Thomas Beecham*. H.M.V. mono XLP 30028.

Schubert wrote his sixth symphony when he was 21, just after the Rossini wave had hit Vienna; and, to judge by the operatic cast of the finale, Schubert was as intoxicated as everyone else by the sunny sparkle and wit of the Italian. The scherzo, on the other hand, is a high-spirited tribute to Beethoven. But the rest of the work is pure Schubert, with a *Rosamunde*-like charm in the first movement and a delicious songlike andante. In a performance dating from 1956, reissued at bargain price in 1964, Sir Thomas Beecham makes the music smile enchantingly, and provides the elegance of line and rhythm that was so characteristic of him, while avoiding, for the most part, the mannerisms that sometimes crept into his latter-day performances of his favourite classics. The Grieg pieces are enjoyable trifles, exploiting the vein of pastoral lyricism which so irritated Debussy but which Sir Thomas could turn into tone painting of the most delightful order. The first piece, a very early work, is an orchestral expansion of a song Grieg had written called *Autumn storms* (but the high-spirited coda suggests that the harvest is successfully gathered); the second, dating form 25 years later, has its inspiration in a folksong, *Sigurd and the troll bride*. The recording has its rough moments; not, however, the performance.

SCHUBERT: Rosamunde, incidental music—Overture, Entr'acte No. 3 in B flat major, Ballet in G major, D.797. MENDELSSOHN (1809-1847): A Midsummer Night's Dream, incidental music—Overture, Scherzo, Nocturne. *Concertgebouw Orchestra conducted by Eduard van Beinum.* Decca mono ACL 85.

Schubert wrote his incidental music for a play by the incompetent Helmine von Chezy, the librettist of Weber's *Euryanthe*. The play is now forgotten; but the melody, as they say, lingers on. Or rather melodies, for Schubert poured some of his sunniest ideas into these pieces, known to generations of would-be pianists in versions for four hands. The overture was composed, in fact, for another play; but it has long been known as *Rosamunde*, and, with its wonderful exuberance and bubbling tunes, it is perfectly in keeping with the rest of the music.

Mendelssohn's incidental music to a much better play is as evergreen as the Schubert. The overture, a youthful masterpiece, was composed at the age of seventeen—a few months after the equally miraculous string octet. The other pieces date from sixteen years later, towards the end of his life, but they manage to recapture the same atmosphere of youthful enchantment. The Dutch recording, which includes three favourite pieces from each work, was first issued in the early days of LP. Now available at bargain price, it still sounds well; and the performances have a warm-heartedness and a natural beauty of detail, typical of their conductor.

SCHUBERT: Great C major symphony, D.944. *Halle Orchestra conducted by Sir John Barbirolli.* H.M.V. stereo ASD 2251, mono ALP 2251.

In the months before his death, Schubert poured out at breakneck speed some of his greatest masterpieces. Among them was the symphony we have come to know as the "Great C major," to distinguish it from his earlier, lighter symphony in the same key. Schubert himself never heard it played. When rehearsed by the Vienna Philharmonic Society, it was deemed too long and complicated and was promptly shelved. Not until Schumann and Mendelssohn championed it ten years later did it receive its first, abbreviated, performance. Schumann declared its length to be "heavenly"; but in fact, not all performances make it seem so. Even more than with most symphonies, the conductor must treat the music as one vast coherent span, and not as a series of episodes. This is the strong point of Toscanini's famous N.B.C. recording (R.C.A. mono RB 16079), but the ruthlessness with which he achieved his ends deprives the symphony of some of its essential lyricism. Sir John Barbirolli, in a warmer-toned modern recording, gives us lyricism in abundance, without allowing the rhythm to sag or the music to lose its sense of forward progress. The tempo changes of the first movement, so full of pitfalls for all but the most perceptive conductor, are carried out discreetly and naturally; and the coda, in spite of including the fashionable slow-up in the closing bars, is convincingly handled.

MENDELSSOHN: Symphony No. 4 in A major (Italian); Overture, the Hebrides. WEBER (1786-1826): Overture, Oberon. *Cleveland Orchestra conducted by George Szell.* Columbia stereo SAX 2524, mono 33CX 1880.

No composer, not even Mozart, has written with greater fluency than Mendelssohn. By the time he was fifteen, he had composed thirteen symphonies—though he later disowned all but one of them. The *Italian* is the finest of his "mature" symphonies: begun during a visit to Italy at the age of 21, it cost him far more effort than usual. He did not complete it until two years later, and even at the time of his death he was contemplating revising it. Yet its effect is as deft and spontaneous as can be. Sparkling, euphonious, and perfectly proportioned, it culminates in a breathless *saltarello* that is one of the swiftest and most exhilarating symphonic finales ever composed.

Under George Szell's conductorship, the Cleveland has become the finest of the American orchestras, with a crisp sense of rhythm and an overall mellowness of tone that sets it apart from its rivals in New York, Boston, Philadelphia, and Chicago. Its performance of the *Italian* is beautifully paced: fast, but never hustled. The sound is clear, alive, immaculately tailored. And in the first movement the vital repeat of the exposition, so often omitted by even the best conductors, is for once included—thus restoring the balance of the movement, as well as 23 important bars of music.

Of the two shorter pieces on side two, *The Hebrides* is a concert overture, a marvellously evocative grey-and-silver tone painting of the northern waters which Mendelssohn visited during his tour of Scotland in 1829. Szell conducts it rather more slowly than is customary, but the lapping pulse of the music is never lost and the relaxed pace allows the orchestra to delight in the delicate detail of the scoring. *Oberon*, too, is a picturesque and lucid overture—this time to an opera whose plot is equally picturesque but rather less lucid. Its action ranges from Fairyland to Baghdad to the court of Charlemagne! Again the performance is as warm and springy as the music deserves.

ROSSINI (1792-1868): La Boutique Fantasque (arr. Respighi).   **DUKAS (1865-1935): The Sorcerer's Apprentice.**   *Israel Philharmonic Orchestra conducted by Georg Solti.*   Decca stereo SDD 109, mono ADD 109.

In his provocative book of musical essays, *Contingencies*, Cecil Gray delivers a ferocious broadside against artists who, at the height of their career, suddenly turn their backs on their art. "This," he exclaims, "is truly insufferable. He who does so is not a hero but a coward, a traitor, a renegade. He is given . . . the rarest and most precious of all gifts, and he throws it away. He has no right to do so, even, for it is not his to dispose of. It belongs to the whole of mankind; he is only a custodian with a sacred trust."

No one knows exactly why Rossini, in his early middle-age, gave up composing operas and devoted most of the remaining 36 years of his life to the less industrious task of being a dilettante, epicurean, and wit (the likeliest reason for his apparent loss of enthusiasm—a severe nervous breakdown at the age of 44—is the one that is least often mentioned). The scraps of music, mainly short piano pieces and songs, that he did find time to write in his spare moments, suggest that his melodic inspiration and his gift for musical epigram were still in good condition; and the ballet music that Respighi concocted out of these pieces, first staged by the Diaghilev company in 1919, is both a delightful and a tantalising memento of Rossini's later years. Georg Solti's vital, alluring performance of the complete ballet has long been the gayest record in the Decca catalogue; and now that it has been reissued at bargain price, it is even more desirable. The filler, immortalised by the Mickey Mouse episode in Disney's *Fantasia*, is both apt and equally brilliantly played and recorded.

BERLIOZ (1803-1869): Symphonie Fantastique. *London Symphony Orchestra conducted by Colin Davis.* Philips stereo SAL 3441, mono AL 3441.

As recently as 1950, the status of Berlioz—freak or genius? —was still a matter of controversy. His more eccentric works, for instance the monodrama *Lélio*, were always good for a gibe. But the spadework of conductors like Sir Hamilton Harty and Sir Thomas Beecham, and writers like Tom Wotton and Neville Cardus, has at last begun to have its effect; and a new generation of Berlioz enthusiasts (in particular the conductor Colin Davis and the critic David Cairns) has arisen to consolidate what had already been achieved. Berlioz, in Britain at least, is now accepted as one of the greatest, most fascinating and moving figures in the history of music. It is a pity that the composer's native France has yet to understand him fully and to treat him with the seriousness and sympathy he deserves.

Berlioz wrote a number of works before his *Symphonie Fantastique*—the *Waverley* and *Francs-Juges* overtures among them. But the five *Episodes in the Life of an Artist*, as he subtitled the symphony, were the first potent manifestation of his romantic and picturesque genius. Just how far the music was inspired by his then unrequited passion for the Irish actress, Harriet Smithson, is uncertain. But prominence has always been given by virtuoso conductors and by programme annotators to the pictorial elements of the music—the young composer's reveries and passions, the scene at the ball where he encounters his beloved, the visit to the country and the distant thunderstorm, the march to the scaffold and the witches' sabbath. And yet for all the extravagance of the symphony's programme, it is also a classical masterpiece, written within three years of Beethoven's death and obeying certain traditional laws of symphonic form.

No recording reminds us more keenly of this fact than Colin Davis's. To begin with, accustomed to more violent performances of the work, we may find his approach rather subdued. The slow introduction is treated, precisely, as a slow introduction, and not as an excuse for a bit of spurious passion; the first movement repeat is included in tribute to the movement's classical balance; the closest attention is paid to the notes Berlioz wrote, and how he marked them and phrased them; the cornet parts, omitted from most performances, are restored to the ballroom scene—and the effect is delightful. Far from seeming pedantic, or less tinglingly exciting than usual, the performance in the end reveals itself as a deeply satisfying and stirring experience. By phrasing the music as Berlioz wanted it, Davis emphasises its extraordinary strength and beauty of line, and sensitively evokes the atmosphere of the notes—in the magical expectancy of the introduction, in the vivid, alive, ideal shaping of the *idée fixe*, in the uneasy tread of the first movement and the pastoral stillness of the *Scène aux champs*, gradually darkening as the composer's sense of loneliness increases.

The performance has been recorded at a low level, which necessitates turning up the volume control, which necessitates, in turn, a certain amount of surface noise. This is a pity; but no one should let it deter him from acquiring, in preference to the many others, this fresh, coherent, and quite unusually convincing account of Berlioz's youthful masterpiece.

BERLIOZ: Harold in Italy.   *William Lincer/New York Philharmonic-Symphony Orchestra conducted by Leonard Bernstein.*   C.B.S. stereo SBRG 72112, mono BRG 72112.

Berlioz wrote very little music for solo instrument and orchestra. Not being a pianist, he was uninterested in the thought of a piano concerto. His *Reverie et Caprice* for violin and orchestra is an early work, delicately conceived but not fully typical of him. And in *Harold in Italy*, the nearest he got to producing a concerto, the writing is reflective rather than virtuosic. The idea of a composition for viola came from Paganini, who asked Berlioz to write him a display piece for a Stradivarius viola he had recently obtained. Berlioz promptly began a work called *Les Derniers Instans de Marie Stuart;* but the solo part was not sensational enough for the Italian showman, and the project fell through. Nevertheless, the seeds had been sown for *Harold in Italy*, which Berlioz composed for the same instrument (though not the same performer) a year later.

The music depicts, with great sympathy and beauty, a series of scenes from Childe Harold's pilgrimage. The first three movements contain some of Berlioz's most exquisitely pastoral writing, and are full of all kinds of sensitive and original touches; only in the finale, an unconvincing *Orgy of Brigands*, is there a splash of Berliozian bombast. Properly enough, when Paganini—nearly twenty years later—finally heard the work he had indirectly inspired, he knelt at the composer's feet and gifted him 20,000 francs. Among present-day performances of it, William Primrose's is justly renowned—though he treats it more like a concerto than Berlioz might have wished. William Lincer's recording has no such defect. Perhaps because he is less of a star name than Primrose, he is content to play his role as if he were a member of the orchestra; and the performance, a fresh and carefully pondered one, thereby gains in unity, especially as Bernstein (a fine and underestimated Berlioz conductor) is here at the top of his form.

BERLIOZ: Romeo and Juliet—excerpts.   *Berlin Philharmonic Orchestra conducted by Lorin Maazel.*   D.G.G. mono 29340.

Berlioz, throughout his life, was fascinated by Shakespeare;

and a number of his works pay eloquent tribute to this fascination. In the case of the long dramatic symphony, *Romeo and Juliet*, the tribute is uneven in quality. Some of the vocal movements are, for Berlioz, uncommonly tedious. Yet there are so many memorable pages—among them the understanding portrait of Romeo alone, the radiant love music, the fine-spun Queen Mab scherzo, and the tumultuous feast of the Capulets—that the work is often played in an abbreviated form. This recording offers a generous measure of the better movements in a dynamic performance under one of the most exciting of the younger Berlioz conductors. In quality, the recording is a little harsh; but, perhaps because of this, it has been released at bargain price. A complete version of the score, with the vocal numbers sung by Regina Resnik and David Ward, is obtainable in stereo and mono in a fine two-disc performance by the London Symphony Orchestra under Pierre Monteux (World Record Club).

BERLIOZ: Overtures—Beatrice and Benedict, Benvenuto Cellini, Roman Carnival, Le Corsaire; Royal Hunt and Storm (from the Trojans). *Boston Symphony Orchestra conducted by Charles Munch.* R.C.A. stereo SB 2125, mono RB 16254.

Berlioz, like Rossini, has the misfortune to be known more by the overtures to some of his large-scale works than by the works themselves. How many people who know the airy overture to *Beatrice and Benedict* have discovered the equally airy opera, based on *Much Ado about Nothing*, to which it serves as introduction (and which is available in a good Oiseau-Lyre performance under Colin Davis; stereo SOL 256-7, mono OL 256-7)? *Beatrice and Benedict* (1862) is an unexpectedly serene, comic product of the composer's old age, comparable in its way to Verdi's *Falstaff; Benvenuto Cellini* (1838) is his first opera, based on the autobiography of the famous Florentine sculptor (a book on which he modelled his own melodramatic *Memoirs*) and concerning, in particular, Cellini's love for Teresa and the creation of the Perseus statue. Out of one of the scenes from this work, Berlioz constructed the brilliant concert overture, *Roman Carnival*, which was also intended to serve as introduction

61

to act two of the opera. The *Corsaire* overture, dedicated to the music critic of *The Times*, is purely a concert piece, of dazzling beauty, and containing, in the slow section that follows the vigorous introduction, one of Berlioz's most eloquent, softly radiant, and characteristic melodies. The *Royal Hunt and Storm* is a magically lovely interlude in *The Trojans* (1858), Berlioz's great two-part opera after Virgil, a work whose presence in the record catalogues is surely as desirable as Wagner's *Ring* and whose absence is a matter of scandal and concern (though a goodish interim recording of scenes from the opera, with Régine Crespin in the roles of Cassandra and Dido, has now been issued by H.M.V.—stereo ASD 2276-7, mono ALP 2276-7).

All these pieces are given the highly-charged treatment we expect from the French conductor, Charles Munch, whose fiercely energetic approach to the composer is in stimulating contrast with the more subtle, refined approach of Colin Davis. The great Boston orchestra plays with tremendous verve, accentuated by a glittering recording.

SCHUMANN (1810-1856): Symphony No. 1 in B flat (Spring); Symphony No. 4 in D minor. *Cleveland Orchestra conducted by George Szell.* Columbia stereo SAX 2475, mono 33CX 1831.

"I often feel tempted to crush my piano," wrote Schumann when he was 29. "It's too narrow for my thoughts. I really have very little practice in orchestral music as yet. Still, I hope to master it." Two years later he composed the first of his four completed symphonies, works whose opaque texture shows clearly enough his amateurishness as an orchestrator. Many of us think of Schumann's symphonies as the poor relations of the German symphony family. Behind their backs we refer to them as a source of musical embarrassment to us. In their presence we tend to listen patronisingly to their attempts to follow in Beethoven's footsteps. But when they are played with sympathy and an alert poetic sensibility, many of our doubts vanish and we realise how much beauty lies behind the seemingly stodgy surface of the music.

This is the sort of playing that Szell obtains from his wonderfully alive and warm-toned American orchestra. He brings a lithe and lyrical approach to each work. In rapid passages, the chording is light and springy, as it has to be if Schumann is to sound successful. And it is hard to imagine a more precise or dazzling account of the rushing quavers that end the D minor symphony—one of the most treacherous passages in all orchestral music. Yet these are far from being mere high-pressure American performances: the slow movement of each work is made to sound truly meditative, luminous, and beautiful; and the delicate detail of each score, which some conductors treat rather brusquely, is always affectionately handled, with woodwind playing of great charm.

SCHUMANN: Piano concerto in A minor. GRIEG: Piano concerto in A minor. *Solomon/Philharmonia Orchestra conducted by Herbert Menges.* H.M.V. stereo ASD 272, mono ALP 1643.

Schumann composed three full-length concertos—one for piano, one for violin, one for cello—but only the first is regularly performed. The reason is not far to seek, for whereas the string concertos are both rather stilted, the piano work has a warmth of melody and happiness of spirit that have endeared it to audiences from the moment it was first performed, by the composer's wife, in 1846. Clara had always hoped for a "big bravura piece" from her husband. What he gave her was something different. In character, and paticularly in its subdued conversational style, it is a descendant of Beethoven's G major piano concerto. But where the Beethoven is at its most sublime (as in its brief andante), the Schumann is homely—though none the worse for that.

Schumann's concerto, too, has had its descendants, of which Grieg's concerto in the same key, composed 23 years later, is perhaps the best and most famous. Here, it forms an appropriate coupling. Debussy, ever antagonistic to Grieg's music (he likened it to a pink bonbon stuffed with snow), complained of the piano concerto that it was broken up by martial trumpet blasts announcing nothing more than languishing cantabiles. Yet it is this very mixture of the martial and the songlike that has given the work its charm.

Many performances, unfortunately, fail to reconcile the one element with the other; they are either too virtuostic or too effeminate. The merit of Solomon's performance is the care and affection with which he binds the music together. Nothing is overdone; nor is any point missed. The same is true of the Schumann, in which exuberance and delicacy could not be more admirably matched.

BRAHMS (1833-1897): Piano concerto No. 1 in D minor.
Clifford Curzon/London Symphony Orchestra conducted by George Szell. Decca stereo SXL 6023, mono LXT 6023.

In the early years of the nineteenth century, Beethoven considerably widened the scope of the classical concerto. Brahms continued the process. His two piano concertos are among the most large-scale ever written—not only in length, but in the power and range of their feeling. The first concerto was composed in 1858 in the shadow of Schumann's attempted suicide and mental derangement, and Brahms's grief at the fate of his friend is reflected in the opening of the first movement, with its grim drum rolls and fierce main theme. The slow movement is elegiac in quality and the finale is an aggressive rondo whose closing pages allow the sun to come out on what is otherwise one of Brahms's most darkly passionate works. Clifford Curzon has long been associated with this concerto, and his sinewy performance is a profoundly exciting experience. The fiendish technical difficulties of the writing hold no problems for him. In the first movement, the piano's trills ring out like alarums, and the octave passages are given a massive splendour that would be hard to surpass. The passages of repose, played with affecting tenderness, are equally convincing, and the whole performance is strongly bound together by a responsive accompaniment from the L.S.O.

BRAHMS: Symphony No. 1 in C minor. *Philharmonia Orchestra conducted by Otto Klemperer.* Columbia stereo SAX 2262, mono 33CX 1504.

Brahms took his responsibilities as a post-Beethoven symphonist with the utmost seriousness. Each of his four works in this form was deeply pondered. The C minor symphony, begun when he was in his early twenties, was not completed until he was middle-aged. Like Beethoven's work in the same key, it is a symphony of conflict, with a dark drama in C minor ultimately resolving itself in a triumphant C major. Unlike the Beethoven symphony, it is inclined to sprawl. It lacks sharpness of rhythm, and of colour. As one of Brahms's biographers has remarked, it is a predominantly dour work—which is why, in the hands of conductors not fully in command of its style, it tends to sound turgid and unrewarding. But it need not be so. Klemperer, as well as being one of the greatest of Beethoven interpreters, is also a great Brahmsian; and in a finely proportioned and clean-limbed performance, he gets straight to the heart of the C minor symphony. In the long and patchy finale, where many conductors attempt to dramatise the music with exaggerated changes of tempo, his sense of propulsion carries the most profound conviction. There is no slow-up for the sake of effect when the majestic chorale theme returns during the coda; and so the flow of the music is preserved, logically and exhilaratingly, to the end. This, surely, is what Brahms wanted. Yet Klemperer is almost alone among conductors to direct the music, at this point, exactly as Brahms wrote it.

BRAHMS: Symphony No. 2 in D major. *Royal Philharmonic Orchestra conducted by Sir Thomas Beecham.* H.M.V. stereo ASD 348, mono ALP 1770.

After deliberating for more than twenty years over his C minor symphony, Brahms composed his next symphony comparatively quickly, during a summer spent on the banks of the Wörthersee, one of the loveliest of Austrian lakes. The beauty of the surroundings seems to have given the music a spontaneity and freshness to some extent lacking in the earlier work; and so sunny is its colouring, so gently contemplative its mood, that this symphony is sometimes called Brahms's *Pastoral.* Sir Thomas Beecham, always more at home in genial than in dramatic music, was particularly fond of this work, and his gracious, serene performances of it were justifiably famous. Here, in a recording made shortly before his death, his interpretation is caught at its most glowingly human. The delicate opening is magically shaped; the scherzo, really a theme and variations, is exquisitely pointed; and at the end of the finale, the trombone scales are unfurled with that mellow exuberance for which we remember Sir Thomas with particular affection.

BRAHMS: Violin concerto in D major. BRUCH (1838-1920): Violin concerto No. 1 in G minor. *Arthur Grumiaux/ Concertgebouw Orchestra conducted by Eduard van Beinum and Bernard Haitink.* Philips stereo SAL 3526, mono AL 3526.

When it was first performed, the conductor Hans von Bulow called Brahms's a concerto "against" the violin—which today may seem an uncharitable description of so warm-hearted a work. Like the D major symphony of a year earlier, it was composed on the banks of the Wörthersee; and, again like the symphony, it is a receptacle for some of Brahms's most radiant thoughts. The first movement mingles passion and repose in almost ideal proportions, and it contains, after the soloist's cadenza, one of the most peaceful passages in all music. The finale is a robust, open-air rondo, with a captivatingly gipsy-like main theme. Almost all the greatest violinists, from Joachim onwards, have included this concerto in their repertoire, and there have been many fine recordings of it. The merit of Arthur Grumiaux's performance is its noble purity of tone, underpinned by a lyrical and intelligent feeling for the music. In addition, room has been found, without loss of quality, for a sizeable filler in the form of Max Bruch's flowery violin concerto—a work whose purple patches, in Grumiaux's hands, take on a new delicacy of colour. Two generations of Concertgobouw conductors (Van Beinum in the Brahms, Haitink in the Bruch) provide excellent accompaniments.

BRAHMS: Symphony No. 3 in F major; Academic Festival Overture. *Philharmonia Orchestra conducted by Otto Klemperer.* Columbia stereo SAX 2351, mono 33CX 1536.

The F major is the most concise of Brahms's symphonies and the hardest to perform. Its argument can sound dismally sluggish; it can also sound excitingly turbulent. Its colouring can seem monotonously grey; it can also blaze with autumn tints. Much depends on the vision of the conductor; and although one does not look to Klemperer for a "colour-ful" interpretation, he nevertheless reveals the essence of the music more vividly and completely than conductors (such as Karajan and Giulini) who prefer a more sensuous approach. His grasp of the structure of each phrase, his understanding of its shape and density and place in each movement, is everywhere compellingly apparent; and like all conductors who appreciate the overall architecture of this symphony (there are not all that many), he includes the exposition repeat in the first movement. The inclusion, also, of the *Academic Festival Overture* is no less welcome. Composed in tribute to Breslau University, which in 1879 made Brahms an honorary Ph.D., it is a handsome, good-natured work, built from a number of traditional student songs and ending with a rousing delivery of the well-known *Gaudeamus Igitur*. Klemperer gives it a broad, firmly-controlled performance, and engineers with complete success the awkward change of gear that marks the arrival of each song.

BRAHMS: Piano concerto No. 2 in B flat major. *Leon Fleisher/Cleveland Orchestra conducted by George Szell.* Columbia stereo SAX 2534, mono 33CX 1890.

Today we revel in the size, vigour, and intensity of Brahms's piano concertos. But originally those were among the features that hampered their popularity. So sourly was the first piano concerto greeted by the public—in Leipzig, Brahms was hissed off the platform—that more than twenty years passed before he tried his hand at another. Then, in 1881, mellowed by a spring spent in Italy and Sicily, and a summer on the Wörthersee in Carinthia, he produced his second and last piano concerto. Like its predecessor, it is conceived on the grandest scale; but otherwise it is as different in feeling as the second symphony from the first. Instead of the grim energy that characterises so much of the D minor work, there is golden sunshine. The broad, eventful first movement immediately captures the imagination with a magical opening horn call, gently echoed by the pianist; the finale is a chain of friendly, playful melodies, some of them with a gipsy allure; between those movements lie an energetic scherzo and a glowing adagio, with an important part for solo cello.

The juxtaposition of masculine vitality and intimate lyricism is hard to achieve in performance. Leon Fleisher's approach is essentially a youthful one, and he is splendidly punchy in the vigorous passages of the first movement and scherzo; but he can also be tender and sparkling when required, and throughout the long work he and the conductor convey the strength and maintain the progress of the music with complete rapport, never overdoing any point to the detriment of the whole design.

BRAHMS: Symphony No. 4 in E minor. *N.B.C.*
Symphony Orchestra conducted by Arturo Toscanini.
R.C.A. mono RB 16100.

Sustained and vital in its inspiration, this is the summit of Brahm's symphonic achievement and one of the great masterpieces of the orchestral repertoire. Like Mozart's 40th, it is a truly tragic symphony, moving from a passionate and searching first movement, through a consoling andante and a vigorous scherzo, to a taut and powerful finale that preserves the minor key in which the work opens. Deserting traditional sonata-form, Brahms here broke new ground by ending his symphony with a passacaglia—a series of thirty cogent, concentrated variations on a climbing theme first sounded by the trombones. Toscanini's famous performance presents the music at white heat. Those who find the pace too great and the approach too ferocious may prefer the more sober virtues of Klemperer's purposeful reading (Columbia stereo SAX 2350, mono 33CX 1591), a worthy companion to his recordings of the other symphonies.

SMETANA (1824-1884): My Country.   DVORAK
(1841-1904): Symphonic Variations. *Royal Philharmonic*
Orchestra conducted by Sir Malcolm Sargent. H.M.V.
stereo SXLP 20064-5, mono XLP 20064-5.

Smetana is often called the father of Czech music; Dvořák and Janáček were his gifted offspring. More an operatic than an orchestral composer, he nevertheless produced, between the ages of 50 and 55, a set of six striking symphonic poems, one of which, *Vltava*, has become a concert favourite. Smetana wrote the pieces, each depicting a Czech landscape or legend, at a time of intense personal crisis. When he began them he was suffering from a disorder of the ear which, before he had got very far, deteriorated into total deafness. Unlike Beethoven, who responded to a similar crisis by composing the *Eroica*, Smetana consoled himself by producing some of his most lovable open-air music. Only an overuse of the brass in certain passages, and a tendency to labour some of his fortissimi longer than necessary, suggest that he was relying entirely on his inner ear while composing these works. But for the most part the result is splendid. Listening to the pieces in close formation, one understands why *Vltava* has become the most popular of them, for, in its impression of the great river rising in the forests of Sumava and flowing on to Prague, it is especially varied and delightful; but *Vyšehrad* and *From Bohemia's Meadows and Forests* have a candid beauty, and *Sarka* an earthy vigour, that are very endearing.

Most of us, at some time, have been guilty of taking Sir Malcolm Sargent for granted. It is easy to cite conductors who can interpret this or that work more profoundly than he; and so it is all the more pleasant to find him, in a recording made in honour of his 70th birthday, conducting music in which he is completely and rewardingly at home. Indeed it is hard to imagine a more sympathetic or spirited account of *Má Vlast*—incisive, finely paced, welcomely unmannered—than he gives with the Royal Philharmonic on these two bargain-price discs. The inclusion of Dvořák's *Symphonic Variations* on side four is a handsome bonus. Though badly neglected, it is one of his happiest inspirations; and the playing is warm-hearted and musical.

BRUCKNER (1824-1896): Symphony No. 4 (Romantic).
Philharmonia Orchestra conducted by Otto Klemperer.
Columbia stereo SAX 2569, mono 33CX 1928.

In spite of Bruckner's long-standing popularity in certain countries—Holland, for instance—his music still meets more resistance than that of any other great symphonist. In Britain, Tovey was among the first to suggest that Bruckner was worth treating seriously; and although the advice he offered about this most misunderstood of composers does not today seem entirely reliable, at least it was well intentioned and came from the heart. "Listen to it humbly," he wrote of the fourth symphony; "not with the humility with which you would hope to learn music from Bach, Beethoven, and Brahms, but with the humility you would feel if you overheard a simple old soul talking to a child about sacred things."

Tovey's advice pays tribute to two of the main aspects of Bruckner's character: his innocence and his deep religious faith. But in his musicianship, his ability to unroll and sustain a vast orchestral panorama, he was far from being a simple old soul. His symphonies have a leisurely, candid beauty—sometimes serene, sometimes pastoral, sometimes grand—that is quite unique in the history of music. Wilfrid Mellers, in *Man and his Music*, put his finger on one of the essential differences between Bruckner and other symphonists when he wrote that "the symphony depends on conflict; and to Bruckner's quasi-medieval mind, conflict might seem extraneous . . . He starts from the liturgy of the church, and transforms the symphony into a confession of faith."

Bruckner's inspiration is heard at its most open-hearted in his fourth symphony, the most accessible of his works and the one best suited for the beginner to tackle. Its title, *Romantic*, was affixed by the composer himself, but should be approached warily—like the story he supplied, on the request of a friend, about the meaning of the music. This had something to do with a medieval township, knights and damsels, hunting parties, morning mists and forest murmurs; and in such descriptions, far more than in the music itself, we recognise Bruckner's simplicity of character. Wisely, he withdrew the explanation later, and its details are best ignored. Bruckner's symphonies are not symphonic poems, and the closest the fourth symphony gets to telling a story is in the creation of a pastoral atmosphere. The text behind the music could just as easily be *All things bright and beautiful*—more easily, in fact, for the words of the hymn, in spite of their triteness, are filled with a sense of wonder at what God created, and this, surely, is what the fourth symphony is all about.

Bruckner spent a year composing it, completing it in 1874 and rewriting parts of it later on the advice of well-intentioned friends who always thought they knew better than

70

he did how his symphonies should go. Whether his revisions —and those by other hands—were improvements or not is still a matter for debate; but present-day scholarship generally prefers performances of the symphonies to stick as closely as possible to what is believed to have been Bruckner's true intentions. Performances should also be in tune with Bruckner's particular rate of breathing, rather slower than that of most composers; with his pauses to gather his thoughts after a long brassy fortissimo; with the huge span of his symphonic movements; and, more basically, with the quintuplet rhythms with which he loved to spatter his music and which can sound so stilted in unspontaneous performances. To hustle a Bruckner symphony is fatal. But to give the music too much elbow-room is equally disastrous. The pulse of each movement should always be detectable, even during the pauses for breath. Neville Cardus has quoted Sir Thomas Beecham's experience with a Bruckner symphony. "In the first movement alone," said Sir Thomas, "I took note of six pregnancies and four miscarriages." It must have been a poor performance he heard. In a good one, there should be no miscarriages, no matter how imminent they may sometimes seem.

Of the conductors who have held the key to Bruckner's symphonies, three of the finest—Walter, Furtwängler, and Van Beinum—are now dead; and a fourth, Horenstein, has so far suffered from inadequate recordings. Klemperer, too, has sometimes been unlucky; but in the case of his recording of the fourth symphony, issued in honour of his eightieth birthday, the E.M.I. engineers have caught his performance in full splendour. Perhaps his conception of the score lacks something of the magic that Walter used to give it, but his understanding of its architecture and the superb logic of his performance may be considered ample recompense.

BRUCKNER: Symphony No. 7.   WAGNER (1813-1883): Lohengrin, prelude; Siegfried Idyll.   *Columbia Symphony Orchestra conducted by Bruno Walter*.   C.B.S. stereo SBRG 72139-40, mono BRG 72139-40.

It is said that when Bruckner attended a performance of a Wagner opera, he preferred to sit at the extreme side of the theatre, where he had almost no view of the stage but could follow every movement in the orchestra pit. Although, for much of his life, he maintained what Ernest Newman called a "doglike devotion" to Wagner, it is nowadays considered insensitive to ask if he was in fact influenced by the stronger-minded composer. If you point to the typically Wagnerian twist of the plaintive little oboe theme near the start of the seventh symphony, you will be told by earnest Bruckner experts that the theme may look Wagnerian all right, but that in its context its effect is entirely different. And so, of course, it is. And nowhere is this more evident than in the above two-disc recording, one of the last to be made by Bruno Walter before his death in 1962, in which the seventh symphony—after the fourth the most eventful of his works—is joined by two of Wagner's most glowing inspirations: the exquisite *Siegfried Idyll*, conceived as a birthday present for his wife and first played early one morning in 1870 at the foot of the staircase in the Wagner home, and the prelude to the first act of *Lohengrin*, which depicts, in the most gentle of orchestral colours, the descent from the heavens of the Holy Grail. The music of the symphony—whose slow movement was intended as an elegy for Wagner, who had just died—has obvious Wagnerian fingerprints, which it would be foolish to deny. The vocabulary of the two composers was very similar; the scherzo of the symphony has a whiff of *Die Walküre* about it; but whereas Wagner's music is often powerfully erotic in feeling, Bruckner's tends to look back to the outdoor Austrian world of Schubert, to the spaciousness of Beethoven's ninth—and it has a hint, too, of the organ loft in its long brassy fortissimi that end so often in a sudden, hushed pianissimo.

Bruno Walter, who championed Bruckner's symphonies at a time when they were far from widely accepted, obtains a performance of wonderful eloquence, humanity, and intensity from his American players, and gives the music a warm, poetic, at times almost yearning beauty that few other conductors have achieved so tenderly; and the Wagner pieces, caressingly moulded, are no less successful.

BRUCKNER: Symphony No. 9 in D minor. *Berlin Philharmonic Orchestra conducted by Wilhelm Furtwängler.* D.G.G. mono LPM 18854.

Bruckner's detractors often claim that he wrote the same symphony nine times over. It is true that the scale, the character, and the layout of his symphonies remained pretty much the same throughout his career, and anyone expecting to find in Bruckner a development comparable to Beethoven's is bound to be disappointed. But the reason his last symphony is a richer emotional experience than his first is because the material and the feeling he put into his works deepened and intensified with the years; and the power of his invention is nowhere stronger than in his unfinished ninth symphony, in which the writing has an apocalyptic splendour that is quite overwhelming. The vast span of the first movement is set on its course by soft, mysterious calls from the brass; then come a ferocious scherzo, with a quicksilver trio, and the great final adagio, culminating in a Brucknerian glimpse of heaven and a gradual, radiant fading of the vision.

Wilhelm Furtwängler, like Bruno Walter, was a great Bruckner conductor, with the vital ability to handle the tempo changes convincingly and to sustain an adagio at a really slow pace without letting it sag. His recording of the ninth symphony, made in 1944, was one of his greatest achievements, with a grandeur unequalled by any of the more recent recordings. Reissued on LP (with an unfortunate turnover in the middle of the scherzo) it makes a very presentable sound, but listeners desiring a hi-fi recording may prefer the 1965 Decca one by the Vienna Philharmonic under the Indian conductor Zubin Mehta (stereo SXL6202, mono LXT 6202), though the performance has not quite the authority and spaciousness of Furtwängler's.

JOHANN STRAUSS (1825-1899) and JOSEF STRAUSS (1827-1870): Waltzes, polkas, etc. *Vienna Philharmonic Orchestra conducted by Clemens Krauss.* Decca mono ACL 49.

Sifting the output of the Strauss family is nearly as complicated as sifting that of the Bach family. For most people, the Viennese waltz is synonymous with Johann II—and not without reason, for he composed nearly four hundred of them as well as about a hundred polkas and sixteen operaettas. Melodies, he said, gushed out of him like fresh water (an appropriate simile from one whose most famous work was destined to be *The Blue Danube*). Wagner declared

Strauss waltzes to be a narcotic more potent than alcohol, and on one occasion, succumbing to the drug, he asked an orchestra to regale him with a programme of Strauss's music. Richard Strauss (no relative—though he, too, knew how to write a good waltz) hailed Johann II as "the most endearing of all the God-gifted dispensers of joy." Brahms good-naturedly envied him *The Blue Danube*, and added a violin descant to Strauss's *Waldmeister* overture when he came upon a copy of the score at a rehearsal.

But although Johann II was "The Waltz King," Johann I, the father of the Strauss dynasty, was also a substantial composer, who learnt his trade as a violinist in Lanner's travelling orchestra and whose music was a link between the sophisticated waltzes of his sons and the earlier, more rustic Austrian dances so loved by Schubert. the third famous Strauss, Josef, brother of Johann II, was a reluctant musician but in some ways the most interesting of the three. A shy, introspective man, he was by profession an architect and engineer (he invented a street-cleansing machine) and at first he wanted no part of the "waltz fever" that raged in Vienna in the second half of the nineteenth century. But when overstrain caused Johann II to give up some of his duties as conductor and director of the Court Balls, Josef agreed to help out, took a course in musical instruction, and went on to write nearly three hundred works of a sensitivity often deeper than that of the other Strausses. Always an intensely nervous man, he was never really happy conducting, and died at the age of 43 after falling from a concert platform.

Of all the many Strauss concerts issued on LP, this one is among the oldest; but for wit and magic, understanding and beauty of tone, it has yet to be surpassed. Clemens Krauss, like Bruno Walter, was a great conductor who had time, and the lightness of touch, for delicious trifles such as these. Especially welcome in this collection is the rarely-heard complete version of *Tales from the Vienna Woods* by Johann II, with its exquisitely dreamy introduction and gentle zither. The *Pizzicato Polka* is also included, in a performance of the utmost artistry, and there are some beguiling lesser-known items, among them an *Excursion Train Polka* by Johann II and a waltz by Josef charmingly entitled *My life is filled with love and pleasure*. The recording still sounds good. But readers wishing something more modern are recommended to a similar if more expensive concert, containing only one duplicate (the *Pizzicato Polka*), by the same orchestra under Willi Boskovsky—who con-conducts while leading on the violin, just as Johann II himself liked to do. Here *Vienna Blood* is the best-known piece, and there are others with enticing titles like *Champagne* and *Explosions*, and also the Brahms-amended *Waldmeister* overture (Decca stereo SXL 2082, mono LXT 5432).

Earlier days of Viennese dance music are explored in another enjoyable Boskovsky disc, in which he directs not the Vienna Philharmonic but his own small ensemble of nine players. Here the senior Strauss, Johann I, is repre-presented by a waltz for three violins and bass, there are galops by Lanner and Schubert, an early *Joke Polka* by Johann II, and a melodious chain of *contredanses* by Beethoven, including an airy version of the theme that was later to be ennobled in the finale of the *Eroica*. Beautifully recorded, this sells at bargain-price (Philips stereo SGL 5682, mono GL 5682).

BIZET (1838-1875): Jeux d'Enfants, suite.   IBERT (1890-1962): Divertissement.   SAINT-SAËNS (1835-1921): Danse Macabre; Omphale's Spinning Wheel. *Paris Conservatoire Orchestra conducted by Jean Martinon.* Decca stereo SDD 144, mono ADD 144.

Every record collection should contain a few *jeux d'esprit*, and here, in a well-compiled French salad, we have no fewer than four. Bizet's *Children's Games* (1871) first saw life as a set of piano duets, some of which the composer later orches-trated and which, in the present century, have been turned into a charming ballet ending with a merry *galop*. Ibert's *Divertissement* for chamber orchestra was written as incidental music for *The Italian Straw Hat*, and is one of the few really good, succinct, and repeatable musical jokes, full of deliberately fruity melodies and gags and even a jaunty quotation from Mendelssohn's wedding march. Saint-Saëns's symphonic poems are among the sharpest and most concise of his orchestral works. The *Danse Macabre* is a witty French equivalent of the more hair-raising *Night on the Bare Mountain* by Mussorgsky, and offers the sound of Death tuning up his fiddle, the rattle of bones, and the *Dies Irae* masquerading in waltz-time. *Omphale's Spinning Wheel*, more subtle in its material, is distantly concerned with the story of the enslaving of Hercules by the Lydian Queen. Jean Martinon conducts all these pieces with the crispness and deftness of touch they need, and the hilarious performance of the Ibert is also available separately on a 45 r.p.m. disc, mono CEP 681.

DVORAK: Symphony No. 7 in D minor. *Czech Philharmonic Orchestra conducted by Zdeněk Košler.* Supraphon stereo SUA AT 50647, mono SUA 10647.

Like several other famous symphonists, Dvořák wrote nine symphonies; but it was not until recently that he was credited with more than five. Since then, four prentice works have been accepted into the official canon, and receive occasional performances (they have been recorded by Supraphon); and the better-known works, formerly numbered 1-5, have been rearranged in correct chronological order and numbered 5-9. Thus the D minor symphony, long known as No. 2, has now become No. 7. But no matter how it is numbered, it is in many ways the finest of Dvořák's symphonies, the most sombrely powerful and dramatic in its argument, and the least "local" in its language and colouring. Tovey hailed it, along with Schubert's Great C major and the four symphonies of Brahms, as one of the greatest and purest examples in this art-form since Beethoven. Zdeněk Košler, a young Czech conductor who in 1963 won the Mitropoulos Prize in New York, obtains a fresh, natural, spacious performance from his Czech players, with warm string tone, and clean, poetic woodwind playing. The recording, despite a rather heavy surface, is one of the most imposing to come from Czechoslovakia's national record company, and sells at bargain price.

DVORAK: Symphony No. 8 in G major; Scherzo Capriccioso. *London Symphony Orchestra conducted by Istvan Kertesz.* Decca stereo SXL 6044, mono LXT 6044.

If, in his D minor symphony, Dvořák speaks Brahmsian language, in his G major he prefers to use Czech dialect. The result is enchanting, a pastoral symphony of bird calls

76

and village bands and gentle landscapes. The writing, apart from some moments of bombast in the finale, is airy and lyrical; and although it does not, perhaps, add up to everyone's idea of a symphony, it silences criticism with its warmhearted exuberance and the richness and fecundity of its melodies and counter-melodies (for some years Dvořák played the viola in the Czech National Theatre Orchestra and knew how it was when symphonies had uninteresting middle parts.) Istvan Kertesz, one of the brightest of the younger generation of conductors, is well-known for his vital and sympathetic handling of Dvořák's music. He conducts the symphony with relish; and if, like most conductors in this work, he occasionally presses forward or holds up the action in order to admire the view, the liberties he takes are never serious enough to distort Dvořák's intentions. The inclusion of the *Scherzo Capriccioso*, a tightly knit and grossly neglected masterpiece, is particularly welcome. Tovey thought a possible reason for its neglect was the difficulty of its dangerously exposed opening theme for horns. The London Symphony makes it sound child's play, and gives a captivating and high-spirited account of a work in which—as Tovey remarked on another occasion—all Dvořák's characteristics are summed up with complete mastery and strength.

DVORAK: Symphony No. 9 in E minor (From the New World). ROSSINI: William Tell, overture. *N.B.C. Symphony Orchestra conducted by Arturo Toscanini.* R.C.A. stereo VICS 1187, mono VIC 1187.

Dvořák's most popular symphony owes its title to his two-year visit to America, where he taught at the National Conservatory of Music in New York. While there, he absorbed the idiom of American, and particularly Negro, folk music so deeply into his personality that it is hard to tell to what extent the symphony is Bohemian and to what extent American (a similar cross-fertilisation between Central European and American idioms was to occur half a century later in a famous work by another expatriate composer—Bartók's Concerto for Orchestra). Certainly, the largo conjures up an impression of wide-open spaces, and it is said that, in writing this movement, Dvořák was inspired by *Hiawatha's Wooing*; but at the same time, the music is intensely and nostalgically Czech in character.

Of the thirty-odd available recordings, Toscanini's has certain special virtues: it is wonderfully strong and vital, avoiding the exaggerated tempo changes and sentimentality that mar so many performances of this glowing work; its rhythmic incisiveness does not sound too clipped (as happened in other products of the maestro's later years); and the recording is, for this conductor, remarkably vivid, though more so in mono than in stereo. The record sells at bargain price, and includes a vital account of the *William Tell* overture as filler. A gentler, more lyrical and sparkling reading is available on a bargain Supraphon record by the Czech Philharmonic under the great Dvořák conductor Vaclav Talich, but the sound is rather under-nourished (mono SUA 10128). Listeners wanting a more up-to-date recording than either of these are recommended to Karajan (Columbia) and Kertesz (Decca), though both are more self-consciously "poetic" in their treatment of the music.

DVORAK: Cello concerto in B minor. *Mstislav Rostropovich/Royal Philharmonic Orchestra conducted by Sir Adrian Boult.* H.M.V. stereo ASD 358, mono ALP 1595.

Dvořák began writing his cello concerto in New York in 1894 (a few days after hearing the premiere of a similar work by his friend Victor Herbert, better known for operettas) and completed it the following year in Prague. As with the *New World* symphony, the music has been closely scanned for American influences; but for the most part, it seems redolently Bohemian. It is one of the few really great, large-scale, full-blooded cello concertos, and consequently it has become firmly established in the repertoire. Each movement is rich in warm-hearted melodies, imaginatively sung by the orchestra and tenderly adorned by the cello. So lyrical, indeed, is the solo part that many players succumb to the temptation of pulling it around like plasticine. In an early recording, still available at bargain-price on Supraphon, Rostropovich was decidedly wayward; but here he has tightened up his performance considerably, without losing any of its poetry and beauty of line; and the lovely orchestral accompaniment, so often dimly recorded by engineers intent on spotlighting the cello, is shaped with sensitive understanding by Sir Adrian Boult.

A famous 78 recording of this concerto, made by Casals in 1937, has been reissued on LP in H.M.V.'s *Great Recordings of the Century* series (COLH 30). Although the sound quality is inevitably antique, the performance has a fierce, inimitable majesty—Casals playing, as the *Record Guide* put it, "with a sword rather than a bow." Readers who can afford alternative performances will find the comparison between two generations of cellists a rewarding one.

MUSSORGSKY (1839-1881): Pictures at an Exhibition. *Chicago Symphony Orchestra conducted by Fritz Reiner.* R.C.A. stereo SB 2001, mono RB 16072.

Several composers have attempted to set paintings to music (one thinks of Rakhmaninov's *Island of the Dead* and the slow movement of Mahler's first symphony), but none has done so more successfully than Mussorgsky in his *Pictures at an Exhibition*, which he wrote in 1874 after visiting a retrospective show of paintings and carvings by his friend Victor Hartmann, who had died the previous year. Ten of the exhibits, linked in places by a "promenade" theme, are depicted with great imagination; and indeed Hartmann, who seems to have been a fairly minor artist, is now known to us mainly through Mussorgsky's music—just as the minor poet Müller has been immortalised by Schubert's *Schöne Müllerin* and *Winterreise*.

Mussorgsky wrote the work for piano solo (for which version Sviatoslav Richter states a powerful case on a Philips record, mono GL 5752); but a number of more recent composers, acting on the assumption that Mussorgsky did not know what he was doing, have set about orchestrating the monochrome original into glorious Technicolor. Ravel's orchestration has been generally deemed the most effective, and is the only one currently available on record. He uses a wide range of colours, calling on the services of an alto saxophone, gong, whip, rattle, bells, celesta, glockenspiel, and xylophone, in addition to all the usual instruments, so that the result has become an orchestral, and thus a hi-fi, showpiece. A number of recordings have been made of it, and each very vividly has its points.

79

But the enthusiasm with which Fritz Reiner takes us on tour of the exhibition, from the sinister grotesquerie of *Gnomus* to the spectacular glitter of the *Great Gate of Kiev*, makes him the most exciting of guides.

BORODIN (1833-1887): Symphony No. 2 in B minor; Symphony No. 3 in A minor. *Philharmonia Orchestra conducted by Nicolai Malko.* H.M.V. mono XLP 30010.

Surgeon, scientist, lecturer, and mushroom hunter, Borodin was a spare-time composer who, like Mussorgsky, left his best music to be completed by other people. In the circumstances, his achievement was an impressive one—"no composer less derivative ever lived," asserts Gerald Abraham—and it is tantalising to think how much more he might have written had he not been such a lad of parts. His melodic sense was strong and colourful, his ideas bold and piquant. His masterpiece, the opera *Prince Igor*, still awaits a worthy recording; but his three symphonies, heroic in character and concentrated in layout, give a good impression of his powers. Of the two included here, the popular B minor uses material originally intended for *Prince Igor*, and opens with a long, eloquent call to attention whose grandeur is in no way let down by the rest of the work; the unfinished A minor is less well known, but has the same irresistible drive, especially in its scherzo in 5/8 time, a most original movement. Nicolai Malko was clearly completely at ease in both these works; and his bargain-price performance of them, issued two years after his death in 1961, moves with intoxicating verve.

SAINT-SAËNS: Carnival of the Animals.   FAURE (1845-1924): Dolly Suite.   POULENC (1899-1963): Sonata for two pianos. *Cyril Smith and Phyllis Sellick with Chamber Ensemble.* H.M.V. stereo CSD 1624, mono CLP 1904.

Not all Saint-Saëns's prolific output has worn well, and a musical joke such as the *Carnival of the Animals* is just the sort of work one would expect to have bitten the dust long ago. But the various birds, beasts, and fishes are all so deliciously portrayed, especially the imaginative and elegant study of the aquarium, that the popularity of this "zoological fantasy", as the composer called it, has never staled. It has been recorded many times and with a variety of couplings, but this 1965 issue has special virtues: it forms part of an attractive French programme of particular appeal to children (the first movement of Fauré's ravishing *Dolly* suite for two pianos has long served as the signature tune of the BBC radio programme, *Listen with Mother*); and the performance of the Saint-Saëns, instead of using the standard version for two pianos and full symphony orchestra, reverts to the composer's original accompaniment for chamber ensemble—which greatly increases the point and wit of the music. The whole record is played with the utmost affection.

TCHAIKOVSKY (1840-1893): Symphony No. 2 in C minor (Little Russian). *Vienna Philharmonic Orchestra conducted by Lorin Maazel.* Decca stereo SXL 6162, mono LXT 6162.

A long-prevalent theory about Tchaikovsky is that he did not "find" himself as a symphonist until he had made several unsuccessful attempts at the form. "Don't listen to his first three symphonies," we are told, "for they are weak and dull and flabbily written." In fact, if these works contain faults, they are caused more by youthful inexperience than by lack of inspiration. Each is full of good things; and indeed, with their strong whiff of the theatre, and their enchanted atmosphere which has more in common with his ballets and operas than with the symphony in the Beethovenian sense, they might even be thought more characteristic of him than his later, more famous and determinedly symphonic works. The mistake many of us make in approaching Tchaikovsky is that we tend to forget that he was so very much a man of the theatre. It is perhaps a natural mistake, because, in Britain at least, we have been given scant chance to get to know any of his ten operas. A small handful of his works are played again and again, the rest ignored. Tchaikovsky, in many ways, is an absurdly neglected composer; and if it were not for the gramophone, our knowledge of him would be very limited indeed.

Of the three early symphonies, the *Little Russian*, composed at the age of 33 and revised six years later, is the most masterly, a work of great originality and beauty whose failure to establish itself in the concert repertoire is a mystery. Its first movement shows Tchaikovsky exper menting with a motto theme more spontaneously than he was to do in some of his later works. The slow movement is a jaunty march with a wit which at times seems to anticipate Prokofiev. The scherzo glitters entrancingly. The finale begins like a majestic piece of Mussorgsky, then suddenly alters course to become a series of dazzling, kaleidoscopic variations on a catchy Ukrainian folk-song called *The Crane*. Lorin Maazel, who has recorded all six of the numbered symphonies for Decca, gives it a vital and coherent performance, a particularly happy feature of which is that he plays the slow movement quickly and lightly enough to give it the crisply processional character which Tchaikovsky surely intended and which other recordings, even Beecham's, have completely missed.

A taste for this symphony is likely to produce a taste for the two other early symphonies, and here, too, Maazel makes the music a captivating experience—the *Winter Dreams* symphony (No. 1) a little more so than the *Polish* (No. 3). The former, long thought to be as dead as a dodo, becomes in his hands a work of great charm, gentle in colour, wistful in mood, with a wheeling and faintly Stravinskian first movement, a tenderly lyrical slow movement said to depict a sleigh-ride across the frozen Lake Ladoga, and a frostily sparkling scherzo with a scrumptious waltz as its trio (Decca stereo SXL 6159, mono LXT 6159).

TCHAIKOVSKY: Piano concerto No. 1 in B flat minor. *Sviatoslav Richter/Vienna Symphony Orchestra conducted by Herbert von Karajan.* D.G.G. stereo SLPM 138822, mono LPM 18822.

This is the most glamorous piano concerto in the world. It is a young man's work—Tchaikovsky was 34 when he composed it, though he considerably revised it later—and it combines virtuosity, passion, and lyricism in ideal proportions. Like almost all big romantic concertos, it has its moments of tastelessness; but it has, too, a burning spontaneity of utterance that silences criticism, and so prodigal a supply of inspired melodies that the composer was able to use the opening one (among the finest and most famous he ever wrote) as a mere apéritif: after the first four minutes, it never returns. The slow movement, with its scherzo-like middle-section based on a French folk-song, shows Tchaikovsky's touch at its most delicate; and the finale is a rumbustious Russian dance that finds room for one of those choice Tchaikovsky tunes that extend like bubble-gum.

At one time the record companies' favourite concerto, it is today less frequently recorded than the Beethoven *Emperor*. Even so, there are seldom fewer than twenty performances of it to choose between. Most of them stress the virtuosic elements of the music at the expense of the poetic. The best are those that give us the prodigious glitter, and at the same time probe below the surface. In this respect, Richter's performance is wonderfully understanding. It is full of fire and rhythmic subtlety and the most sensitive beauty of tone; and, by neither overstating nor understating the juicier passages, it ensures that they take their place naturally, yet excitingly, in the overall design.

TCHAIKOVSKY: Symphony No. 4 in F minor. *Vienna Philharmonic Orchestra conducted by Lorin Maazel.* Decca stereo SXL 6157, mono LXT 6157.

Tchaikovsky's fourth symphony was composed in the shadow of his short and disastrous marriage to one of his pupils at the Moscow Conservatory; and at the same time it was intended as a gift for Madame Nadejda von Meck, the rich Russian recluse who became his patroness and confidante, but who never in fact met him. The music, like Beethoven's fifth symphony, depicts a victorious struggle with fate. And in the yearning lilt of the first movement's waltz tunes, the poignancy of the woodwind in the andante, the hysterical climaxes and sudden plunges into despair, the final burst of noisy optimism, it is easy to detect the 37-year-old composer's neurotic frame of mind, which was to become still more pronounced in his later works.

Unless performed with the utmost conviction and warmth of tone, Tchaikovsky's symphonies—for all the glitter and beauty of their orchestration—can sound tiresomely abrasive and inflated. Of the twenty or so recordings currently available of the fourth symphony, only a few can be said to be really satisfactory. Of these, the Maazel record benefits from the presence of a great orchestra at the top of its form, and an interpretation that is youthfully alive to the fire and sensibility and moodiness of the music. From the initial statement of the "fate" motive, with the brass marvellously balanced and eloquent, right through to the vociferous brilliance of the closing pages, the playing never for a moment sags. The slow movement has the brooding beauty of one of the more reflective scenes in a Tchekhov drama; and the pizzicato scherzo has a lithe springiness of touch that is completely captivating.

TCHAIKOVSKY: Violin concerto in D. MENDELS-SOHN: Violin concerto in E minor. *Christian Ferras/ Philharmonia Orchestra conducted gy Constantin Silvestri.* H.M.V. stereo ASD 278, mono ALP 1543.

At one time Tchaikovsky's violin concerto was said to be unplayable. The trouble today is that it is all too playable. Amid the welter of nonchalant, virtuoso, over-rich, throw-away renderings of it, one finds oneself longing for a performance which is not all gloss, which contains even the softest beat of a human heart. Ferras's performance admirably fills the bill. It is not for those who like a whizz-bang treatment of the music; but it catches the lyrical warmth that lies behind the notes and, in its occasional hints of struggle, it reminds us how immense, really, are the technical difficulties of this work. The coupling, another favourite violin concerto of the nineteenth century, is happily chosen; and Ferras, playing with a fresh, light, silvery tone and a sparkling sense of rhythm, gives the music a delicacy that is usually lost in more high-powered performances. If the latter is wanted, then Isaac Stern, on C.B.S., fills the bill.

TCHAIKOVSKY: Symphony No. 5 in E minor. *Leningrad Philharmonic Orchestra conducted by Evgeni Mravinsky.* D.G.G. stereo SLPM 138658, mono LPM 18658.

Even more than its predecessor, Tchaikovsky's fifth symphony is a battle with fate: dating from ten years later,
84

it plumbs gloomier depths, makes greater use of its "fate" motive, is more hysterical in its despair and more exultant in its final paean of victory. And even more than with its predecessor, conductors are often tempted to exaggerate its already over-exaggerated emotions. Violent changes of tempo, brutal fortissimi, and heart-on-sleeve expressiveness are what we are regularly treated to in performances of this symphony, But in fact it does not need exhibitionism of this kind. With natural tempi, and a careful control of dynamics and rhythm, the music speaks vividly for itself. This is how Mravinsky approaches Tchaikovsky; and the result, in the wonderfully lyrical and dignified performance of the Leningrad orchestra, sounds no less thrilling and far more musical than the hothouse kind of performance this work usually receives.

TCHAIKOVSKY: Symphony No. 6 in B minor (Pathé-tique). *Berlin Philharmonic Orchestra conducted by Herbert von Karajan.* D.G.G. stereo SLPM 138921, mono LPM 18921.

The legends surrounding Tchaikovsky's swansong are legion and inevitable—no composer could produce a symphony such as this, and die in faintly mysterious circumstances a week after its unsuccessful premiere, without people adding two and two to make five. Today, perhaps, we are more inclined to accept it for what it is: the work in which Tchaikovsky gave us the emotional masterpiece for which the fourth and fifth symphonies were in many ways rehearsals. Whereas those two works have the happy endings which Russian symphonists (just as much as American film directors) have always felt honour-bound to provide, the sixth symphony closes in dark melancholy—the only possible ending for a work the rest of which has run the gamut of the composer's overwrought emotions. To be fully effective, a performance needs to live the music from moment to moment, and yet have the powerful coherence which this strongest of Tchaikovsky's symphonic structures demands. Herbert von Karajan succeeds on both counts, and obtains from the Berlin orchestra a performance that sounds superbly uninhibited and is at the same time carefully controlled and played with a consistent beauty of tone that brings every detail of the score glowingly to life.

MAHLER (1860-1911): Symphony No. 4. *Elisabeth Schwarzkopf/Philharmonia Orchestra conducted by Otto Klemperer.* Columbia stereo SAX 2441, mono 33CX 1793.

For those who cannot stomach his larger and more apocalyptic symphonies, this is Mahler's masterpiece. It is compactly written (it runs to a mere fifty minutes) and is lightly scored (a mere four horns and no trombones, though this economy is somewhat offset by a variety of exotica, including sleighbells, a gong, and a violin tuned a tone higher than normal); and because it dates from a time (1900) when Mahler felt unusually settled and happy—his health had improved and he had recently been appointed chief of the Vienna *Hofoper*—the music reflects his temporary composure of mind by being, throughout most of its course, sunny and tender and relaxed.

The first movement contains a wealth of radiant open-air melodies, masterfully assembled and worked out. In the scherzo, the spookier side of Mahler's nature does its best to intrude but is dispelled in the magical theme and variations which form the slow movement and lead to the short finale, a setting of a poem from *Youth's Magic Horn* (a collection of German folk poetry that was a favourite source of inspiration for Mahler), describing a child's vision of Heaven. Here the solo soprano makes her appearance in what is interpretatively the most difficult portion of the symphony to bring off, for the music must sound fresh and innocent and contain no hint of sophistication. It is a passage on which many performances have foundered, but Elisabeth Schwarzkopf's approach is ideal—pure-voiced, gentle, infinitely touching in its simplicity of utterance. Klemperer conducts with complete authority, moulding each phrase with a clean, sublime beauty of line, and choosing tempi which allow the orchestra to enjoy the pastoral charm of the music but never hamper its forward progress.

MAHLER: Symphony No. 5; Kindertotenlieder.
*Jennie Tourel/New York Philharmonic Orchestra conducted
by Leonard Bernstein.* C.B.S. stereo SBRG 72182-3,
mono BRG 72182-3.

Mahler's fourth symphony ends with a child's view of
Heaven; the fifth begins with a grim and far from childlike
funeral march. Neville Cardus has called the opening fan-
fare a "sinister trumpet call of fate sounding in a nature-
haunted imagination." And it is this spirit that pervades
much of the work. The second of the five movements is a
feverish, charging allegro; the third is one of the finest of
Mahler's acidly waltzing, outdoor scherzos, full of wood-
notes wild; the fourth is the famous, tenderly consoling
adagietto for strings and harp, sometimes performed as a
separate concert piece; and the finale is a vigorous, at times
eerily humorous, and ultimately magnificently affirmative,
rondo. Leonard Bernstein's recording has been criticised for
sounding a little too carefully calculated. Yet it would be
unfair to what is unquestionably an extremely perceptive
and deeply-felt performance to dwell too much on its faults.
The tone of the New York Philharmonic has great splendour;
the music flickers and blazes and struggles and aches; and
as an appropriate filler on side four, there is an unexag-
gerated and delicate account by Jennie Tourel of the five
songs on the death of children, which Mahler composed,
by one of those sad ironies with which his life was filled,
between the deaths from scarlet fever of three of his
daughters.

MAHLER: Symphony No. 8. *Soloists/University of Utah
Choruses and Salt Lake City Schools/Utah Symphony
Orchestra conducted by Maurice Abravanel.* Philips
stereo SAL 3469-70, mono AL 3469-70.

At one time Mahler's great choral symphony was thought
to be, for all its immense size and weight, one of his lesser
works. But in recent years, carefully prepared and superbly
animated performances by Horenstein in London and
Alexander Gibson at the Edinburgh Festival have made us
better aware of the Faustian splendours of this tinglingly
exciting score. The first and shorter of its two movements is

a headlong setting of a medieval Latin hymn, *Veni Creator Spiritus*, celebrating the descent of the Holy Ghost upon the apostles at Pentecost; the second, by a masterstroke of genius, finds an antithesis to this in the closing scene of Goethe's *Faust*, describing the ascent of Faust's soul into Heaven. Like all Mahler's masterpieces, it explores a whole world of emotion: in the first movement, a prodigious, surging vitality, which makes way, at one place, for a darkly stalking march—one of those sudden, inevitable Mahler visions of death in the midst of life; in the second movement, a slow, wintry, wonderfully poised orchestral introduction, with the woodwind distilling a mood of infinite regret, while down below the strings mutter sadly; and later, soaring, lyrical passages for the solo singers, jingles for the boys' chorus, a final, hushed, ethereal, consoling hymn, rising in the final pages to a pitch of brassy grandeur, with organ sounding and bells pealing.

So far, the symphony has defied recording; and this devoted performance by good American provincial forces, while very enjoyable and quite acceptably recorded, is not yet the definitive issue we have been waiting for. The choirs lack the full necessary radiance of tone and the ability to sustain a true pianissimo; the boys, compared with the wonderfully "boyish" sound produced by Arthur Oldham's choristers at the Edinburgh performance, are rather too sweet-toned; the soloists are very adequate—routine, perhaps, but good routine. But it would be churlish to make too many complaints about a performance which, for all its faults, contains so much that is absorbing. An alternative recording, by Leonard Bernstein, is in the offing as these pages go to press.

MAHLER: Symphony No. 9. *Berlin Philharmonic Orchestra conducted by Sir John Barbirolli.* H.M.V. stereo ASD 596/ASDS 597, mono ALP 2047/ALPS 2048.

Even more than Tchaikovsky's *Pathétique*, which it resembles in layout, Mahler's last completed symphony is one of the great, heart-breaking experiences of music. His champion, Bruno Walter, who conducted the first performance a year after the composer's death, once said that Mahler "never found deliverance in his agonised effort to

88

make sense in human life." Mahler himself confessed that his symphonies exhausted the content of his entire existence —and nowhere is this more overwhelmingly apparent than in the vast, highly-charged, sunset adagio that closes the ninth symphony.

In his outstanding recording—the first to be made by a British conductor with the Berlin Philharmonic since Beecham's pre-war *Magic Flute*—Sir John Barbirolli throws himself as full-bloodedly and understandingly into the music as Mahler would have wished. Instead of being assembled out of short "takes" that characterise so many recording sessions, each movement was recorded straight through, which undoutedly helps to give the performance its powerful conviction and flow. In the finale, the sound of the Berlin strings has a grief-stricken intensity and vibrancy, bringing to mind Neville Cardus's phrase about Mahler's music being a kind of ectoplasm of tone which one can almost see moving. This movement has been recorded complete on the single-sided record that forms part of this two-disc set, and can be bought separately; but as it is the logical outcome of the long, hectic opening movement, and the two savagely sardonic middle movements, only the most faint-hearted Mahler-lover will want to make do with part of the work.

DEBUSSY (1862-1918): La Mer; Prélude à l'après-midi d'un faune. RAVEL (1875-1937): Daphnis et Chloe, Suite No. 2. *Berlin Philharmonic Orchestra conducted by Herbert von Karajan.* D.G.G. stereo SLPM 138923, mono LPM 18923.

Debussy and Ravel tend to be treated just as much as musical Siamese twins as Haydn and Mozart, or Bruckner and Mahler; and they are just as different. But it is useful to have some of their best orchestral works assembled, in superlative performances, on one disc, for the difference between them is the difference between the two faces of a coin. *L'après-midi d'un faune*, the earliest of the three works, is an evocation of the Mallarmé eclogue about the faun daydreaming in the summer warmth. Dating from 1894, its subdued, shimmering, drifting orchestral colours were hailed by the composer's admirers as the advent of a new chapter in the history of music—as indeed they were. The three symphonic sketches, *La Mer*, date from eleven years later, when the composer's ideas had reached full maturity and he was able to create the most vivid, vast (in scope, not duration), and subtle musical seascape ever written.

Ravel, although a less profound composer than Debussy, had the same knack of setting a scene with the most ravishing beauty of sound. *Daphnis and Chloe*, the "choreographic symphony" written in 1910 for Diaghilev's *Ballet Russe*, shows Ravel's style at its most sumptuous and electrifying. Two orchestral suites have been extracted from the ballet, the second of which opens with a dawn scene alive with birdcalls and ends with a tumultuous dance for the Greek shepherd and shepherdess whose love has been the main topic of the ballet.

German orchestras and conductors are often thought to miss the delicate nuances of Debussy and Ravel; but just how wrong we are to make blanket condemnations is proved by this record, in which Karajan draws sounds of miraculous refinement and radiance from the Berlin Philharmonic, clarifying every detail of rhythm and texture, and immersing himself completely, and with total conviction, in the atmosphere of each work.

DEBUSSY: Nocturnes. RAVEL: Mother Goose Suite.
Orchestre de la Suisse Romande conducted by Ernest Ansermet. Decca stereo SXL 2062, mono LXT 5426.

Debussy wrote his three *Nocturnes* between *L'Après-midi* and *La Mer*, at the same time as he was working on *Pelléas et Mélisande*. They are not nocturnes in the Chopinesque sense, but are intended to convey different effects of light—originally he thought of calling them *Twilight Scenes*. The first piece, *Nuages*, is said to have found its inspiration in the sight of thunder clouds from the Pont de la Concorde in Paris and the mournful sound of the hooters of the boats passing below. *Fêtes* is a tingling evocation of a festival in the Bois de Boulogne, through which a mysterious procession advances and recedes. *Sirènes* is a magical seascape in which the waves, as the composer expressively put it, are "silvered by the moonlight." Here, more than in any of his other works, Debussy functions as a musical equivalent of the impressionist painters. *Nuages* is popularly likened to Monet, *Fêtes* to Renoir, and *Sirènes* to Turner.

Ravel first wrote his *Mother Goose* suite as a piano duet for the children of some friends, but later orchestrated it and extended it into a ballet. A series of short, ravishing studies of fairy-tale characters, it inspired in Ravel (as did *L'Enfant et les Sortilèges*) a vein of tenderness quite unusual in his music. The picture of Petit Poucet lost in the forest, in particular, is an exquisite miniature of great feeling and beauty, with a theme that keeps going back to where it started and an imaginative portrayal of the birds eating up the trail of bread the little boy has left behind. Although some conductors have been known to give the rhythm more "snap", no one catches the refined, luminous colours and tenuous beauty of these works more sensitively than Ernest Ansermet; and the Ravel side has an unexpected bonus in the form of a prelude and spinning-wheel dance not normally included in the concert suite.

ELGAR (1857-1934): Enigma Variations.   BRAHMS: Variations on a Theme of Haydn. *London Symphony Orchestra conducted by Pierre Monteux.*   R.C.A. stereo VICS 1107, mono VIC 1107.

At one time Elgar was thought to be the musical epitome of all that is grandiose and patriotic in the British character. He composed marches with titles like *Pomp and Circumstance* and *The Crown of India;* the slow movement of his second symphony is an elegy on the death of Edward VII; and, in order that no one should mistake his intentions, he had a habit of spattering his music with such directions as *nobilmente* and *allargando*. To begin with he was admired for the imperial splendour of his writing; later he was reviled for it; today his fortunes seem to have changed once again, and instead of liking or disliking the vein of Edwardian self-assurance that runs through his music, we now sometimes deny that it even exists—so much so that a contributor to *The Listener* in 1964 was able to write, without arousing controversy, that Elgar never really conceived a confident vision in his life.

The present-day view of Elgar—encouraged by the touching and sensitive television film on the life of this sad, complicated man—is no doubt nearer the mark than the original one, but it still does not give a completely balanced picture. The *nobilmente* qualities, whether conceived confidently or otherwise, are undeniably there in the music; and another generation may pass before we can get them satisfactorily into focus. The *Enigma Variations*, the earliest and most popular of Elgar's major orchestral works, contains its share of them: in the variation entitled *Nimrod*, which is often performed out of context on occasions that demand noble music, and in the long and martial finale, which brings in a booming organ to bolster the harmony. But the rest of the work—consisting of sharp, intimate sketches of some of Elgar's friends, each referred to by initials or a nickname—contains some of the composer's most delicately expressive and fastidious writing. There is an old and rather foolish belief that only British conductors can ever hold the secret of Elgar's music. a nonsense successfully scotched in this deeply-felt and wonderfully alive performance under the veteran French conductor, in which every phrase is shaped with love and inner parts glow with beauty. In addition, the record usefully complements those listed in the Brahms section of this book, for it includes, in an equally lively, springy, and satisfying performance, the *Variations on a Theme of Haydn*, perhaps the most radiant of all Brahms's orchestral works.

ELGAR: Introduction and Allegro for strings; Serenade for strings.   VAUGHAN WILLIAMS (1872-1958): Fantasia on a theme of Thomas Tallis; Fantasia on Greensleeves.
Sinfonia of London conducted by Sir John Barbirolli.
H.M.V. stereo ASD 521, mono ALP 1970

Here, conveniently assembled, are two major masterpieces of British string music, and two minor ones. The earliest is the lovely little serenade (1892), whose pensive slow movement touchingly anticipates the great Elgar works to follow. Elgar, himself a violinist, wrote particularly perceptively for strings, and nowhere more so than in his sublime *Introduction and Allegro*, conceived on a clifftop in Cardiganshire in 1902 and completed three years later, with a quotation from *Cymbeline*—"A smiling with a sigh"—inscribed on the title page. The quotation is apt; the music, in which a solo string quartet is contrasted with the rest of the orchestra, has the spirit and the good tunes we expect of Elgar, and also a sadness lurking behind every phrase.

Vaughan Williams's *Tallis Fantasia* dates from 1910, and is his first important orchestral work. The theme to which it owes its inspiration is called *Why fumeth in fight*—a sentiment as appropriate to Vaughan Williams's personality as the Shakespeare quotation to Elgar's. As in the *Introduction and Allegro*, solo instruments mingle with a large body of strings to richly expressive effect. The announcement of the theme, divided between different sections of the orchestra beneath a sustained high note from the violins, is magical; so, too, the gentle intertwining of solo violin and viola later. In his official study of Vaughan Williams's music, Michael Kennedy compares parts of this work with sunlight flooding through the arches and coloured glass of the cathedrals in which it is often played. The *Greensleeves Fantasia* (1934) is shorter and simpler, is adapted from the opera *Sir John in Love*, and uses, in addition to the evergreen tune, another peaceful folk-song entitled *Lovely Joan*.

Sir John in Love would also be an appropriate title for this record, every moment of which radiates the conductor's love of the music. The Elgar *Introduction and Allegro*, which he first recorded on two plum labels in the early nineteen-thirties, has long been one of his favourite works. This latest recording (1963) is mellow and expansive; the themes are encouraged to bloom, and the lively fugato section is not raced off its feet—a trait of conductors less sensitive to the gait of the music. The other works are similarly treated, with lyrical ardour, humanity, and beauty of tone.

ELGAR: Symphony No. 1 in A flat major. *Philharmonia Orchestra conducted by Sir John Barbirolli.* H.M.V. stereo ASD 540, mono ALP 1989.

Like Brahms, Elgar waited until his middle years before producing a symphony; he then wrote two in quick succession. The first, dating from 1908, was originally to be a portrait of General Gordon; but in the end the composer preferred to describe it as the expression of "a wide experience of human life with a great charity and a massive hope in the future." It is written, like its successor, on the broadest scale; and the grandeur of its thought can be gauged at once by the noble tread of the huge theme with which it opens. This theme serves as the *motto* of the work; and there are other themes no less rich, such as that of the scherzo, which gradually transforms itself, in one of the most haunting passages of all symphonic music, into the beautiful theme of the slow movement.

At its premiere, conducted in Manchester by Hans Richter, the work was an instant success, and it was performed no fewer than a hundred times in its first year (no new work today has such luck). After a period of neglect, it is now once again recognised as a masterpiece; and the 1963 recording by Sir John Barbirolli, another conductor with Manchester connections, is the second he has made of it in recent years. His performance is that of a profoundly committed Elgarian; it has, in abundance, all the spaciousness, the poetry and plaintiveness, and the ripe eloquence that the music requires.

ELGAR: Symphony No. 2 in E flat major; Symphonic study, Falstaff. *Hallé Orchestra conducted by Sir John Barbirolli.* H.M.V. stereo ASD 610-1, mono ALP 2061-2.

Elgar wrote his second symphony in tribute to Edward VII; and it is often looked on as a memorial to the whole Edwardian era, during which Elgar produced many of his greatest works. Grandeur the music inevitably contains: in the muscular unfurling of the first movement, as exhilarating an opening page as a symphony could hope to possess, and in the broad, flowing tune from which so much of the long finale is built. But there is also, as always in Elgar, pathos beneath the pageantry; and the slow movement, a golden elegy for the late king, reveals clearly and movingly the fundamental melancholy of the composer's mind.

Falstaff, which followed two years later, is in many ways Elgar's masterpiece, though is has never achieved the popularity it deserves. In nature and style, it has something in common with Strauss's *Don Quixote*: a warmly human character study, packed with incident and yet marvellously concentrated and convincing as a whole, richly comic in a way that Elgar unfortunately seldom allowed himself to be, picturesque, dreamy, wistful, tender, full of the composer's

94

love for London and for the peaceful fields of Gloucestershire, and finally, with the old knight's downfall, intensely touching.

Sir John Barbirolli's 1964 recording of the symphony is even broader than his previous (and now deleted) one—which has necessitated the music spilling over on to a second record. It may seem a pity that the symphony and *Falstaff* have thus been turned into Siamese twins, but the performances are so red-blooded and spontaneous that it would be curmudgeonly to grumble. Sir John shapes the music with great elasticity; and although we know that Elgar liked his works to be flexibly played, some listeners may find the Barbirolli treatment too much of a good thing. For them, Sir Adrian Boult's more straightforward approach will be preferable, but the lack of body of both his recordings (one with the Scottish National Orchestra, the other with the London Philharmonic) diminishes the nobility of his performance.

Although scarcely a "key" record, a collection of Elgar's shorter pieces performed by the Royal Philharmonic under the veteran conductor Lawrance Collingwood is a peculiarly endearing issue (H.M.V. stereo CSD 1555, mono CLP 1766). Entitled *The Miniature Elgar* and inspired by the touching television profile of the composer, it reveals the most gentle side of his nature. Here are excerpts from the *Wand of Youth* suites, music he wrote as a boy for private theatricals; some pieces from *The Starlight Express*, and other attractive odds and ends, all played with appropriate intimacy and sympathy. Elgar's miniatures, as we are coming to realise, shed as much light on his intricate personality as his large canvases. Some more of them, including the melodious and fanciful *Nursery Suite*, composed towards the end of his life, are conducted by Collingwood on a bargain record (Music for Pleasure mono MFP 2046) that deserves a treasured place in every Elgar-lover's collection.

ELGAR: Cello concerto; Sea Pictures. *Jacqueline du Pré/Janet Baker/London Symphony Orchestra conducted by Sir John Barbirolli.* H.M.V. stereo ASD 655, mono ALP 2106.

"This is the best of me," wrote Elgar of *The Dream of Gerontius*. In fact, something still finer was to come eighteen years later, in 1918, with the composition of the cello concerto, the most subtly poetic and touching and elusive of his works. Not all cellists, not even the most gifted and mature, have managed to catch the deeply felt, inward, pessimistic beauty of this late, great masterpiece, composed in the twilight of his career. But here, in a performer only 20 years old, it seems to have found its ideal interpreter. Jacqueline du Pré's amazingly profound, searching, and absolutely assured performance may deepen still more in the years to come, but it is hard to imagine anything more stirring than the amber glory of her playing, caught in its full youthful spontaneity on this record.

DELIUS (1862-1934): Brigg Fair; Fennimore and Gerda (intermezzo); Marche-caprice; On hearing the first cuckoo in spring; Sleigh-ride; A song before sunrise; Summer night on the river. *Royal Philharmonic Orchestra conducted by Sir Thomas Beecham.* H.M.V. stereo ASD 357, mono ALP 1586.

Sir Thomas Beecham, more than any other conductor, held the secret of Delius's music: and his death in 1961 left a void that still shows no sign of being filled. It may be that, in the future, another figure will appear who can capture the essential Delius magic. The time is certainly ripe for a reappraisal of his music, which to some ears is too sweet and formless and nostalgic (Cecil Gray claimed that the Delius "style" had its origin in syphilis, and said it was just the same with the lush Tahiti paintings of Gauguin—an interesting, if debatable, theory) but which is much wider in range and feeling than is commonly supposed.

Beecham's efforts on behalf of Delius, whom he considered the only really original English composer since Purcell (though in fact he was born of German-Dutch parentage and lived very little of his life in England), have fortunately left us with a wealth of fine recordings, starting with the famous pioneering Delius Society volumes on 78, and ending with some LP performances made by Sir Thomas in his last years. Unhappily, not all his records are at present available, and we must hope that the more serious deletions will be restored to the catalogue. The seven pieces in the above record form an admirable introduction to the gentler, dreamier side of Delius's nature. *On hearing the first cuckoo in spring* is the most popular, and perhaps the most expressive, of all his country idylls; the items are scarcely less poetic and all are beautifully played, the pensive stillness of *Summer night on the river* in particular being exquisitely sustained.

RICHARD STRAUSS (1864-1949): Don Quixote; Don Juan. *Pierre Fournier/Cleveland Orchestra conducted by George Szell.* Columbia stereo SAX 2495, mono 33CX 1852.

Strauss's main contribution to the concert repertoire was his series of sumptuous symphonic poems, in which he used the orchestra with a richness, vividness, and panache that had never before been achieved and has never since been surpassed. Sometimes, as in parts of *Ein Heldenleben*, he unleashed his vast orchestral forces on insignificant material; but at other times, with inspiration aflame, the ends fully justified the elaborate means. *Don Juan* (1888) was his first symphonic poem to become popular; in it, the amorous adventures and final downfall of the rake are portrayed with a youthful exuberance and glitter, and with a chain of glowing melodies, which, however well we know them, remain irresistibly alluring.

If the compact *Don Juan* is Strauss's most approachable work, *Don Quixote* (1897) is his masterpiece—a longer symphonic poem in variation form, with important parts for cello and viola (representing the Don and Sancho Panza), with extravagant pictorial effects (the episodes of the flock of sheep and the flight on the wooden horse), and with a wit and deep psychological insight into the characters of the Cervantes tragi-comedy. The many reflective passages, especially those of the closing pages, are intensely beautiful and sad and touching. Pierre Fournier has twice recorded this work on LP, and his earlier performance—a magical one with Clemens Krauss and the Vienna Philharmonic—is still available (Decca mono LXT 2842). But the 1954 recording is not quite equal to the delights of the music, and readers will find the 1963 version a more satisfying choice, for Fournier's performance has the same poetic feeling and beauty of tone, and the orchestral playing, though it lacks a little of the love that the Vienna orchestra poured into the music, has marvellous clarity and point. So, too, the sizzling account of *Don Juan*, which certainly tips the balance in favour of the newer disc.

SIBELIUS (1865-1957): Symphony No. 2 in D major.
Concertgebouw Orchestra conducted by George Szell.
Philips stereo SAL 3515, mono AL 3515.

There are few composers whose childhood compositions give much clue to their future developments. Mozart's earliest minuet, produced at the age of three or thereabouts, was no doubt a remarkable achievement; but no one would recognise in it the seeds of the *Jupiter* symphony. Sibelius's first work, on the other hand, seems to have been peculiarly significant. Composed when he was ten, it was called *Drops of Water* and was a pizzicato duet for violin and cello. Pizzicato passages were to become one of his most regular fingerprints; and the equation of his music with water has become standard practice among programme annotators at a loss for words. The second symphony, dating from 1901, was his first major work to present both features in full strength. The rushing pizzicato of the massed strings in the first movement, the sinister pizzicati of the double basses and cellos in the andante, these sound just as individual today as they must have done when they were written; and the clear pure water imagery, which after all had the composer's own sanction, is surely the most apt description of the sober clarity and beauty of the orchestral colouring.

Yet dedicated Sibelians usually reveal suprise and dismay that this, of all his symphonies, is the one that has become most popular with the public. They point to weaknesses, both melodic and structural, in the finale; and add, in vain, that a dose of the fourth and sixth symphonies would be the best corrective. Those, unquestionably, are the more subtle and masterly works—sparse, elliptical, concentrated, uncompromising pieces, the first of them fierce in its icy intensity, the other sparkling like winter sunshine. But they are caviare to the general; and the public's preference for the more accessible second symphony, with its clearly-etched dramatic progress and final mighty paean, is perfectly understandable. Of the seven symphonies, it is the most frequently recorded. Some conductors have allowed the drama of the music to tempt them into gimmicky, exaggerated readings, italicising each point so that it loses its interest and surprise. This is the fault of the high-powercd Maazel performance on Decca—he just won't let the music alone. George Szell, on the other hand, encourages it to sweep forward clearly and naturally; the playing of the great Dutch orchestra (un-accustomed to Sibelius though the musicians must be) is wonderfully strong and eloquent; and the only controversial feature of the performance is the conductor's decision to broaden the tempo at the climax of the finale.

As a possible alternative to Szell, impecunious collectors are recommended to the bargain-price Decca performance by the London Symphony Orchestra under Anthony Collins (mono ACL 34). Collins recorded all the symphonies in the early days of LP, and most of them still sound well. Their main faults are occasionally rushed tempi and too much emphasis on the percussion—the performance of the second symphony, for instance, uses an alternative ending in which the brass's peroration is supported by some dis-turbing thwacks on the timpani.

SIBELIUS: Symphony No. 4 in A minor; Symphonic poem, Pohjola's Daughter. *London Symphony Orchestra conducted by Anthony Collins.* Decca mono ACL 184.

"Nothing, absolutely nothing, of the circus about it," wrote Sibelius of his fourth symphony. In this grim landscape with-out figures, composed when he was in his middle forties, we reach the heart of the Sibelius country. Robert Layton, in his admirable book on the composer, relates that the austerity of the music earned it the title of the *Barkbröd* symphony—a reminder of the hard days in nineteenth-century Scandinavia when starvation compelled some of its victims to eat the bark of trees. Certainly, it is a work on which there is no surplus vegetation, a symphony stripped to its essentials. Its strange, chilly beauty never becomes softened by familiarity, though the harsh intensity of its feeling is sometimes sugared by conductors intent on beautifying the line of the music. This, Collins takes care not to do. His performance is strong and sane; and although it does not manage to give us the full truth about what is arguably the greatest symphony of the century, it has yet to be surpassed by another LP performance. Like his other Sibelius records, it sells at bargain-price; and it includes also an admirable account of *Pohjola's Daughter*, composed five years earlier. As with many of Sibelius's other works, this symphonic poem has its inspiration in Finnish folk-lore. Its programme concerns a northern hero who is asked to prove his love for the maiden Pohjola by performing a series of magical feats—including tying an egg in invisible knots. All this is closely followed in the music, which nevertheless manages to retain a coherent and impressive symphonic structure. In recent years, a school of thought has arisen that deems Sibelius's symphonic poems to be greater than his symphonies; but a more balanced judgment would surely be that he composed great masterpieces in both forms, and that we still do not hear the greatest of them often enough.

SIBELIUS: Symphony No. 5 in E flat major; Karelia suite. *London Symphony Orchestra conducted by Alexander Gibson.* R.C.A. Victrola stereo VICS 1016, mono VIC 1016.

Emotionally, Sibelius's fifth symphony is more a successor to his second than to his fourth. Like the second, it is clear-cut and affirmative; and, not unexpectedly, it has become very nearly as popular. The powerfully sculptured first movement culminates in a concentrated, swirling scherzo that is one of the most exhilarating passages in twentieth-century music; the short, swaying slow movement is built from a mesmerically-repeated theme; and the finale, in Tovey's memorable phrase, opens with a rushing wind, through which Thor can presently be heard swinging his hammer. The peroration, ending with six incisive, widely-detached hammer-blows, is Sibelius at his most grandly sonorous.

For all its directness, the symphony has not always fared well at the hands of its interpreters, too many of whom regard it as a handy vehicle for their own self-glory. But Alexander Gibson, perhaps the most sensitive and sensible of the younger generation of Sibelius conductors, never thrusts himself in front of the music. To begin with, perhaps, one slightly misses the fierceness that other conductors bring to this work; but one quickly grows to enjoy the milder climate of Gibson's reading, which conveys the drama of the music with a grave and natural eloquence, never underlining points unnecessarily or pressing on the accelerator to the detriment of articulation. Why R.C.A. has not asked him to record some of Sibelius's other orchestral works, of which fully convincing and idiomatic performances are few and far between, is a mystery.

The three *Karelia* movements included as a filler are minor Sibelius, dating back to the earliest years of his career; but they are crisp, melodious, and excitingly worked up, and it is easy to see why one of them was chosen as the signature-tune of the television documentary, *This Week*. The recording, first issued in 1958, is now available at bargain price.

SIBELIUS: Symphony No. 6 in D minor; Pelléas and Mélisande, suite. *London Symphony Orchestra conducted by Anthony Collins.* Decca mono ACL 228.

The sixth (1923) is the most serenely reticent of Sibelius's symphonies—and it has paid for this by being played perhaps even more rarely than the fourth. Cecil Gray, that eloquent Sibelius advocate, wrote admiringly of its "softly luminous pearl greys and light browns"; and its pale, restrained colouring is matched by a subtle symphonic strength that grows more and more fascinating the better one gets to know it. Indeed, one can hardly think of any other twentieth-century symphonic masterpiece, unless it be Sibelius's fourth symphony, in which ends and means are more ideally suited to each other. Anthony Collins's performance, though a little more perfunctory than his account of the fourth symphony, nevertheless gives a good impression of the wintry, pastoral beauty of the music; and to complete the record there are four of the nine, cool, imaginative pieces Sibelius wrote in 1905 as incidental music to the Maeterlinck tragedy.

The seventh symphony (1924), in which Sibelius sonsolidated his structural ideas into a single movement, has never fared well on LP. But as no Sibelius collection would be complete without this noble valedictory work, readers are recommended with reservations to the Saga recording of it by Alexander Gibson and the Scottish National Orchestra (stereo and mono STXID 5284), a performance whose defects are a lack of thrust in the orchestra and a lack of richness in the recording, which was made in 1965 in the dry acoustics of the Usher Hall, Edinburgh. Yet Gibson's poetic, thoughtful interpretation contains much to admire; and it is coupled with an excellent, crisp, cogent, unhurried account of the superbly muscular and underrated third symphony (1907), a much more satisfactory performance than the overdriven Collins one, which has reigned in the catalogue since 1954, and which costs twice as much.

SIBELIUS: Tone poem, Tapiola. Pieces by DELIUS, DVORAK, FAURE, and GRIEG. *Royal Philharmonic Orchestra conducted by Sir Thomas Beecham.* H.M.V. stereo ASD 518, mono ALP 1968.

Although he wrote some minor pieces after it, *Tapiola* was to all intents and purposes Sibelius's swansong. He was 61 when he composed it; he was to live on for another 31 years; but, wise after the event, we now find in this grim, lonely, concentrated music such an air of finality that it is hard to imagine where Sibelius might have gone from there. Elgar, it is said, was once so shaken by a performance of Berlioz's *March to the Scaffold* that the hairs of his moustache stood on end as he listened to it. *Tapiola*, too, is a terrifying score— but here the terror stems not from hostile humanity but from hostile nature. The music, which grows almost entirely from the brooding theme heard at the beginning, explores the same territory as the fourth symphony, but here everything is even darker and bleaker. The score is prefaced by some lines describing the Northland's dusky forests and the mighty god (Tapio) who dwells within them. There are long-held chords and sudden silences, eerie skirls from the woodwind and menacing interjections from the brass. Towards the end, in one of the most chilling passages in all music, a great storm arises. When it dies away, there is no hymn of thanksgiving à la Beethoven, only a feeling of overwhelming space and solitude.

Sir Thomas Beecham, like Kajanus and Koussevitsky, was one of the great first-generation Sibelians; and it is a

102

pity that the recordings he made did not always catch him at his finest. In the concert hall, his performance of *Tapiola* could be a more intense experience than the one we have here. Even so, it is good to have this souvenir, eked out with a number of the odds and ends he loved to conduct and which have come to be known as "Beecham lollipops." Those on hand comprise Delius's *A Summer Evening* and the prelude to *Irmelin*; Dvořák's third *Legend*; Grieg's second *Symphonic Dance*; and perhaps the pick of the bunch, Fauré's sad, drooping *Pavane* (this played by the French National Radio Orchestra).

RAKHMANINOV (1873-1943): Piano concerto No. 2 in C minor; Preludes in B major, Op. 23, No. 2; D major, Op. 23, No. 4; G minor, Op. 23, No. 5; C minor, Op. 23, No. 7; C major, Op. 32, No. 1; B minor, Op. 32, No. 2. *Sviatoslav Richter/Warsaw Philharmonic-Symphony Orchestra conducted by Stanislaw Wislocki.* D.G.G. stereo SLPM 138076, mono LPM 18596.

Rakhmaninov's second piano concerto vies with Tchaikovsky's first for the title of the most popular concerto ever written. Tchaikovsky was 34 when he composed his concerto; Rakhmaninov was 28, and in the process of recovering from a nervous breakdown that had shattered his confidence as a composer. Both works use similar, rich ingredients: lavishly abundant, juicy melodies, often yearningly eloquent in quality, and a piano part of the utmost splendour and virtuosity. Although dating from before the birth of the talkies, the Rakhmaninov has subsequently become a film-maker's paradise, turning up on the soundtrack of many films (*Brief Encounter* sticks especially in the memory), being used as the subject of the hilarious mock-seduction scene in *The Seven Year Itch*, and having the main theme of its finale turned into a popular song called *Full moon and empty arms*. But it has survived all the raids that have been made on it; and although, since his death, the characteristics of Rakhmaninov's style have been emulated by many composers, none of them has possessed the particular lyrical and melodic inspiration that has given the master's best works their staying power.

Among innumerable recordings, Richter's stands out as

the one that most overwhelmingly catches the nervy, melancholy intensity of the music, and space has been found on side two for half a dozen of the 24 preludes for solo piano, concentrated, sharply inventive pieces which Rakhmaninov wrote as a follow-up to the Chopin set.

RAKHMANINOV: Piano concerto No. 3 in D minor.
Vladimir Ashkenazy/London Symphony Orchestra conducted by Anatole Fistoulari. Decca stereo SXL 6057, mono LXT 6057.

Rakhmaninov's third piano concerto (1909) explores the same vein of romantic melancholy as his second, but in construction it is much more subtle. From the veiled rhythm intoned by the woodwind at the start of the first movement (a rhythm that is to haunt the whole work) right through to the huge, soaring theme at the end of the finale, there is a feeling of growth and logic which its more straightforward predecessor lacks. Although just as difficult to play, the piano part is less obviously "virtuoso" in quality: instead of being spotlit, it is intricately woven into the orchestral texture. The young Russian pianist Vladimir Ashkenazy stresses this aspect of the writing by giving a performance which is refreshingly unostentatious, yet always absolutely assured. In the fast movements, his playing is elegant and aristocratic; and in the intermezzo, he catches with wonderful naturalness all the poetry of what John Culshaw, in his study of the composer, has called the saddest music Rakhmaninov ever wrote.

HOLST (1874-1934): The Planets. *Vienna Philharmonic Orchestra conducted by Herbert von Karajan.* Decca stereo SXL 2305, mono LXT 5669.

The full stature of Holst has yet to be discovered. Perhaps the element of mysticism in his make-up has made us suspect his worth as a composer. Perhaps, because he often wrote for amateurs and was prone for much of his career to turn out cosy folk-song settings, he has come to be looked on by many people as something of an amateur himself, But he was far from being that. Like Dvorak, he started as an orchestral player—a trombonist in ensembles ranging from the Scottish Orchestra to Wurm's White Viennese Band—and his understanding of the orchestra is revealed at its most brilliant and startling in his one really popular work, *The Planets* suite he composed in 1913 in tribute to his enthusiasm for astrology. Each of its seven movements portrays a different planet; and although the inspiration is uneven (the shoe-horning of the school-songlike *I vow to thee my country* into the *Jupiter* movement was a glaring gaffe), the best of it is strong and original. *Mercury, the winged messenger* is depicted with a whirling, gleaming, faintly Russian beauty; and the mysterious calm of *Venus, the bringer of love* and *Saturn, the bringer of old age* anticipates the austere, inward, often fascinating works of the composer's last years.

That *The Planets* is of more than local British interest is proven by the fact that it has been taken up by conductors and orchestras in other countries. A recording by Stokowski was a misfire, for it tampered with the orchestration and character of the music; but Karajan's, marvellously recorded, is a distinct success, performed with the utmost clarity and beauty of tone, and recommended to all but extreme anglomaniacs who believe that only an English conductor can hold the key to Holst. All the same, a new recording by Sir Adrian Boult would be welcome, for he has long been associated with this work, and the two attempts that have been made to capture his performance on LP have failed to convey the splendour of his reading.

HOLST: Hammersmith, prelude and scherzo; Suite No. 1 in E flat major; Suite No. 2 in F major. VAUGHAN WILLIAMS: English Folk Song Suite; Toccata Marziale. *Eastman Wind Ensemble conducted by Frederick Fennell.* Philips mono GL 5840.

Holst's Hammersmith pieces were the result of a B.B.C. commission to write a work for military band. The result, one of the most imaginative products of his last years, never received the performance for which it was commissioned; and it was not until a quarter of a century later, in America, that the music had its first performance in the form in which Holst envisaged it. It is a masterpiece—a poetic, atmospheric evocation of the Thames and the bustle of the part of London that Holst knew best and where he lived for much of his life. No city, surely, has had a finer tribute paid to it, in music of extraordinary feeling and vitality, variety and originality. Here a virtuoso American ensemble, closely associated with this work, gives it a superb and deeply stirring performance on a bargain-price disc crammed with other crisp wind pieces by Holst and his friend and contemporary, Vaughan Williams. The F major suite ends with the *Fantasia on the Dargason* better known in its string version as the finale of the *St. Paul's Suite*.

JANACEK (1854-1928): Sinfonietta; Taras Bulba.
Czech Philharmonic Orchestra conducted by Karel Ancerl.
Supraphon stereo SUA ST 50022, mono SUA 10380.

It is only recently that Janáček's greatness has begun to be recognised outside his native Czechoslovakia. True, the majestically sonorous sinfonietta, with its opening and closing fanfares of trumpets, tubas, and drums, and the epic rhapsody *Taras Bulba* have made intermittent appearances in British orchestral programmes ever since the days of Sir Henry Wood; Rafael Kubelik and Charles Mackerras (who studied under the great Czech conductor Vaclav Talich) have introduced some of his operas to London; but it was, more than anything, the visit of the Prague Opera to the 1964 Edinburgh Festival, with its vibrantly sympathetic and authentic Czech performances of *Katya Kabanova*, *From the House of the Dead*, and the *Glagolitic Mass*, that established Janáček, for many of us, as a major and deeply stirring composer, whose fusion of terseness with tenderness, and whose extremely personal style, made him one of the most endearing and fascinating figures in musical history.

The sinfonietta, composed for a Czech gymnastic festival in 1926, is one of the stream of masterpieces he poured out, with new spontaneity and freshness, towards the end of his long life. Apart from the fanfares that have made it famous, the music is lyrical and melodious, and includes a burlesque dance that anticipates the haunting riverbank scene in his opera *From the House of the Dead*, when the prisoners,

106

allowed briefly to forget themselves, perform amateur theatricals.

Taras Bulba, an earlier work, has its inspiration in Gogol. Janáček called it "a musical testament"; and it was written, as an expression of his nation's struggle for survival, during the First World War. Although its style is broader and fruitier than that of the sinfonietta, it clearly comes from the same hand; and between them, these two works form a varied and admirable introduction to his music. The Czech performances are warm-hearted and idiomatic, alive to the sudden changes of tempo and key that are so much a characteristic of this composer. The recording, another of Supraphon's bargains, is generally clear without being quite the last word in hi-fi.

NIELSEN (1865-1931): Symphony No. 5. *New York Philharmonic Orchestra conducted by Leonard Bernstein.* C.B.S. stereo SBRG 72110, mono BRG 72110.

The Danish composer Carl Nielsen, like the Czechoslovakian Janáček, is one of those quirkily individual, national figures of the past hundred years whose music, though greatly admired in his homeland, has failed to win wide favour abroad. A Nielsen boom in Britain during the nineteen-fifties, partly brought about by the visit of the Danish Radio Orchestra to the Edinburgh Festival, soon went off the boil; but it left many listeners with a taste for his music—and with an intense feeling of annoyance at the fickleness of our concert promoters, who allowed those powerful and exciting works, so bristling with vitality, so varied and absorbing in their argument, so richly melodious and direct and personal in their voice, to drop so quickly from our lives before we had a proper chance to get to know them. The release, in 1963, of this recording by one of America's most popular conductors therefore brought new hope to Nielsen-lovers; and the performance, vital and idiomatic, is in no way disappointing. The music, composed in 1922, unrolls with the inevitability of all great symphonies, and sounds more imposing every time one hears it; and for anyone who does not already know Nielsen's six symphonies, but is curious to hear what they are like, this work makes an ideal introduction. The argument is presented, and resolved, with characteristic bluntness—nowhere more so than in the famous passage where the side-drum is given an *ad lib* cadenza and instructed to do his utmost to disrupt the performance.

Since recording this work, Bernstein has gone on to tackle another Nielsen symphony, the sunnier and less neurotic *Espansiva* (No. 3); but the performance, while agreeably lyrical, has not quite the verve of his earlier effort, nor is the recording (C.B.S. stereo SBRG 72369, mono BRG 72369) quite so clear. Nevertheless, the music, with its enjoyably punchy opening movement, its airy and imaginative slow movement (which makes haunting use of two wordless human voices), and its broadly flowing finale, is so striking and lovable that readers are urged to give it a try.

VAUGHAN WILLIAMS: A London Symphony.
London Philharmonic Orchestra conducted by Sir Adrian Boult. Decca mono LXT 2693.

Like others before him, Vaughan Williams composed nine symphonies. In his lifetime, at least four of them were thought to be masterpieces, and he to be the greatest British composer of his generation. Since then the tide has turned with a vengeance, and for some years his music has been suffering from the period of neglect—and even, in some quarters, of disparagement—that is apt to come to even the best composers immediately after their death. The Howard Hartog survey of modern European music, published in 1957, pointed the way. It dismissed Vaughan Williams in a few lines as a nationalist composer who had arrived ninety years too late. Although, to those who cherish his music, barbs like this may be irritating, they will probably do no harm in the long run. There seems little doubt that Vaughan Williams's reputation will rise again quite soon, just as Sibelius's, which suffered a similar decline, is now doing. It may be that his ultimate position on the musical Parnassus will be lower than was once hoped; but he will have his place nevertheless, and the recent absence of his music from the concert hall makes one eager to savour it again, and to assess it anew. Its flavour, of course, is obstinately English. At worst it has a tweedy, pastoral quality, which Michael Kennedy has aptly described as "an oboe with muted strings as background." At best it has a grave beauty, and sometimes a pugnacity and gruff humour, that make it a strong and rewarding experience.

The *London Symphony* (1914, revised 1920) is not, perhaps, the greatest of his works in this form, but its vitality and poetry easily outweigh a number of passages where inspiration threatens to descend to the level of a J. Arthur Rank travelogue. At the start, the gradual emerging of the city from its early morning haze is wonderfully sensitive, with an impressionistic beauty that reminds us that Vaughan Williams studied briefly under Ravel. The serene, regretful slow movement, which the composer likened to Bloomsbury Square on a November afternoon, and the nocturnal, rustling scherzo evoke nostalgically a London we shall never see again—a London of hansom cabs rather than diesel fumes. In the finale comes a slow, dignified march, which shuns all elements of pomp and circumstance; and at the end the vision gradually fades, even more magically than it appeared.

Sir Adrian Boult recorded all but one of Vaughan Williams's symphonies for Decca in the nineteen-fifties, and these warm-hearted, alive, and authoritative performances have fortunately been retained in the catalogue all through the years when the music has been largely absent from the concert hall. One cannot imagine a better account of the *London Symphony*: the stirring of the city from its slumber, the sense of enjoyment Boult brings to the perky tunes of the first movement, the marvellously sustained, soft, rapt, poignant beauty of the slow movement, the dark and light of the scherzo, the stillness of the closing pages—these, surely, are riches enough to make the record survive changes of fashion and to give profound enjoyment for many years to come. The clarity of the recording, outstanding in 1952 when it was issued, still sounds perfectly satisfactory today.

VAUGHAN WILLIAMS: Symphony No. 4 in F minor.
London Philharmonic Orchestra conducted by Sir Adrian Boult. Decca mono LXT 2909.

Written in the early nineteen-thirties, this is, for Vaughan Williams, an unexpectedly violent and restless work in which programme annotators like to find a musical anticipation of the holocaust of the Second World War. In fact, as

Michael Kennedy has pointed out, we should be wary of interpreting it as a political warning. Its tautness of style and stark harmonic idiom were really the outcome of a vigorous decade in the composer's career; he himself showed awareness of this in his celebrated remark, "I don't know whether I like it, but this is what I meant", and, having got this work off his chest, he moved on to a more reflective and relaxed period in his output. Whether or not one likes it, it is certainly a key work in the history of British music, which Sir Adrian Boult's commanding performance catches with splendid vitality. The crackling rhythms bite deep, without being made to sound exaggerated or neurotic; and the grinding dissonance of much of the writing does not prevent Sir Adrian from finding, and cherishing, some passages of repose which more aggressive conductors ride roughshod over.

VAUGHAN WILLIAMS: Symphony No. 5 in D major.
London Philharmonic Orchestra conducted by Sir Adrian Boult. Decca mono LXT 2910.

This symphony, begun just before the Second World War and completed in 1943, reveals the more contemplative side of Vaughan Williams's nature. It is the most personal of all his symphonies and the most beautifully fashioned, a work of great serenity and character: in fact, his masterpiece. The music, especially the slow movement, shares material with his opera *The Pilgrim's Progress*, and the spirit of Bunyan seems to pervade the whole work. "None of Vaughan Williams's symphonies requires such polished playing as this," says Michael Kennedy. "Its pellucid textures, its finely calculated balance between orchestral sections and its rhythmical elasticity require careful rehearsal, especially in the scherzo." In Sir Adrian Boult's noble performance, all these details are lovingly attended to; the catalogues contain no finer testimony of Vaughan Williams's greatness than this.

VAUGHAN WILLIAMS: Symphony No. 6 in E minor.
London Philharmonic Orchestra conducted by Sir Adrian Boult. Decca mono LXT 2911.

Whereas the fourth is predominantly assertive and the fifth

predominantly tranquil, Vaughan Williams's sixth symphony (1944-7) is less clearly defined in mood. The first movement is tart and brash, but with flashes of stomping jocularity and pastoral lyricism; the slow movement is grim and sinister throughout; the scherzo is angry, with the saxophone in places pouring oil on troubled waters; and the finale, a *locus classicus* of twentieth-century music, is an eerie pianissimo sustained for nearly quarter of an hour, full of strange, shifting harmonies, enigmatically murmuring strings, forlorn phrases from the woodwind. Again, Sir Adrian Boult's performance is all that could be desired—strong and sharply chiselled in the first three movements, wonderfully controlled in the veiled epilogue. As a charming postscript, the record includes a characteristic little speech from the composer himself, thanking conductor and orchestra for their achievement, praising their endurance over the three hours that were spent on recording the finale, and pointing out that the results were so clear that all the faults of the music came to the surface.

STRAVINSKY (born 1882): The Firebird (complete).
London Symphony Orchestra conducted by Antal Dorati.
Philips stereo SGL 5827, mono GL 5827.

No modern composer is better represented in the record catalogues than Stravinsky. All but his most minor works are now available, in excellent performances, often under the composer's own direction (about which he once wrote that "everyone who listens to my records hears my music free from any distortion of my thought"); and since Stravinsky is, for many listeners, the greatest, most fascinating, most varied and yet most consistent composer of our time, it is good that future generations (always assuming that his reputation does not tumble, like Meyerbeer's and Cimarosa's) will have these authoritative readings to study and marvel at.

The Firebird (1910) was the first work he wrote for the Diaghilev Ballet, and indeed his first work of any significance. Based partly on Russian folk-songs, it is his most shimmering and immediately attractive score, both indebted to and surpassing the music of Rimsky-Korsakov, with a fairy-tale story about a young Prince who ventures into a magic garden, meeting there a beautiful princess, a malevolent ogre, and a dazzling bird with plumage of fire, which acts as *deus ex machina* at the prince's moment of need. The special virtues of Antal Dorati's performance are that he is stunningly recorded (at bargain price), and that he gives us not just the standard concert suite but the complete ballet—which, apart from containing many little-known passages of rare loveliness, is far more coherent and gripping in its overall effect.

STRAVINSKY: Petrushka. *Orchestre de la Suisse Romande conducted by Ernest Ansermet.* Decca stereo SXL 2011, mono LXT 5425.

From a ballet about an enchanted garden, Stravinsky turned to one about a puppet that comes to life. For a 28-year-old composer, *Petrushka* is a work of almost insolent assurance; and its premiere by the Diaghilev Ballet in Paris, with Nijinsky in the title-role, was—unlike the *Rite of Spring* two years later—an instant success. For some listeners, *Petrushka* is still the *ne plus ultra* of Stravinsky's music. Certainly, it is among the most endearing and striking of his scores. Never has the brash and colourful atmosphere of a fairground, and of the frost and snow of a Russian winter, been more sharply or melodiously caught in music. The veteran Swiss conductor Ernest Ansermet, who has received the composer's personal accolade ("one of the most reliable and understanding executants of my compositions"), has twice recorded *Petrushka* for Decca. His first recording (1953) was one of the early triumphs of LP; his second manages to surpass the previous achievement, and brings the whole scene even more vividly to our imagination.

STRAVINSKY: The Rite of Spring. *Columbia Symphony Orchestra conducted by Igor Stravinsky.* C.B.S. stereo SBRG 72054, mono BRG 72054.

The Rite of Spring, which followed two years after *Petrushka*, marked the culmination of Stravinsky's first "period." This time the subject was earth worship; and the music Stravinsky wrote to depict a series of primitive pagan rites (ending with a female victim dancing herself to death in honour of

112

the god of Spring), as well as the scandal caused by the
Diaghilev Ballet's first performance of it in Paris, have made
it a milestone in musical history. Today we take its motoric
rhythmic violence and its harmonic asperities quite easily in
our stride, and see beauty in it where none was detected in
1913—will listeners in the year 2000 feel the same about
Stockhausen? The popularity of *The Rite* is affirmed by
the number of recordings of it that now exist. The two best
are those that have been made by Pierre Boulez (but this,
being a Concert Hall Record Club issue, is not readily
available) and by Stravinsky himself, the latter performance
having a bone-hard rhythmic strength, a clarity of line and
texture, and a fierce, unrelenting concentration that make it
among the most overwhelming experiences the gramophone has to offer. A short spoken commentary by the
composer completes the record.

STRAVINSKY: Apollo; Orpheus. *Columbia and
Chicago Symphony Orchestras conducted by Igor
Stravinsky.* C.B.S. stereo SBRG 72355, mono BRG
72355.

At one time, Stravinsky's successive stylistic changes were
thought to signify a lack of creative potency. Today we can
see that the works which followed the explosion of *The Rite*,
in which he pared his style down to the bone, were just as
characteristic of him, and just as fascinating and inspired,
as anything else he has poured out in his long and extraordinarily fertile career. The ballet *Apollo*, a title the composer now prefers to the original *Apollon Musagetes*, was
written for a festival of contemporary music in Washington
in 1928; and its severely classical subject, describing Apollo's
election as leader of the muses, is reflected in music of grave
serenity, scored throughout for strings and ending with
some of the most sheerly beautiful pages Stravinsky has
ever produced. His own intensely revealing recording of it
is coupled, aptly, with his more recent classical ballet,
Orpheus (1948), composed, not for Diaghilev (who died in
1929), but for the great present-day choreographer, George
Balanchine. Perhaps the most tender of all his scores (even
the composer, who for so long opposed the idea that his
music could be "expressive," more or less admits to its

113

plaintiveness), it receives from him a performance that is a masterpiece of keen clarity and feeling.

STRAVINSKY: Greeting prelude; Eight instrumental miniatures; Circus polka; Dumbarton Oaks concerto; Two suites for small orchestra; Four études for orchestra. *C.B.C and Columbia Symphony Orchestras conducted by Igor Stravinsky.* C.B.S. stereo SBRG 72299, mono BRG 72299.

Entitled *Stravinsky Conducts Favourite Short Pieces*, this record consists mainly of shavings from his workshop; but the music, covering forty years of his career, is so delectable and the performances so spirited that they deserve to take their place alongside more important Stravinsky issues. They are written in his most approachable vein, with a wittiness for which he is not always given credit, and form a perfect introduction to various aspects of his style. The *Greeting prelude*, for instance, is a brilliant and characteristic canonic reworking of *Happy birthday to you*, written in honour of Pierre Monteux's eightieth birthday. The *Circus polka*, written for a Barnum and Bailey elephant called Bessie, is the one that ends with a raucous outburst of Schubert's *Marche militaire*. There is a good deal of the circus, or fairground, about the rest of the record, too; and students of Stravinsky will detect, in the waltz from the second suite for small orchestra, a link between *Petrushka* and the neo-classical works of the nineteen-twenties.

BARTOK (1881-1945): Piano concerto No. 2; Piano concerto No. 3. *Geza Anda/Berlin Philharmonic Orchestra conducted by Ferenc Fricsay.* D.G.G. stereo SLPM 138111, mono LPM 18611.

Bartók is one of the key figures of twentieth-century music, a composer of the utmost integrity and imaginative vigour, a nationalist who worked out his ideas with a fierce and concentrated logic, whose works preserve the flavour of Hungarian folk-music without ever lapsing into the kind of pastiche that was written by Liszt and Brahms when they wanted to sound Hungarian. His three piano concertos, composed over a period of twenty years, show a gradual

114

refining of his style. The first (1926), dating from his most abrasively experimental years, is a hard, clattering, unfriendly work, as forbiddingly difficult to play as it sounds; the second (1931), though no less energetic, shows greater awareness of tonal beauty and contains, in its slow movement, some magical passages of "night" music—the outcome of Bartók's intense fascination for insects, birds, and plants; the third (1945), written just before his death, is predominantly lyrical, opening with a long and ravishing theme, sharply picked out by the soloist in octaves, and including another of Bartók's nocturnal slow movements. Geza Anda and Ferenc Fricsay, both outstanding authorities on the music of this great pianist-composer, here combine to give performances of exhilarating spontaneity and suppleness. As a basis for one's Bartók collection, this record is indispensable.

BARTOK: Music for strings, percussion, and celesta; The Miraculous Mandarin, suite. *London Symphony Orchestra conducted by Georg Solti.* Decca stereo SXL 6111, mono LXT 6111.

The "essential" Bartók is to be found in his six string quartets, which were his most personal works and spanned most of his career. But they are not pieces that yield their secrets immediately; and anyone who finds them tough-going is recommended to approach them by way of the *Music for strings, percussion, and celesta,* in which the writing has the same concentration and intensity but the sonorities have a more immediately appealing range of colour. Indeed, this work—composed in 1936 for the tenth anniversary of the Basle Chamber Orchestra—is perhaps the most striking of all Bartók's experiments in orchestral timbre, and a live performance, with the two sections of the string orchestra separated by the celesta, harp, piano, xylophone, drums, and other percussion instruments, can be a subtle and memorable experience. Today, thirty years after it was written, the music sounds as strange and imaginative as ever; and the adagio, with its high-pitched, other-worldly tapping of the xylophone, its muted glissandi on the timpani, its rustling strings and shimmering celesta and sudden glancing chords on the piano, is one of the most haunting of all Bartók's pieces of night music.

The Miraculous Mandarin represents the more ferocious side of Bartók's character. Although the sordid plot of this pantomime-ballet—concerning a prostitute who entices men to her room in order that they can be beaten up and robbed by her accomplices—has stood in the way of its popularity, the violently emotional music has gained its place in the concert repertoire in the form of an orchestral suite. Georg Solti's performance is typically highly-charged and dazzlingly put over; and in the other work, ideally suited to the wide-spacing of stereo reproduction, he relaxes the tension just long enough to catch the softer, more delicate shades of the music.

BARTOK: Violin concerto No. 2. *Yehudi Menuhin/New Philharmonia Orchestra conducted by Antal Dorati.* H.M.V. stereo ASD 2281, mono ALP 2281.

Dating from 1938, when he was at the height of his powers, this is one of Bartók's most masterly inspirations. The writing has all his fingerprints—the tough strength and concentration of the material, the mysterious sonorities, the poignant lyricism of the slow movement, with its meditative main theme. Yehudi Menuhin has long been associated with this work, and plays it with great understanding. This recording replaces his older one, conducted by Furtwängler, and it finds space (as its predecessor did not) for a welcome encore in the form of six of Bartók's duos—sharp, characteristic little pieces in which Nenuhin is joined by Nell Gotkovsky.

BARTOK: Concerto for Orchestra. *Philadelphia Orchestra conducted by Eugene Ormandy.* C.B.S. stereo SBRG 72282, mono BRG 72282.

Ask a Bartók aficionado how he feels about the enormous popularity of the Concerto for Orchestra, and he will probably reply that he thinks it regrettable. The sternness of his attitude, he will hasten to add, does not stem from snobbery but from sorrow that Bartók's most frequently-heard work is one which is not fully typical of him; its inspiration, compared with that of the second piano concerto, is sugar-coated; its thought is less profound; its popularity, like that

116

of Sibelius's second symphony, is an obstruction that prevents his more subtle works from being performed as often as they deserve. All this is true enough. Yet the enduring success of the Concerto for Orchestra is understandable. Its lucidity of texture, its straightforwardness, its energy, its mysterious sounds, its melodic strength, its pungent but not nerve-fraying discords, its variety of mood, and the effect it gives of being extremely difficult and at the same time extremely exciting to play, all these factors contribute towards making it the most accessible of his works. Furthermore, it is through this concerto that many of us—including some of the pundits who are loudest to condemn it —have graduated to Bartók's deeper and more masterly inspirations.

It is a work one can love even after one has grown to recognise its faults. The signs it contains that Bartók was a sick and dying man when he composed it, in America in 1943, are not necessarily a reason to dismiss it; they may even be a reason to admire it the more, and to tolerate those passages where inspiration dwindles and the technician takes over. The weakest movement, the motoric finale, makes a pretence of vivacity while remaining all too obviously rooted to the spot. Yet is there not something intensely moving about the mixture of American and Hungarian idioms employed in this movement, in which Bartók's present and past come touchingly together?

In the hands of a sympathetic conductor, who views the music as more than a vehicle for virtuosic display, the many beautiful moments of this uneven work can be made immensely telling; and in Ormandy, another Hungarian who settled in America, it seems to have its ideal interpreter, who is from start to finish on the same wavelength as the composer. In the elegiac slow movement, which is the emotional heart of the work, the strange soft whorls from clarinet and flute, the tiny flecks from the piccolo, the sudden and painfully stabbing entry of the theme previously heard in the introduction to the first movement, and the plashing of the harps are all exquisitely woven into a magical fabric of sound. There have been many recordings of the Concerto for Orchestra, but it is hard to imagine one in which instrumental brilliance and sensitivity are better combined.

PROKOFIEV (1891-1953): Symphony No. 1 in D major (Classical): Lieutenant Kije, suite; The Love for Three Oranges, suite. *Philadelphia Orchestra conducted by Eugene Ormandy.* C.B.S. stereo SBRG 72185, mono BRG 72185.

Prokofiev was 26 when he composed his *Classical* symphony, declaring it to be the sort of symphony Haydn would have written had he lived in recent times. In fact it is little more than a brilliant pastiche, but so deliciously melodious and succinct, so crisply orchestrated and buzzing with life, that one can easily understand why it has remained Prokofiev's most popular work, even although it gives no hint of the deeper music to follow. Here it shares a record with two colourful suites—one from the opera, *The Love for Three Oranges*, a Prokofievisation of a fantastic tale, by Carlo Gozzi, that would have appealed to Rimsky-Korsakov; the other from music he wrote for the satirical film *Lieutenant Kije*. It was the chance to write the latter which, surprisingly, lured him back to Russia after his fifteen years of wandering in America and Europe. The result of the commission was film music of superb beauty and atmosphere—not just background music but an integral part of the film. Eugene Ormandy obtains splendidly lively and striking performances of all three works, the *Lieutenant Kije* pieces being especially successful. Readers wishing only the *Classical* symphony are recommended to a sprightly D.G.G. recording by the Berlin Radio Symphony Orchestra under Ferenc Fricsay, in which the music is neatly contained on a 45 r.p.m. disc (mono EPL 30212).

PROKOFIEV: Violin concerto No. 1 in D major; Violin concerto No. 2 in G minor. *Isaac Stern/Philadelphia Orchestra conducted by Eugene Ormandy.* C.B.S. stereo SBRG 72269, mono BRG 72269.

Prokofiev's two violin concertos are predominantly lyrical works, though each is sprinkled with his own particular brand of ginger. The first, roughly contemporary with the *Classical* symphony, has a frosty, fairy-tale beauty that is quite enchanting and very Russian. The second dates from nearly twenty years later, but stylistically is much in keeping with its predecessor, if slightly less obviously Russian;

indeed, as the composer himself pointed out, it is a very international work, whose first movement was written mainly in Paris, part of the second movement in Voronezh, the orchestration in Baku, and the premiere given by a French violinist in Madrid.

Isaac Stern's performances are predictably high-powered, but do not lack sensitivity. Heart and mind, as well as fingers, are involved, and whether in the shimmering and mysterious sonorities of the first concerto, or the broad *cantabile* passages of the second, he sounds completely in love with the music—as, too, does Eugene Ormandy, in an accompaniment beautifully geared to the solo part.

PROKOFIEV: Romeo and Juliet—Suite No. 1 (excerpts); Suite No. 2 (complete). *Czech Philharmonic Orchestra conducted by Karel Ancerl.* Supraphon stereo SUA ST 50009, mono SUA 10104.

Like Tchaikovsky before him, Prokofiev was not only a symphonist of stature, but also a superb and instinctive man of the theatre. *Romeo and Juliet*, the greatest of his ballets, was written in 1935, soon after his return to Russia; but, because it was at first thought too difficult to dance to and listen to, it did not reach the stage until 1940—when, with Ulanova in the role of Juliet, it was an instant success at the Leningrad Kirov Theatre. Today, with Kenneth MacMillan's new choreography, it is one of the most stirring ballets in the repertoire of Covent Garden. The music, much of it in Prokofiev's richest and most imaginative vein, catches the spirit of the drama with a sharp lyricism which, even in the concert hall, is wonderfully telling.

Of the three suites Prokofiev drew from the ballet, the second is the most often performed and is widely considered to be the best-compiled. Unfortunately, many conductors treat it as little more than an orchestral showpiece, and, by exaggerating the tempi and intensifying the surface glitter, they rob the music of its feeling. Karel Ancerl never makes this mistake. Under his eloquent, perceptive direction, the Czech Philharmonic produces colours that are bright but never garish, and rhythms that are incisive but never over-pressed. The recording is up to Supraphon's highest standard. A slightly more generous amount of music (but at a slightly less generous price) is available in an alert,

equally well-recorded performance by Stanislaw Skrowac-
zewski and the Minneapolis Symphony Orchestra on
Philips stereo SAL 3463, mono AL 3463. This includes the
whole of the first suite (Ancerl give only three of the seven
movements) and all but one movement of the second suite.

PROKOFIEV: Symphony No. 6 in E flat minor.
Philadelphia Orchestra conducted by Eugene Ormandy.
C.B.S. stereo SBRG 72149, mono BRG 72149.

Of Prokofiev's seven symphonies, only the first and fifth
are performed with any frequency; yet it is the sixth that has
the greatest claim to be his masterpiece. Composed in the
wake of the Second World War, at a time when the music
of Soviet composers, and of Prokofiev in particular, was
coming under increasing surveillance by Zhdanov for signs
of neuropathic decadence, it is ostensibly an "optimistic"
work, celebrating victory over the Nazis. But it also reflects,
as the composer himself said, the feelings of the thousands
who "have been left with wounds that can't be healed—
health ruined for life, dear ones gone for ever." The music
has a dark power and brooding intensity that may come
as a surprise to those who think of Prokofiev mainly in
terms of astringent wit. The first of the three movements
has the character of a grim funeral march; the second
continues the mood of bitterness; and although the finale
begins in the jaunty circus vein so favoured by Russian
composers at this point in their symphonies, the mood of
levity is shattered from time to time by ominous interrup-
tions in the bass, and the work ends as sombrely as it began.
   The cushioned tone and underlying flabbiness of rhythm,
which are sometimes a defect of the Ormandy-Philadelphia
relationship, are impressively replaced in this performance
by a tension and incisiveness appropriate to the music on
hand. The epic breadth of the work is splendidly conveyed;
so, too, the undertones of tragedy.

**BERG (1885-1935): Violin concerto. BARTOK: Two
rhapsodies.** *Isaac Stern/New York Philharmonic conducted
by Leonard Bernstein.* C.B.S. stereo SBRG 72070, mono
BRG 72070.

Perhaps the most hopeful sign that Berg's music is at last
120

establishing itself in the affection of ordinary listeners is the current intellectual snobbism that deems him to be the "Puccini of the second Viennese school." Of all Schönberg's disciples, he has proved the most humane, the most lyrical, the most red-blooded. His masterpiece *Wozzeck* remains one of the most shattering experiences the opera-house has to offer; and in the concert-hall, his violin concerto is surely the most moving work in the form to be composed this century. Berg dedicated it "to the memory of an angel"—the angel being the extremely beautiful nineteen-year-old Manon Gropius, daughter of Mahler's widow and the architect Gropius, who had just died in great pain of spinal paralysis. The first of the concerto's two movements depicts the girl's character; the second, marked *Catastrophe* and *Resolution*, consists of a violent, bitter allegro followed by a sublime adagio based on the Bach chorale, *It is enough*. Composed in 1935, the concerto was Berg's last work. A few days after completing it, he was stung on the back by an insect and four months later died of an abscess caused by the bite. He never heard his concerto performed.

Now that the fine old Andre Gertler recording has been withdrawn by E.M.I.—one hopes only temporarily—Isaac Stern's is the best of the available issues. A little less sensitive and "committed" than Gertler's, this is nevertheless a stirring and impressive performance, richly recorded, with Bartók's two attractive rhapsodies (1928) as a happily-chosen filler.

WALTON (born 1902): Facade suites Nos. 1 and 2; Johannesburg Festival Overture; Portsmouth Point Overture; Crown Imperial; Orb and Sceptre. *Philharmonia Orchestra conducted by Sir William Walton.* H.M.V. mono HQM 1006.

Like Elgar, Walton has written confident martial works but (again as with Elgar) those works show only one side of a personality more complex and less confident that it at first seems. On this record, one of a valuable series of bargain-price H.M.V. issues of twentieth-century music, it is mainly the more extrovert side of Walton that appears, with sharp, sprightly, enjoyable performances, under the composer's direction, of some of his shorter pieces. *Facade*,

121

written at the age of 20, was originally intended for performance in conjunction with poems by Edith Sitwell; but the music, wittily satirical and melodious, has established itself in its own right as one of Walton's most popular works. The two overtures, one composed for the 70th anniversary of the city of Johannesburg, the other a picturesque evocation of the Portsmouth waterfront in the eighteenth century, have a similar high-spirited vivacity; and the two coronation marches that complete the record are stirring examples of Walton in his most patriotic vein.

The performances, which date as far back as 1953, are perhaps not models of high fidelity; but they still sound very fresh. Good recordings of Walton's more reflective works, in which the lyrical and melancholy sides of his nature come to the surface, are not so easy to find. New issues of the first symphony and the viola concerto, arguably his finest works, are long overdue. Meanwhile, readers are recommended to Zino Francescatti's rich account of the 1939 violin concerto—an uneven work, but with some splendid pages—coupled with an equally large-limbed performance of the Sibelius violin concerto on C.B.S. stereo SBRG 72351, mono BRG 72351.

SHOSTAKOVICH (born 1906): Symphony No. 1 in F major; Cello concerto in E flat major. *Mstislav Rostropovich/Philadelphia Orchestra conducted by Eugene Ormandy.* C.B.S. stereo SBRG 72081, mono BRG 72081.

Shostakovich's first symphony, written at the age of twenty, is an even more striking prentice work than Prokofiev's *Classical.* Varied in feeling, it encompasses pungent humour, rather tense high spirits, and tragedy—all within half an hour, and with extraordinary success. The cello concerto, a work of the composer's maturity, shows the fulfilment of that early promise. One of his richest and most darkly passionate inspirations, it was written in 1959 for Rostropovich, whose performance of its fiendishly difficult solo part —like his performance of Britten's cello symphony, written for him five years later—has such fierce authority and breadth of tone that few other cellists have risked comparison with him. Here, his playing is caught at full splendour; and he receives a grave, finely integrated accompani-

122

ment from Eugene Ormandy, whose treatment of the youthful symphony is equally assured.

SHOSTAKOVICH: Symphony No. 5 in D minor. *Czech Philharmonic Orchestra conducted by Karel Ancerl.* Supraphon stereo SUA ST 50423, mono SUA 10423.

For Western listeners, this is the most compelling and convincing of Shostakovitch's symphonies. Dating from 1937, its material is not so overworked as that of some of his later symphonies; and the slow movement is a highly original conception, hauntingly elegiac and deeply Russian in feeling, and orchestrated with a delicate frostiness that is very lovely. Karel Ancerl's conception of the music is unhurried, thoughtful, and splendidly coherent—so much so that even the noisily high-spirited finale, which in so many performances is something of a let-down, is made to take its place more logically than usual in the scheme of the work. An equally impressive, though rather more expensive, performance is given by André Previn and the London Symphony Orchestra on an R.C.A. disc, stereo SB 6651, mono RB 6651.

COPLAND (born 1900): Appalachian Spring; The Tender Land, suite. *Boston Symphony Orchestra conducted by Aaron Copland.* R.C.A. stereo SB 2104, mono RB 16232.

Although born in a drab street in Brooklyn, Aaron Copland has captured in his music—more successfully perhaps than any other composer—the atmosphere of the American countryside, and of rural life, whether it be among the pioneers of Pennsylvania or the cowboys of the wide-open spaces. Several representative recordings, some of them under the composer's own direction, are now available in Britain. The airily lyrical clarinet concerto, written for Benny Goodman and one of the best of the "abstract" works, can be found on a C.B.S. record (stereo SBRG 72218, mono BRG 72218), played with serene authority by its dedicatee and coupled with the delightful *Old American Songs*, handsomely sung by the coloured baritone, William Warfield. *Billy the Kid* (1938), the earliest of Copland's ballets, an endearing hymn to the Old West, romantic yet incisive, strikingly orchestrated, full of enchanting metamorphoses of tunes one vaguely recalls from the films of John Ford, has been enjoyably recorded by Bernstein and the New York Philharmonic, and is coupled with the slightly more obvious *Rodeo* dances. But perhaps the loveliest of all Copland's orchestral works is *Appalachian Spring* (1944), a sensitive evocation of a wedding ceremony at a farm-house in the Pennsylvanian hills in the early days of last century. The music makes poetic use of the gentle Shaker tune, *'Tis the gift to be simple;* and the whole work radiates peace and goodwill. The composer's own performance of it with the Boston Symphony Orchestra magically conveys its spirit; and the coupling, a suite of extracts from his folk-opera *The Tender Land* (1954), has a similar touching simplicity.

GERHARD (born 1896): Dances from Don Quixote; Symphony No. 1. *B.B.C. Symphony Orchestra conducted by Antal Dorati.* H.M.V. stereo ASD 613, mono ALP 2063.

More than half a century after its birth, "serialism" is still for many listeners a name loaded with suspicion. Often they are given good cause to suspect; but anyone who rejects serial music on the ground merely that it is serial, is throwing out the baby with the bathwater. Better to listen to it simply as music, than to worry over which particular modern "-ism" it conforms to. This seems to be the philosophy of Roberto Gerhard, the Spanish composer and pupil of Schönberg who has lived in Cambridge since 1938. "There is no substitute for listening," he writes as an introduction to this recording. "A work of art is not something to be explained. Only growing familiarity with it will lead to true participation." Wise words; and happily his music lives up to them, for it is well worth listening to. Few composers have made a more red-blooded case for serialism than he, in a chain of masterpieces which we have allowed ourselves wantonly to neglect.

This recording, made in 1964 with financial support from the Gulbenkian Foundation, is the first example of Gerhard's orchestral music to find a place in the British catalogues. It offers a powerful and enthralling experience,

124

recommended to all who have considered themselves so far unfortunate in their sampling of the present-day musical scene. Gerhard's music is complex, but not forbiddingly so. The pungent, colourful vigour of his writing stems to some extent from his Catalan origin; but he avoids the picturesque "Spanishness" that has been the bane of so much Spanish music just as successfully as he avoids the cold rhythmic stagnancy that has been the bane of so much serial music.

The suite of dances from *Don Quixote*, a ballet he composed in 1941, before his music had become completely atonal, make a lively and easily approachable introduction to his style—and to contemporary music in general. It is a work that engages both mind and heart. So, to an even greater degree, does the first symphony (1953), a work of great intensity and originality, in whose argument one immediately feels involved even if one does not wholly understand what is being said. The composer has summed up this work with a quotation from Dante—"A single melody continuing right up to the end without any melodic repetition and without a break"—which, he claims, expresses his intention so well that he could have adopted it for a motto. Antal Dorati, who has done more perhaps than any other conductor to further the cause of Gerhard, obtains an eloquent and exciting performance, which vividly realises both the strength and the sharp sonorities of the music. The record, supplied with copious notes, is one of a salutary H.M.V. series entitled "Music Today."

BRITTEN (born 1913): Young Person's Guide to the Orchestra; Serenade for tenor, horn, and strings. *Peter Pears/Barry Tuckwell/London Symphony Orchestra conducted by Benjamin Britten.* Decca stereo SXL 6110, mono LXT 6110.

Britten's orchestral music has a fairly small place in his output, but is stamped with the fastidious craftsmanship that characterises all his work. And nowhere is this craftsmanship more approachably displayed than in the *Young Person's Guide to the Orchestra*, a diverting and brilliant music lesson in the form of a series of variations and a fugue on a hornpipe by one of his favourite composers, Henry Purcell. Composed in 1945, directly after *Peter Grimes*, it is

125

one of the first and finest of the many pieces he has written
with young people in mind; and apart from providing a
superb survey of all the main orchestral instruments, in
solo and in chorus, it provides also a useful vade-mecum of
Britten's idiom as it then was.

The serenade, dating from two years earlier, is an
equally successful work of the period, and perhaps the most
popular of all his song-cycles. The music is full of delightful
fantasy, and includes a burnished setting of Tennyson's *The
splendour falls on castle walls*, a sharp and sombre treatment
of a fifteenth-century dirge (*This ae night*), and an ecstatically
coruscating *Hymn*, to words by Ben Jonson. Like so much
of Britten's vocal music, it was written for the clear, expressive voice of his friend and colleague, Peter Pears (the
horn part was for another prodigiously gifted performer,
Dennis Brain). An earlier LP recording of the serenade, with
Pears and Brain as soloists, is still in the catalogue. But the
merit of the newer one is that it is conducted by the composer himself; and since he is a superlative conductor of his
own music, not only the intimate serenade but also the
virtuoso orchestral piece are given performances of outstanding clarity, beauty, and understanding.

**BRITTEN: Cello symphony. HAYDN: Cello concerto in
C.** *Mstislav Rostropovich/English Chamber Orchestra
conducted by Benjamin Britten.* Decca stereo SXL 6138,
mono LXT 6138.

Britten's cello symphony is the most formidable of the chain
of works he has composed in recent years for Rostropovich.
At first acquaintance, its grimness of mood and complexity
of argument prove rather daunting, yet the music is so
obviously rich in promise, so disquieting and challenging,
that one senses its greatness from its first notes and becomes
quickly eager to know and understand it. The first of the
four movements, though cast in traditional sonata form, is
the most elusive to grasp; but gradually—and how useful a
recording is in this respect—one gets to recognise the sign-
posts and generally gets the feel of its desolate beauty. The
other movements are more straightforward, though no less
inspired, in thought: a swift, icy scherzo, full of wisps of
melody and strange petrified chords that nightmarishly
recall the fairy music of Mendelssohn's *Midsummer Night's*

Dream; a rich and passionate adagio, introduced by ominous drum taps and ending with a haunting cadenza that links it, both dramatically and thematically, with the final passacaglia, a movement of impressive strength and grandeur built from a swinging trumpet tune. So finely integrated is the music that one realises why Britten chose to call it a cello symphony rather than a concerto.

Rostropovich has the solo part so deeply in his heart and fingers that he plays it as if he were creating it as he goes along. It is surely one of the great performances of our time, an act of total dedication backed up by superhuman musicianship and with an absolute sense of communication with the other players and their inspired conductor. Haydn's recently discovered cello concerto in C, on side two, makes a delightful makeweight, and benefits from a performance of wonderful point and clarity.

TIPPETT (born 1905): Concerto for double string orchestra. PROKOFIEV: Fugitive Visions. *Moscow Chamber Orchestra/Bath Festival Chamber Orchestra conducted by Rudolf Barshai.* H.M.V. stereo ASD 512, mono ALP 1961.

Less intricate than most of his later music, and more immediately captivating in its dancing tunefulness, Tippett's double concerto has long been his most popular composition. Written in 1939, it was one of the first works that this richly gifted, intensely self-critical and still underrated composer allowed to be published; and with its swinging rhythms, marvellous clarity of texture, and nostalgic lyricism, it finds a link between the seventeenth-century English madrigal (one of the foundations of Tippett's style) and American Negro music. The first movement and finale are bright and blithe; the slow movement a kind of blues, built from a melody of haunting tenderness.

Tippett, who lives in a picturesque Elizabethan house in Corsham, on the southern edge of the Cotswolds, has been closely associated in recent years with the Bath Festival; and this clean-limbed performance, in which a Russian and a British chamber orchestra come together under Rudolf Barshai, is one of the fruits of that connection. The pithy Prokofiev pieces on the reverse were written for solo piano between 1915 and 1917. In Barshai's arrangement for strings, the more percussive pieces perhaps lose something of their effectiveness; but on the whole the music takes surprisingly well to its new medium, especially when played with such conviction.

TIPPETT: Concerto for Orchestra. *London Symphony Orchestra conducted by Colin Davis.* **GOEHR (born 1932): Little Symphony.** *London Symphony Orchestra conducted by Norman Del Mar.* Philips stereo SAL 3497, mono AL 3497.

Tippett composed his concerto for the 1963 Edinburgh Festival, where it was played—as on this record—by Colin Davis and the L.S.O. At first acquaintance a rather stark work, it begins to yield its secrets quite quickly on repetition, especially in so lucid and loving a performance as this. Apart from its great individuality of construction and texture (in the first movement, scored for wind and percussion, the instruments parade in groups of three), the music has one feature that should endear it to all—memorable melodic interest. The short opening theme, for instance, exquisitely laid out for flute and harp, need be heard only once to fix itself naggingly in the mind. In the slow movement the strings make their first appearance, passionate and eloquent; and the lithe finale, which introduces with great subtlety some material from Tippett's opera, *King Priam*, has a salty main theme, to which the trumpet contributes an open-air vigour.

In a happily-chosen coupling, this important work by one of Britain's senior composers is joined by an equally fascinating score by a younger figure on the British scene. Alexander Goehr composed his *Little Symphony* in 1963 in memory of his father, the conductor Walter Goehr, who died three years before. In spite of its name, it is a full-scale symphony in four movements; the diminutive refers to the fact that the music is scored for chamber orchestra. Built from a slow, impassioned, chorale-like theme, played first by the strings, it is largely atonal in idiom, but listeners should not allow themselves to be put off by this knowledge. With its conflicting impressions of utter stillness and of tremendous movement, it is a work that makes an immediate emotional impact, even although full comprehension does not come at the first or second hearing.

128

QUARTET Nº 77

Joseph Haydn, Op. 76. Nº 3.
(1732-1809)

BACH (1685-1750): The Well-Tempered Clavier, Book I.
Ralph Kirkpatrick (*clavichord*).   D.G.G. Archive stereo
SAPM 198311-2, mono APM 14311-2.

No work demonstrates Bach's greatness, and the staggering
fecundity of his invention, more clearly than the 48 preludes
and fugues he composed in defence of equal temperament.
The system of tuning keyboard instruments was a controversial topic in Bach's time. The old system, as H. C. Colles
remarked, was a mixed blessing: it made the instruments
sound beautifully in tune in certain keys, but unbearable in
others. The new system, while it meant compromising on
pitch, had the advantage of laying open the entire cycle of
major and minor keys to the composer and performer.
Bach wrote his eloquent manifesto in two parts, each comprising 24 preludes and fugues, and each beginning in C
major and working upwards through every major and minor
key. Although often used as such, the pieces are no mere
exercises. They are the well-spring of all subsequent keyboard music—which is why they are often called the "Old
Testament of Music." They are an inexhaustible joy to play
(Tovey said we should play them for an hour every day of
our life). And they encompass every facet of his personality.
They are the quintessence of Bach: serene, sombre, intimate,
intense, racy, spiritual, brilliant, majestic. They are also
virtually indestructible, having been sumptuously orchestrated by Stokowski and others, turned into jazz (no
difficult feat, this, for some of them are jazzy already),
played on every conceivable form of keyboard instrument,
and, in the case of the opening C major prelude, meta-
morphosed by Gounod into his sugary *Ave Maria*.

Bach himself did not specify what instrument the music
was intended for. The word clavier means, simply, keyboard.
But the clavichord and harpsichord are widely considered
the most suitable, though in the present century pianists of
the stature of Edwin Fischer and Rosalyn Tureck have
stated a strong case for the more modern instrument. The
harpsichord catches best the flashing brilliance of the music,
and the clavichord the intimacy. For home listening, the
latter is ideal—especially if the performer can command the
full wealth of nuance which this delicate instrument offers.
Ralph Kirkpatrick is alive to all its possibilities, and his
playing is one of the most abidingly satisfying experiences
the gramophone can offer. So far, only Book I of the 48 has

been released. Bach waited 22 years before starting work on Book II. One hopes Kirkpatrick will not wait so long to record it.

BACH: Goldberg Variations. *Ralph Kirkpatrick* (*harpsichord*). D.G.G. Archive stereo SAPM 198020, mono APM 14135.

Bach called his *Goldberg Variations* "an aria with different variations for harpsichord with two manuals, designed for the refreshment of music-lovers." Its history is curious. Composed for one of Bach's pupils, a brilliant harpsichordist called Goldberg, it was used by him to sooth a rich patron (Count Kaiserling, a former Russian ambassador at the Court of Saxony) who suffered from insomnia and neuralgia. So successful, it seems, was the treatment that the count sent Bach one hundred *louis d'or* in a golden goblet. The theme on which this vast masterpiece is based is a slow and richly ornamented one, of great beauty. There are thirty variations, including nine canons and a final *quodlibet*, a medley of popular melodies of the day. To the scholar, intent on unravelling its contrapuntal intricacies, the music provides endless fascination; to the average music-lover, content merely to listen, it is also fascinating— and just as refreshing as its composer claimed it to be. Ralph Kirkpatrick's performance carries impressive authority: it is pure and silvery, is finely built, and employs the two manuals of the instrument with the most delicate variety of tone.

BACH: Partita in B flat major. MOZART: Piano sonata in A minor, K.310. SCHUBERT: Impromptus in G flat major and E flat major. *Dinu Lipatti.* Columbia mono 33CX 1499.

Apart from the 48 preludes and fugues, and individual works such as the *Goldberg Variations* and the *Italian Concerto*, Bach composed also a number of keyboard partitas and suites, no less fertile in their inventiveness and variety of mood. Dinu Lipatti's performance of the first of the partitas is one of the regrettably few souvenirs we have of this enormously gifted young Rumanian pianist who died in 1950 at the age of 33. Although less scholarly than some other Bach players, he was a perfectionist and a musician of rare poetic sensibility, with an extraordinary beauty of touch and the ability to bring every phrase eloquently and naturally to life.

Coupled with the Bach is perhaps the finest of all Mozart's piano sonatas. These are works which, if we have struggled through them in childhood, we grow up to think of as "teaching" material. That they can be much more than that is amply demonstrated in Lipatti's performance, where the discords of the opening movement, and the moments in the finale where A minor turns to A major and then shifts back again, strike straight to the heart. Two of Schubert's shortest and most lyrical pieces complete the disc. The recording, a transfer from 78, is good enough to convey the magic of the occasion.

Lipatti's most famous performance, a transcription of Bach's *Jesu, joy of man's desiring*, which he recorded again and again until he was satisfied with it, is available as part of a rather longer Columbia recital (mono 33CX 1386). Here, in addition to several pieces by Bach, are performances of two Scarlatti sonatas, Ravel's *Alborada del Gracioso*, and Chopin's wonderful barcarolle, to the last of which he brings an inimitable simplicity and twilight beauty.

BACH: Sonatas and partitas for unaccompanied violin.
Arthur Grumiaux.   Philips mono AL 3472-4.

Bach wrote six masterpieces for solo violin and six for solo cello. They are the high Alps of his instrumental music, and should be attempted by only the best equipped, most perceptive and tireless performers. The sonatas, each in four movements, follow a standard slow-quick-slow-quick layout; the partitas are more flexible and less austere, with a greater number of dancing movements. In earlier days of the gramophone, Yehudi Menuhin recorded five of the six works on a series of 78 r.p.m. discs. They were wonderful, monumental performances; but his more recent LP recording of the complete set has not quite the purity of tone and precision and classical feeling of Arthur Grumiaux's, which uses facsimiles of Bach's manuscripts and is in every way a model performance, beautifully recorded.

Collectors wishing to buy the records piecemeal, and who do not already know the music well, are advised to start with AL 3474, which contains the brilliant and tuneful E major partita (whose prelude used to be heard weekly in the early days of television as the signature tune of the charming *Animal*, *Vegetable*, *Mineral* programme) and the deeper, more serious C major sonata, a tougher—but in the end very rewarding—nut to crack. The D minor partita, with its magnificent arching chaconne, is coupled with the A minor sonata on AL 3473, and the B minor partita and G minor sonata are on AL 3472.

BACH: Suites for unaccompanied cello. *Janos Starker.* Saga mono XID 5167 (Suite No. 1 in G major, Suite No. 4 in E flat major); mono XID 5161 (Suite No. 3 in C major, Suite No. 6 in D major).

Bach's six suites for solo cello are less immediately appealing than his works for solo violin. The contrast between the reflective movements and the sprightlier ones is less easily conveyed by the heavier-toned instrument; and unless the performer is fully at home in the music, both spiritually and and technically, the effect can be rather grumpy and monotonous. During the nineteenth century the apparent plainness of these works led other composers, notably Mendelssohn and Schumann, to attempt to "complete" them by adding a piano accompaniment. It was not until Casals made his solo flight in the present century that we recognised them for the superbly concentrated masterpieces they are. Since then, other great cellists have taken them up and have shown us that these works, far from being narrow, can be played convincingly in a variety of ways. Some performers concentrate on the robust, dancing qualities of the music; others prefer a more subdued, self-communing approach, in which the rhythmic gavottes and gigues become dances of the spirit.

Janos Starker, in these records of four of the suites, gives us the best of both worlds. His playing has a youthful energy which is extremely exciting, and which reminds us

134

that Bach himself was a young man when he wrote the works; and at the same time he is able to give the slow, intense, eloquent sarabandes all the poetry they need. The records, although they date from the early days of LP, still sound wonderfully clear; and since they cost only a few shillings each, they are among the most desirable bargains on the market.

BACH: Organ recital. *Helmut Walcha.* D.G.G. Archive mono APM 14509.

The church organ does not take happily to gramophone records, partly because the atmosphere and acoustics of a church are impossible to obtain by one's fireside, and partly because, without that atmosphere, the sound tends to become monotonous. Nevertheless, every record collection should contain some of the glories of organ music, which means, in particular, a selection of works by Bach. Of the many recordings made by the blind German organist, Helmut Walcha, the above is perhaps the first to choose, since it contains the most popular of all Bach's organ works, the Toccata and Fugue in D minor, along with three of his great series of preludes and fugues. Walcha plays on two organs—the noble Schnitger organ in Cappel and the small organ of St. Jakobi in Lubeck—and the relaxed intimacy of his approach makes his recital better suited than most to reproduction in home surroundings. Readers who find this record to their taste will no doubt wish to nibble at some of the others Walcha has made for D.G.G.

Toccata C Maj.

DOMENICO SCARLATTI (1685-1757): Twenty sonatas. *Wanda Landowska (harpsichord).* H.M.V. mono COLH 304.

Apart from producing Bach and Handel, 1685 was an *annus mirabilis* that yielded also Domenico Scarlatti, the Italian-born, Spanish-domiciled master of the harpsichord, in whose 500 sonatas lie the stylistic roots of Chopin and other piano composers of the nineteenth and twentieth centuries. The gifted son of an equally gifted father

135

(Alessandro Scarlatti was a leading figure in the development of Italian opera), he liked to call his pieces *Esercizi* (exercises); but they are generally known by the more ambitious title of sonata, even although each consists of only one short movement. Brevity, in Scarlatti's case, is synonymous with greatness—just as it is in Chopin's music, which also compresses big events into small packages. And although the general shape of Scarlatti's packages was fairly constant, the music he put into them was wonderfully fanciful, catching much of the atmosphere of his adopted country. Here are crisp Spanish rhythms, employed far more imaginatively than in the work of Spanish "national" composers of more recent times; the sound of guitars and castanets, of drums and processions, of voices in the night air, all magically evoked with an irresistible spirit and sense of adventure.

No performer has caught the feeling of these pieces more sharply than Wanda Landowska, the great Polish harpsichordist who, more than anyone else, has been responsible for the revival of interest in this instrument in the present century. Happily, some of her finest performances were caught for posterity in a series of recordings she made in Paris on her Pleyel harpsichord in the nineteen-thirties, when she was around sixty years of age. The last of these, gathered on this LP, coincided with the outbreak of the Second World War (a thudding noise at one point is said to be gunfire). The pieces are well chosen to reveal the composer in all his moods. One of them (the D major, L.14) is a wild Spanish dance, another (F major, L.228) a gentle pastoral, and a third (F minor, L.382) is darker and more introspective. A companion record, containing another twenty sonatas recorded a few years earlier, is no less enchanting (H.M.V. mono COLH 73).

Although the harpsichord is the ideal instrument to bring out the sparkle and incisiveness of Scarlatti's music, the pianism of the writing makes it suitable also for performance on the more recent instrument. Readers wishing to sample some of the pieces on the piano are recommended to Horowitz's 1965 recording of twelve of them (C.B.S. stereo SBRG 72274, mono BRG 72274), performed with tremendous allure, and duplicating only one of the sonatas included on COLH 304 and none of those on COLH 73.

SOLER (1729-1783): Six concertos for two organs.
E. Power Biggs and Daniel Pinkham. C.B.S. stereo
SBRG 72382, mono BRG 72383.

The Spanish composer Antonio Soler was a minor figure
in the history of music, who spent most of his life as an
organist at the monastery of the Escurial, near Madrid.
For five years, however, he studied under Domenico
Scarlatti, and something of the exuberance of the
Italian master can be detected in these six enchanting
concertos, with quick movements that dance and march to
exhilaratingly percussive rhythms, and slow movements
that are more reflective, with delightful contrasts of colour
and sometimes a tinge of Spanish melancholy. Playing on
two Dutch organs at Harvard University, E. Power Biggs
and Daniel Pinkham catch the light and shade and intimacy
of the music effectively; and, in the stereo recording, a
successful attempt has been made to recreate the atmosphere of the Escurial, where the two original organs, on
which Soler and a royal pupil played these works, fronted
each other across the choir.

**HAYDN (1732-1809): String quartet in F major, Op. 3,
No. 5; String quartet in E flat, Op. 33, No. 2 (Joke);
String quartet in D minor, Op. 76, No. 2** *Janacek
Quartet.* Decca stereo SXL 6093, mono LXT 6093.

Haydn is popularly known as the father of the symphony;
but he could be called, just as aptly, the father of the string
quartet. He was the first composer fully to realise the poten-
tialities of this intimate form of music-making, and he
brought to it a mastery of invention that none of his
predecessors, and few of his successors, could rival. He
composed more than eighty quartets, spanning most of his
working life. The early ones were intended to be serenades
(and Tovey relates how Haydn once played an amiable
practical joke by arranging for several serenade parties to
perform different music in earshot of each other, to the
annoyance, not only of a respectable neighbourhood, but
of an adjoining police station). The later ones were increasingly profound, and increasingly varied in their feeling and
in their use of the four instruments. "Art," Haydn once wrote,

"is free, and should be fettered by no mechanical regulations." Haydn's quartets never sound fettered. In their wealth of melody, their sparkle, their poise, their beauty of form and texture, they are among the most refreshing masterpieces ever written. One listens and listens, and rejoices in their purity and humanity. The mystery, and the tragedy, is that so few of them are regularly played and even fewer are recorded. It is surely a strangely frivolous industry that is willing to record Tchaikovsky's sixth symphony again and again, yet ignore some of Haydn's most important works.

Of the three quartets on this record, the first is of a serenade type and includes as its slow movement one of the most famous pieces of chamber music in the world— the delicate *andante cantabile*, sung by a solo violin over a pizzicato accompaniment, long the signature tune of the B.B.C. programme, *Music in Miniature*. Ironically, it now seems possible that this work was not composed by Haydn at all, but by a monk called Romanus Hofstetter. Either way, it is charming. The other two works are authentic Haydn, and date from different periods in his life. In the E flat major, which he wrote in his late forties, a sunlit opening movement and a piquant finale (ending with the joke of the title) encase a tenderly grave *Largo sostenuto*. In the D minor, dating from his old age, joy gives way to a brooding, sardonic energy that is dark, powerful, and disturbing. The Janáček Quartet—one of the finest ensembles from that glorious land of string quartets, Czechoslovakia— catches the spirit of all three works most successfully, conveying the exquisite lightness of Op. 3, the epigrammatic crispness of Op. 33, and the bit eof Op. 76 with complete spontaneity and a heart-warming beauty of tone.

HAYDN: String quartets Op. 54 (complete). *Allegri Quartet*. H.M.V. stereo CSD 3502, mono CLP 3502.

Just as Mozart composed his six Haydn quartets after a deep study of Haydn's chamber music, so Haydn composed his three opus 54 quartets after a deep study of the six works Mozart dedicated to him. Like all Haydn's best works, they are packed with brilliant and surprising touches that retain their freshness no matter how well one knows them; in addition the music conveys its feelings with a

138

V.G.

Haydn

Piano Sonata in E flat
H XVI 49 — Emmanuel Axe

new richness and mastery surely produced by Haydn's knowledge of the Mozart works. The slow movements—especially the dark modulations of the G major quartet and the florid, passionate adagio of the C major—reveal Haydn's widening emotional range the most powerfully. But the other movements, too, all contain things to marvel at, such as the great climbing arpeggios for the cello in the finale of the C major. "The E major quartet," wrote Tovey in 1929, "is one of Haydn's greatest works, and should be better known." Today the third of the opus 54 series is no better known than it was; but at least we can savour its beauties again and again in the Allegri Quartet's lively and understanding account of it and its two eventful companion-pieces. A second record from the same players, consisting of the three Op. 55 quartets, is scarcely less enjoyable (H.M.V. stereo CSD 3503, mono CLP 3503).

HAYDN: Piano sonatas Nos. 20 in C minor, 23 in F major, 40 in G major, 48 in C major. *Artur Balsam.* Oiseau-Lyre stereo SOL 275, mono OL 275.

Haydn's sonatas, like his symphonies and string quartets, span almost the whole of his career. Some are intimate masterpieces, others are attractive teaching pieces, and almost all are neglected. Everyone who plays the piano should discover the pleasure of thumbing through a volume of these works—there is scarcely a page that does not contain musical adventures and delights. But they are also a pleasure to listen to—more so, on the whole, than Mozart's—and this record has been compiled with a keen ear for the contrasts they contain. The C minor is one of the finest of the series, a passionate work from the same period as his early *Sturm und Drang* symphonies. To this, the F major and G major sonatas act as light-hearted foils, and the selection is completed by the striking C major sonata, a concentrated two-movement work that Haydn wrote for a *Musical Potpourri* published by Breitkopf and Härtel in 1789.

Artur Balsam's performances form part of what is to be a comprehensive recording by him of the fifty-odd works. They are strong and lively, emphasising more the masculinity of the music than the grace. A gentler and more flowing account of Nos. 20 and 40, along with Nos. 31 in

E major and 46 in A flat major, is to be found in an equally
enjoyable recital by Kathleen Long (Decca mono LXT
5144).

Serenade Nº 3 in D M jv (K.185) G

MOZART (1756-1791): Serenade in B flat major, K.361.
*London Wind Quintet and Ensemble conducted by Otto
Klemperer.* Columbia stereo SAX 5259, mono 33 CX 5259.

Music for wind instruments, like music for organ, does not
lend itself entirely happily to the gramophone. What is
needed is the atmosphere described by Leopold Mozart,
who, recalling the performance of one of his son's serenades
in the open air on a summer evening outside the house of a
friend, wrote that "we knew nothing about it until we heard
it deliciously in our rooms from across the water." Yet every
record collection should include at least a little wind music,
and there is no better starting point than Mozart's sublime
B flat major serenade for thirteen wind instruments, a
large-scale and deeply emotional work which (Blom
conjectures) was probably written for members of the
Munich orchestra at the time when Mozart was preparing
for the premiere of *Idomeneo* there. Klemperer, with some of
the cream of London's wind players to support him, explores
the full range of the music, from the wit of the theme and
variations that form the sixth of the seven movements to the
murmuring sadness of the great adagio.

MOZART: Oboe quartet in F major, K.370. *Leon Goossens/
Members of the Lener String Quartet.* H.M.V. mono
7ER 5232.

Here a single wind instrument is blended with three strings
in a small-scale work of entrancing beauty, composed for
the leading Munich oboist, Friedrich Ramm, around the
same time as the big serenade in B flat. Einstein, quoting a
contemporary source, has given this description of Ramm's
playing: "It is not too much to say that no one has yet been
able to approach him in beauty, roundness, softness, and
trueness of tone on the oboe, combined with the trumpet-
140

like depth of his *forte*. He plays, for the rest, with a delicacy, a lightness, and a power of expression that enchant the listener; he handles this instrument wisely, according to its true, individual nature, and with a practical skill possessed by few oboists; in an Adagio his interpretation is full of feeling, but he also knows how to express spirit and fire, if the effect and the inspiration demand them."

The above description could be applied, with almost equal aptness, to this performance by a great oboist of the present century, supported by three members of a great (though now, alas, defunct) string quartet. Recorded in 1934, it has been effectively transferred to a 45 r.p.m, disc, and remains one of the most sheerly delightful Mozart performances in the catalogue.

MOZART: String quartet in B flat major, K.458 (Hunt). HAYDN: String quartet in C major, Op. 76, No. 3 (Emperor). *Amadeus Quartet.* D.G.G. stereo SLPM 138886, mono LPM 18886.

No record is better designed to show the differences, and the similarities, between Haydn and Mozart than this. In 1781, when Haydn was 49 and Mozart 25, the two composers met and became friends. Four years later, after studying Haydn's set of six quartets, Op. 33, Mozart poured out his own six *Haydn* quartets, dedicated to and inspired by the older composer. He wrote them extremely carefully, and the manuscript contains, for Mozart, an unusually high number of alterations. The result is a consummate beauty and artistry, a maturity and an inexhaustible subtlety of inspiration that caused Haydn, when he attended the premiere of three of these works (including the one on this record), to declare to Mozart's father: "Before God and as an honest man, I tell you that your son is the greatest composer known to me either in person or by name. He has taste and, what is more, the most profound knowledge of composition."

The *Hunt* quartet owes its nickname to the swinging horn-like tune with which it opens. A tune like this, at the start of a Haydn work, would immediately create a robust out-of-doors feeling; but Mozart, and this is an essential difference between the two composers, seems to go no farther than his window. As in all his most deeply-felt masterpieces, the polish of the writing and the passion of the thought are combined in such a way that the one enhances the other. The minuet is a model of gracefulness; but it is a gracefulness punctured by tiny stabs of pain. The slow movement embodies, to quote Andrew Porter's expressive phrase, "a trembling sense of the mystery of beauty"; but it is a beauty behind which sadness lurks.

Haydn, in his later years, learnt just as much from Mozart as Mozart did from Haydn; and the premature death of his young friend in 1791 moved him deeply. Haydn is popularly depicted as the most genial of composers, and the un-buttoned high-spirits of much of his music has helped to further this idea. Yet in his youth he knew poverty as agonising as Mozart's; his marriage was a failure; and his old age, despite the fame and respect he had won all over Europe, was shadowed by loneliness and ill-health. For all the outdoor vigour of so many of his works, one can perceive, as with Mozart, the skull beneath the skin, the suffering behind the fluency. The slow movements of his mature quartets have a compassion that touches the heart, and some of the faster movements a contrapuntal fierceness that can be overwhelming in its intensity. The slow move-ment of the *Emperor* quartet is a series of straightforward, but glowingly harmonised and decorated, variations on the noble theme of the Austrian Imperial National Anthem, which Haydn himself had composed only a few months earlier. The finale is an unexpectedly stormy outburst in C minor, whose impact is made all the more powerful by the fact that the rest of the work has been substantially in the major.

Both works find the Amadeus Quartet in its best form, alive not only to the surface beauty of the music but to the feeling below. On a technical level, it is seldom that one hears the opening of the finale of the Mozart quite so pithily turned and so neatly graded; and on a spiritual one, it is seldom that the adagio of the Haydn is so meaningfully unfolded.

MOZART: String quartet in G major, K.387; String quartet in A major, K.464. *Amadeus Quartet.* D.G.G. stereo SLPM 138909, mono LPM 18909.

Mozart's string quartets fall conveniently into two groups:
142

those composed between 1770 and 1773, which contain much of interest but little of profound inspiration, and the maturer works of 1783 onwards, when he had come under the influence of Haydn and gained a stronger grasp of the possibilities of the form. The two works on this record belong to the latter group, and come from the set of six quartets that Mozart dedicated to the "dear friend" from whom he had learnt so much about the art of writing for the four instruments. And yet, as Einstein has pointed out, scarcely any of Mozart's works are more "personal" than these, which seem so sunny and gracious but which are full of inner tension—and nowhere more so than in their minuets, where the popular dance of the eighteenth century suddenly gains overtones of despair. The Amadeus's performance of each work is a model of inspired ensemble playing—crisp, pure, and infinitely tender in its shaping of the sighing chromaticisms with which Mozart from time to time revealed his sadness.

MOZART: Piano quartet in G minor, K.478; Piano quartet in E flat major, K.493. *Pro Arte Piano Quartet.* Oiseau-Lyre stereo SOL 285, mono OL 285.

The combination of a piano and a trio of strings inspired Mozart, in the two works he wrote for these forces, to produce some of his richest and most strikingly contrasted ideas. The G minor work, whose boldness and complexity so alarmed Mozart's publisher that he asked him not to compose another like it, its mainly sombre and brooding; the E flat is open-hearted and brilliant, with a theme in its rondo finale which Einstein described as "the purest, most childlike, most godlike melody ever sung." Although Lamar Crowson, the pianist of the Pro Arte Quartet, lacks a little of the magic Curzon brought to his famous 1954 recording, the string playing in this newer issue is more eloquent, the texture more beautifully blended, and the recording more vivid. An equally fine recording of Mozart's great E flat piano quintet, K. 452—in which strings are replaced by wind instruments, and which Mozart declared to be the best work he had ever composed—has been made by Lamar Crowson and the Melos Ensemble, coupled with the youthful companion piece Beethoven wrote in the same key and for the same instruments (H.M.V. stereo ASD 2256, mono ALP 2256).

MOZART: String quintet in G minor, K.516; String quintet in C minor, K.406. *Griller Quartet with William Primrose (viola).* Philips stereo SGL 5841, mono GL 5841.

Mozart's string quintets are among the glories of chamber music. In his piano quartets, he added a piano to a trio of strings. Here he adds a second viola to the traditional string quartet, and the dark tones offered by this combination are ideally suited to the intensity of the G minor quintet which (with the G minor symphony of the following year) is one of his most troubled works. The C minor quintet is a transcription, which he made himself, of his powerful wind serenade in the same key. In theory the wind version is the better; but the string adaptation brings out new aspects of the music, and, for home listening, has much to commend it. A good comprehensive recording of all five quintets is long overdue. This bargain-price issue lacks the ultimate beauty of tone, but is played with a tension that admirably catches the introspective passion of the music.

MOZART: Clarinet quintet in A major, K.581; Clarinet trio in E flat major, K.498. *Gervase de Peyer (clarinet) and members of the Melos Ensemble.* H.M.V. stereo ASD 605, mono ALP 2056.

Mozart was the first composer to discover and reveal the full beauty of the clarinet. He called it a "lordly" instrument, and lavished on it some of his most serene and intimate thoughts. The quintet for clarinet and strings is a gracious companion piece to the clarinet concerto he composed, towards the end of his life, for the Viennese clarinettist Anton Stadler. The trio for clarinet, viola, and piano, which dates from slightly earlier, is scarcely less delicious. Gervase de Peyer and his colleagues give each work a performance of unruffled beauty. The start of the first movement of the quintet—than which there is no more magical *open sesame*—is irresistibly played, and the sublime slow movement is given a celestial radiance and stillness.

MOZART: Divertimento in E flat major for violin, viola, and cello, K.563. *Jean Pougnet* (*violin*), *Frederick Riddle* (*viola*), *Anthony Pini* (*cello*). H.M.V. mono CLP 1861.

According to box-office receipts, no form of chamber music is less popular than the string trio—which explains why this, one of Mozart's most sublime instrumental inspirations, is still a rarity in our concert programmes. Anyone who thinks of a trio as no more than a depleted quartet, and of a divertimento as no more than "entertainment" music, will be astonished at the richness and profundity of this long work, in which, throughout the six movements, the players cast a spell as intense as that of the more famous quartets and quintets. Since recordings of this mature and deeply serious masterpiece are about as rare as live performances, this issue is particularly desirable, especially as it is played with great feeling for the thoughtful beauty of the music, and with a fine sense of rapport.

BEETHOVEN (1770-1827) 32 piano sonatas. *Artur Schnabel*. H.M.V. mono COLH 51-63.

Just as Bach's 48 preludes and fugues have been nicknamed the Old Testament of the keyboard, so Beethoven's 32 piano sonatas have become known as the New Testament. They fall, along with the rest of his works, into three distinct periods: the early one, in which he adapted, to his own purposes, the forms and style of Haydn and Mozart; the middle one, in which he widened the whole scope of music, giving it a range and intensity of expression it had never before known; and the late one, when deafness and failing health served to inspire a more "inward" and philosophical stream of masterpieces, which, at the time of their composition, must have sounded just as austere and strange as did much of Bartók's music in the first half of the present century.

Artur Schnabel was the most searching of Beethoven pianists. His complete series of the sonatas, recorded over a number of years on 78, was one of the gramophone's noblest achievements; and it is good to have these performances available again, with a substantial reduction in surface noise and cost, on thirteen LPs, in H.M.V.'s *Great Recordings of the Century* series. Schnabel did not make records willingly. He believed, rightly, that his playing was in a constant state of development, and was unhappy that any of his performances should be captured for posterity and regarded as his last word on the music. Yet without these souvenirs of him our insight—which is his insight—into Beethoven's keyboard music would be infinitely poorer. Schnabel, in his time, had his detractors, who branded him "over-intellectual" and "under-emotional". Today it is hard to understand how anyone could come to that conclusion. If Schnabel's playing had a fault, it was that it was sometimes too impulsive; it was seldom too cerebral. His spiritual profundity, his grasp of the overall structure and line of a movement, the subtlety of expression he could bring to a phrase, to a single chord or note, these were his supreme virtues; and it is these that make his records such an enthralling experience. True, his technique was not always up to the demands that Beethoven placed on it. But no matter. As another Beethoven performer, Denis Matthews, has written of him: "If his mind sometimes outstripped his fingers, how much better that it should be this way round."

Since the records are available separately, collectors can acquire the set piecemeal. Perhaps the best starting point is the middle, with the disc containing two of the grandest sonatas, the *Waldstein* and the *Appassionata*, plus the lesser-known and more relaxing F major sonata, Op. 54, which Beethoven composed between these two giants (COLH 59). From here one can work forward and backward, discovering how much more than other pianists Schnabel was able to find in the early works, and marvelling at the sustained meditative beauty and control of his handling of the great variation movements of the late sonatas. Among the early works, the *Pathétique* and the two gracious Op. 14 sonatas make a particularly happy group (COLH 54); among the late ones, the finale of the last sonata, the C minor, Op. 111, is magnificent, and is—or should be—ample recompense for some blurred passage-work in the first movement (COLH 63, with the A flat major sonata, Op. 110, as coupling).

Readers who prefer a more modern sound quality than is found in these reissues are recommended to the series of records made by Wilhelm Kempff for D.G.G. Here, too, is a rare poetic insight into the music, and a fine feeling for the scale and argument of each of the works recorded. Another great Beethoven pianist, Rudolf Serkin, is scandalously under-represented in the catalogues. His recording of the three most famous "titled" sonatas, the *Pathétique*, *Moonlight*, and *Appassionata*, matches nobility of utterance with a technical command more powerful than either Schnabel's or Kempff's (C.B.S. stereo SBRG 72148, mono BRG 72148).

BEETHOVEN: Eleven piano trios. *Beaux Arts Trio.* Philips stereo SAL 3527-30, mono AL 3527-30.

The modern passion for completeness, which leads to marathon recitals of all Bach's cello suites or all Beethoven's cello sonatas, is even more prevalent in the record industry than on the concert platform. No one, surely, would wish to hear whole programmes of Beethoven piano trios, especially as these pieces are much more uneven in inspiration than the string quartets and sonatas; but musical magpies may find it an attractive idea to be able to collect the eleven works neatly on four discs, so that they can dip at leisure into music ranging from the delightfully high-spirited, confident E flat major trio, Op. 1, No. 1, in which, at the age of 25, he gave the Viennese public a glimpse of what they were in for, to the profound and noble Archduke trio, Op. 97, which he composed sixteen years later, around the same time as the seventh symphony.

In these lissom American performances, the players remind us that Beethoven did not score the music for piano with a background of strings, but gave each instrument—piano, violin, and cello—something important and beautiful to say. Readers wishing to sample the set (the records are available separately) are recommended first to volume three, which includes the powerful *Ghost* trio, Op. 70, No. 1, with its sinister slow movement, and its more felicitous companion-piece, Op. 70, No. 2 (stereo SAL 3529, mono AL 3529); and to volume four, most of which is devoted to a spacious but lively account of the *Archduke* (stereo SAL 3530, mono AL 3530).

BEETHOVEN: Violin sonata in F major, Op. 24 (Spring); Violin sonata in A major, Op. 47 (Kreutzer).
Yehudi and Hephzibah Manuhin. H.M.V. stereo ASD 389, mono ALP 1739.

Beethoven's ten violin sonatas have never enjoyed quite the popularity of those he wrote for piano alone—just as violin recitals in general do not have quite the drawing power of piano ones. Yet these works for two players contain some of the splendours of Beethoven's instrumental music, and no record collection would be complete without at least a few of them. They are true duo sonatas; the instruments are treated throughout as equal partners, and not, as was the case in the eighteenth century, with the violin in the subsidiary role. The *Spring* and *Kreutzer*, perhaps because they are the only ones with nicknames, have often been coupled on records, and there are several good performances to choose from—including a remarkable bargain issue by Alan Loveday and Leonard Cassini (Fidelio stereo TLS 6011, mono ATL 4060), yours for the price of two packets of cigarettes. But perhaps the most lasting satisfaction comes from the playing of the Menuhins, who treat the youthful *Spring* sonata with sparkling sunniness and wit, and give a superbly coherent and vital account of the sombre, thrusting *Kreutzer*. Beethoven described this music as "in a highly concerted style, just like a concerto"; and it was not, in fact, written for the great violinist Rodolphe Kreutzer (who apparently could never abide the work and declared it outrageously unintelligible) but for the British one, George Augustus Polgreen Bridgetower, who, at the first performance, had practically to sight-read the music from Beethoven's hastily-written and almost illegible manuscript.

A companion record by the same players contains the *Kreutzer's* powerful predecessor, the C minor, Op. 30, No. 2, and the last and most serene of the sonatas, the G major, Op. 96, composed for Pierre Rode, famous for the calmness of his playing (H.M.V. stereo ASD 510, mono ALP 1959).

BEETHOVEN: Five cello sonatas. *Mstislav Rostropovich/ Sviatoslav Richter*. Philips stereo SAL 3453-4, mono AL 3453-4.

Beethoven composed chamber music throughout his career, and nowhere is his development more sharply illustrated than in his five sonatas for cello and piano. As in the violin sonatas and piano trios, the instruments are treated as equals; and the task of matching their voices here seemed to fire his imagination even more strongly. The youthful vigour and far-flung spendour of the first two, composed when he was 26, owe something perhaps to the fact that they were written for Jean Pierre Duport, the leading cellist in the court of King Frederick William II of Prussia. The next sonata, the sublime and beautifully proportioned A major, is a "middle period" work dating from 1808—the same year as the *Pastoral* symphony. The pair of sonatas that form Op. 102 are introspective products of his last period—concentrated, experimental works, which can sound irritatingly gruff or nobly visionary according to who is playing them. None of the sonatas, surely, has ever sounded nobler than in these intense, cogent performances by Russia's two leading instrumentalists. If the music seems longer than usual, it is because each of Beethoven's repeats has been scrupulously included, and because these two great musicians play, where appropriate, with such breadth. Yet it is hard to imagine performances more alive, or with more sweep, than these—performances shaped and balanced with the kind of beauty one dreams of when reading the score, but seldom finds in practice.

BEETHOVEN: Six string quartets, Op. 18. *Amadeus Quartet*. D.G.G. stereo SLPM 138531-3, mono LPM 18531-3.

Beethoven composed fewer quartets than Haydn; but, like those of the older composer, they are among his most masterly and personal utterances, and span almost his whole career. They fall into three main groups, of which the earliest is the opus 18 set, Haydn-ish in size and spirit, completed when he was thirty years old and first aware that he was going deaf. The writing, is lithe, youthful, aphoristic, with sudden plunges into dark melancholy, as in the slow movement of the F major work, No. 1, said to be a tone painting of the tomb scene in *Romeo and Juliet*, and in the mysterious slow introduction to the finale of the B flat major, No. 6, a section actually entitled *La Malinconia*.

Although these quartets are not related in their material the way some of the later works are, it is nevertheless an advantage to buy them as a set, recorded by one group of players. The performance by the Amadeus gives us an admirable uniformity of approach. The playing is beautifully poised, and speaks in every bar of loving familiarity with the music.

BEETHOVEN: String quartets in F major, Op. 59, No. 1; in E minor, Op. 59, No. 2; in C major, Op. 59, No. 3; in E flat major, Op. 74; in F minor, Op. 95 *Amadeus Quartet*. D.G.G. stereo SLPM 138534-6, mono LPM 18534-6.

These are Beethoven's "middle period" quartets, written when he was approaching forty years of age and in the process of reconciling himself to the deafness that had overcome him in 1800. "Let your deafness no longer remain a secret, even in art," he jotted on one of his sketches for these works. The music is fiercer and more ambitious than the opus 18 quartets, less visionary than the great final group that was to follow. The three works comprising opus 59 are the *Rasumovsky* quartets, which, in tribute to the Russian count who commissioned them, make subtle use of Russian themes. The F major work is broad and singing, the E minor plaintive and passionate, the C major brilliant and athletic—together they make a kind of Beethovenian equivalent of Mozart's last three symphonies. But the boldness of their writing did not win immediate approval. One cellist, when faced with the scherzo of the F major work, threw the music on the floor and jumped on it in rage; and so many people considered these quartets to be the ravings of a madman that Beethoven felt impelled to

150

say "Not for you, but for a later age." Opus 74 is the *Harp* quintet, a more lilting work, which owes its nickname to the pizzicato arpeggios of its first movement. Opus 95, sometimes called the *quartetto serioso*, is grim, wiry, and concentrated; it cuts, says Marion Scott, "like an acetylene flame."

A variety of recordings are available of these works. That of the Amadeus, apart from being sympathetically performed, has the merit of being economic—it gives us the five works on three records. And since, like the opus 18 group, they date from one short period in Beethoven's life, there is much to be said for having them as a set performed by a single team of players who are completely at ease in the style.

BEETHOVEN: String quartets in E flat major, Op. 127; in B flat major, Op. 130; in C sharp minor, Op. 131; in A minor, Op. 132; in F major, Op. 135; Grosse Fuge, Op. 133. *Amadeus Quartet.* D.G.G. stereo SLPM 138537-40, mono LPM 18537-40.

Fourteen years separate Beethoven's late quartets from their predecessors. It was a period that brought him new sufferings, new tensions, and new worries, from which these last great visionary works served as a release. Like the opus 59 set, some of them are dedicated to a Russian patron, a rich amateur musician called Prince Galitzkin, who wrote to the composer that "At present there is scarcely one hearer who would be sufficiently enlightened to enjoy the full beauty of this music, but posterity will pay homage to you and bless your memory more than your contemporaries are able to do." Time has given proof to his words. Beethoven's last quartets changed the face of chamber music. Their effect was far reaching—as far as the present century, for it is possible to find in the quartets of Bartók and the symphonies of Sibelius (as well as, earlier, the music dramas of Wagner) the influence of this austere, spare, powerful, closely-reasoned music.

Of these five masterpieces, the middle three—the B flat major, the C sharp minor, and the A minor (with the *Grosse Fuge* as an alternative finale to the B flat)—form a triptych, vast in scale, exalted in thought, and related in

151

material. The A minor bears the highest opus number of the three, but was in fact the first to be finished. While composing it, Beethoven suffered a serious illness that left its stamp on the music, particularly the slow movement, on whose manuscript he inscribed the words "Holy Song of Thanksgiving to God from one healed of sickness, in the Lydian mode." But little more music was to be written. Less than two years later, Beethoven was dead.

In the concert hall, Beethoven's late quartets impose a heavy strain, physical, intellectual, and spiritual, on their performers; and in the studio, where the music can be recorded piecemeal, the difficulties are only fractionally less formidable. Consequently, it is understandable that few performances are fully successful. Not even the Amadeus, renowned for its Beethoven playing, here emerges unscathed. An alert Beckmesser would be able to chalk up a number of flaws in intonation, balance, and style; and, on a deeper level, the performances do not give us the whole truth. Even so, there is much to admire. The grief-stricken cavatina of the B flat quartet—about which Beethoven said "Never did music of mine make so deep an impression upon me, even the remembrance of the emotions it aroused always costs me a tear"—is perhaps not quite slow enough, but is played with great intensity. The sunnier opus 127 quartet is beautifully done. The short, crisp final quartet, opus 135, is given the sort of clarity and spontaneity that are so delightful in the Amadeus's treatment of the early opus 18 set. The performances are economically pressed on four records—one fewer than usual.

Collectors not wishing the complete set, or who would prefer a change of performer, are recommended to the Smetana Quartet's excellent bargain-price account of opus 127, coupled with the *Grosse Fuge* on Supraphon stereo SUA ST 50039, mono SUA 10372; to the Vlach Quartet's of opus 131 on Supraphon stereo SUA ST 50044, mono SUA 10365; and to the Janacek Quartet's coupling of opus 135 and opus 18, No. 6 on Supraphon stereo SUA ST 50415, mono SUA 10415. Of the other works, the Budapest Quartet's recordings on C.B.S. are perhaps the best bet, although the performances are less accurate and less profound.

**SCHUBERT (1797-1828): String quartet in E flat major,
D.87; String quartet in D minor, D.810 (Death and the
Maiden).** *Vienna Philharmonic Quartet.* Decca stereo
SXL 6092, mono LXT 6092.

Schubert's chamber music has all the lyricism and intimacy
one would expect of the composer of more than 600 songs.
The early quartets, like the early symphonies, are little
more than student exercises—though with some enchantingly Schubertian touches. The last three, written shortly before
his death, are indispensable masterpieces. Here, neatly
contained on one record, are works from the extremities of
his career. The little E flat major quartet, written when he
was sixteen, is a polished tribute to Mozart and Beethoven;
the D minor, dating from eleven years later, is pure Schubert,
with, as its slow movement, a series of tender variations on
the song that has given the work its nickname. Although
Arthur Hutchings, in his book on the composer, advises us
to beware of reading too deep a meaning into the choice of
this tragic song to form the heart of the quartet, the prevailing atmosphere of the work nevertheless has a pathos which
is maintained right through to the relentless tarantella that
forms the finale. Some performers take every opportunity
to over-dramatise the music, attacking its bold rhythms
with ferocity and making the slow movement sound as
tearful as can be. The Vienna Philharmonic Quartet,
composed of four players from the famous golden-toned
orchestra, recognise that the work does not need to be
browbeaten in this way; and in a wonderfully light and
flexible performance, they encourage it to speak eloquently
for itself.

SCHUBERT: Piano quintet in A major, D.667 (Trout).
Clifford Curzon/Members of the Vienna Octet. Decca
stereo SXL 2110, mono LXT 5433.

1819 was one of Schubert's happier years, in the summer of
which the 22-year-old composer went on a carefree holiday
with his baritone friend Vogl. Their tour took them to the
Austrian Alps, a stopover being made on the way at Steyr,
Vogl's birthplace. Schubert was apparently enchanted by the
countryside, and remarked on it in a letter as "inconceivably

153

lovely"—though he was, in any case, seeing life through rose-coloured glasses just then, for in his board residence there lived five girls, and in the house next door an additional three. "Eight girls," he wrote, "and nearly all pretty." It was in that idyllic atmosphere that this idyllic work was planned. In a lull between girls, Schubert had met and talked to a local amateur musician called Paumgartner, who played the cello and admired Schubert's song, *The Trout*. Paumgartner, it seems, had been practising Hummel's piano quintet with some friends and was on the lookout for another work that used the same unusual combination of instruments (piano, violin, viola, cello, double bass). Such a work proving unavailable, Schubert was invited to write one and the result was the *Trout* quintet, completed the following year in Vienna and containing, in tribute to Paumgartner's good taste in music, a set of variations based on *The Trout*.

It has been said that the Steyr countryside was as much the composer of this quintet as Schubert; and indeed, of all his works, it is perhaps the most peacefully pastoral in nature, a series of sunny landscapes with occasional plunges into some deep pool. If one wishes to introduce somebody to the charms of chamber music, this is the work with which to do so. If one wishes to switch off the gramophone and play some chamber music, this again is a work to tackle, provided that one's cellist is better than Paumgartner, who, after all his trouble, found his part too difficult. We all have our musical deaf spots, but it is hard to imagine anyone being unresponsive to the beauties of the *Trout* quintet.

Curzon and his Viennese companions give it a delectably zestful performance, catching all the sparkle of the bouncing scherzo and pouring out a beautifully paced account of the famous theme and variations, which they treat so lovingly one would think they had just that minute discovered its charms. The recording, just as it should be, is as warm and clear as a summer's day at Steyr.

SCHUBERT: String quartet in A minor, D.804. *Janacek Quartet.* Supraphon mono SUA 10480.

Schubert composed his A minor quartet—the only one of his last quartets to be published while he was alive—

154

around the same time as the D minor. Again the slow movement sheds new light on music he had used elsewhere—this time a familiar, easy-going theme from *Rosamunde*. Again the prevailing atmosphere is poignant. No music is more wistfully Schubertian than the start of the first movement, with its long, lonely opening theme sung by the first violin. Only in the finale, a sturdily dancing movement with a dash of paprika, is the sadness more or less dispelled. The Janáček Quartet gives it an ideal performance—deeply-felt, beautifully phrased, spontaneous. And although the recording has the slightly harsh edge that characterises a number of Supraphon's bargain-price issues, this scarcely detracts from one's enjoyment of the playing.

SCHUBERT: String quartet in G major, D.887.
Juilliard Quartet.   Columbia stereo SAX 2535, mono 33CX 1891.

This, still familiarly known as "Op. 161", is the crown of Schubert's quartets, a long and fiercely dramatic work which obviously marks the start of what would have been a powerful new phase in his quartet writing, had he not died too soon to fulfil it. It is a work which, at every turn, seems to be bursting the bounds of quartet writing. The pages are spattered with savage tremolo passages, double and triple stopping, hurtling rhythms and audacious harmonies. In his useful little handbook, *Playing String Quartets*, Athol Page exclaims about the tunes the cello is given to play, and the opportunities it receives to lead the whole quartet. None of Schubert's previous quartets is so led "from the bottom up," and it is this that serves to give the music much of its sombre intensity—nowhere more so than in the slow movement, which at times has an almost Bartókian explosiveness.

The Juilliard Quartet, a leading American ensemble with a special fame for its performances of present-day music, particularly stresses the "daring" features of this work. Seldom do performances make it sound quite so violently rhythmic and modern; yet the players do not ignore the passages of lyricism, and in the trio of the third movement the pace is relaxed so that the cellist can savour to the full the Ländler-like beauty of the melody.

SCHUBERT: Piano trio in B flat major, D.898.
HAYDN: Trio No. 1 in G major. *Alfred Cortot/Jaques*
Thibaud/Pablo Casals. H.M.V. mono COLH 12.
SCHUBERT: Piano trio in E flat major, D.929. *Rudolf*
Serkin/Adolf Busch/Hermann Busch. H.M.V. mono
COLH 43.

Schubert's two great and wonderfully contrasted piano trios
date from the year before his death. The first (long known as
Op. 99) was described by Schumann as "passive, feminine,
and lyrical," the second (Op. 100) as "active, masculine,
and dramatic." The B flat, perhaps because its material is a
little more joyous and a little less protracted, has always
been the favourite with the public. But the slow movement
of the E flat, with its forlorn, trudging rhythm that reminds
us that it was composed in the same year as *Die Winterreise*,
is one of Schubert's most profound inspirations; and anyone who says he "prefers" the B flat trio is surely neglecting
one of the supreme experiences of music.

Happily, both works are available in inimitably beautiful,
if elderly, recordings. In both cases, three great performers
came together to play music they loved; and their love
shines through every note of their performances. The first
was made in London in 1926; and in its excellent LP
transfer, room has been found for a performance by the
same players of Haydn's earliest piano trio, whose spirited
Gypsy rondo has given it a fame not shared by the thirty other
works he wrote in this form. Here, violin and cello play
merely a subsidiary role—but how rewarding to hear an
accompaniment performed by Thibaud and Casals!

The other Schubert trio was recorded nine years later,
also in London. And here again one marvels at the life of
the playing, in which every phrase speaks more eloquently
than in any subsequent recorded performance.

SCHUBERT: String quintet in C, D.956. *Budapest*
Quartet with Benar Heifetz (cello). C.B.S. stereo SBRG
72187, mono BRG 72187.

Because it needs the services of an extra cellist, Schubert's C
major quintet is not heard so often as some of his quartets—
which is a pity, for it is a glorious work, a masterpiece vast

in its proportions, wide in its emotional range, rich in its melodic and textural interest. It is one of several works that Schubert composed in a final, intense burst of inspiration just before his death in 1828; and we have come to regard it as the artistic, as well as the literal, culmination of his music for chamber ensemble.

Like many of his larger scores, it shows signs of hasty construction, The main theme of the finale comes round rather too often; the parts are not always comfortably laid out for the players; the two cellists have to keep their noses to the grindstone practically from start to finish; and Professor Hutchings has black-marked two pages of the first movement's development section because they merely repeat the previous two pages a tone lower. Yet when the sea is coming at us, we should not criticise some of the waves for being less splendid than others. And so, in listening to Schubert's string quintet, it is better to accept the music in one sweep, and ignore its minor flaws. This performance by the Budapest Quartet, with Benar Heifetz as the extra cellist, makes it easy to do so, for it has great fire and vigour, emphasised by full-blooded recording.

SCHUBERT: Piano sonata in A major, D.959. *Rudolf Serkin.* C.B.S. stereo SBRG 72432, mono BRG 72432.

Schubert's piano sonatas, like those of Tippett in the present century, have often been called "unpianistic," when in fact the fault has usually lain more with the pianist than with the composer. There is no doubt that most of these seventeen works are hard, very hard, to play well. Their style, as the saying goes, is "orchestral"; and the longer sonatas are a mental and physical endurance test for the performer. Yet the feat is not impossible, as Schnabel taught us in the past, and as Serkin is enthrallingly reminding us today. Schubert, like Schumann later, was perhaps excessively aware of what Beethoven had done for the piano and for the sonata. Schumann never quite solved the problem of wedding his lyrical genius to the demands of a vast sonata movement; but Schubert, in his last works, did succeed, and the proof is to be found overwhelmingly in the great A major sonata he completed just before his death. This is the greatest of his keyboard works. Although less well known than its companion-piece in B flat major (whose popularity derives mainly from the lilting tune which haunts the first movement), its melodic and structural invention is more nobly and movingly sustained. Serkin's performance is of the magisterial order that the music needs if it is to be heard in its full splendour. The vast paragraphs of the opening movement are assembled with a superb sense of musical architecture: one has the same feeling of unhurried excitement and satisfaction and wonder that one has on hearing Klemperer conduct the German classics, a feeling that stems less from tonal allure (Serkin is no lilting Schubertian) than from spiritual profundity and intense intellectual concentration. No one who listens to this record can doubt for an instant that this is one of the great masterpieces for piano, just as no one can doubt that Serkin is one of the great pianists of our time, and an ordained interpreter of music such as this.

MENDELSSOHN (1809-1847): String octet in E flat.
Janacek Quartet/Smetana Quartet. H.M.V. stereo SXLP 20071, mono XLP 20071.

Mendelssohn's chamber music is often decried. But those who complain of its over-sweetness usually permit themselves to succumb to one, at least, of his works—the string octet, whose delights are so many and varied it would need a heart of stone to resist them. Mendelssohn was just sixteen when he composed it, and no other composer, not even Mozart, has written so masterly a work at so early an age. Nothing he produced later was to surpass it, nothing was more ravishing, nothing more zestfully spontaneous. From start to finish it moves, delectably, on springs. The first movement is an object lesson in how to make inspired use of arpeggios. The second is a comfortable andante that avoids —as, in his later works, he did not always succeed in doing —sliding into sentimentality. The fleet, silvery scherzo, a well-known concert piece in its own right, anticipates the atmosphere of the incidental music to *A Midsummer Night's Dream*. And the finale is one of the most joyous webs of counterpoint ever spun. Czechoslovakia's two leading string quartets here combine to produce a lively performance. The recording, a bargain one, is beautifully balanced; and in the stereo version there is an exciting, life-like spread of sound.

SCHUMANN (1810-1856): Carnaval, Op. 9; Fantasiestücke, Op. 12. *Artur Rubinstein.* R.C.A. stereo SB 6547, mono RB 6547.

Like so many nineteenth-century composers, Schumann felt compelled to follow in Beethoven's footsteps by writing large abstract works—symphonies, quartets, sonatas—which gave scant opportunity for his lyrical imagination to flower as freely as it needed. To hear the more characteristic Schumann, we must turn to his domestic works, his songs and less consciously "ambitious" piano pieces, in which, away from the strait-jacket of sonata-form, his genius is revealed at its most subtle and spontaneous. *Carnaval*, which he wrote when he was 25, consists of a series of short character sketches, each with its own title, revealing all the aspects of his personality—exuberant, pensive, amorous, melancholy —with a youthful sharpness he was never later to surpass.

Whereas in *Carnaval* Schumann was concerned with people—the music depicts a number of his friends and acquaintances at a ball, along with various characters from the traditional *commedia dell' arte*—in the eight *Fantasiestücke*, Op. 12, dating from the same period, he was concerned more with moods. The pieces bear titles such as *Why?*, *Whims*, and *In the Night*, titles which allowed his lyricism free rein. Artur Rubinstein plays both sets of pieces with a poetic beauty and tenderness, and a freshness that is remarkable when one remembers that he was nearly 80 years old when he recorded them and that he has performed them time and again throughout his long career. But it is this "living" quality of his playing that makes him one of the great pianists of our time.

A delicate performance of the *Kinderscenen*, the most gentle and popular of all Schumann's sets of short pieces, is given by the Hungarian pianist Annie Fischer on a Columbia record, coupled with the deeply introspective and original *Kreisleriana*, a work that deserves to be far better known than it is (stereo SAX 2583, mono 33CX 1944).

CHOPIN (1810-1849): Twelve études, Op. 10; Twelve études, Op. 25. *Gyorgy Cziffra.* Philips mono AL 3427.

Unlike Schumann (his exact contemporary), Chopin knew

159

just where his musical genius lay and seldom attempted to stray outside the world of the short, perfectly proportioned piano piece—a world into which he poured an extraordinary wealth of poetic intensity. Studies, polonaises, mazurkas, waltzes, scherzos, ballades, preludes, nocturnes, impromptus flowed from his pen, linking his nostalgic thoughts for his native Poland with the elegance of the French salons in which he spent most of his career. Chopin was the supreme poet of the piano, and was also a master craftsman; and nowhere is his mastery of his craft more strikingly apparent than in his two youthful sets of studies, each dedicated to a different technical problem of the new piano style he was attempting to perfect. But the pieces are no mere technical exercises: gloriously melodic, graceful, and passionate, they are as much a joy to listen to as they are stimulating to play. Here the Hungarian pianist, Gyorgy Cziffra, performs them as if he believes them to be the greatest music ever written. His playing is breathtaking: dynamic, tender, incandescent, full of entrancing detail; and it is brilliantly captured by the recording engineers.

CHOPIN: 51 mazurkas. *Nikita Magaloff.* Decca mono LXT 5318-20.

Although they conform to the rhythm of the traditional Polish dance, Chopin took care to point out, early in his career, that these pieces are "not for dancing." In fact, they are his most personal works, a kind of private journal in which, throughout his life, he confided all his changing moods, worked out his harmonic and rhythmic experiments, explored the most delicate and various pianistic colours, and paid the most heart-felt of all his tributes to his native Poland. The first mazurka was written before he left his homeland in 1830; the last, a poignant little reflection in F minor, was the last piece he ever wrote. Because of their brevity and complete lack of ostentation, the mazurkas have tended to be less popular with pianists than his other, technically more demanding works. But none of his other pieces requires so much interpretative insight and understanding, none is more essentially Chopin. Nikita Magaloff, playing them in chronological order, catches their spirit with clarity and sensitivity. Of all the sets of pieces by Chopin, this is the most expensive to buy; but the aphoristic, bitter-sweet beauty of the music makes it the most eternally fascinating to live with.

CHOPIN: Four ballades: three studies, Op. posth.
Vladimir Ashkenazy. Decca stereo SXL 6143, mono LXT 6143.

Like the piano mazurka, the piano ballade is a type of piece more or less peculiar to Chopin. It would be too much to call it a "form"; but the four works to which he gave this title do resemble each other in character and scale. And although they do not follow any traditional musical pattern, they are by no means as formless as their name suggests. The G minor ballade, for instance, has a wonderful cogency of construction, and grows from two memorable and characteristic themes—one of them melancholy, rather drooping, in the minor, the other broad, nobly flowing, in the major. By the most subtle changes of mood and colour, Chopin reveals new aspects of these themes on each of their appearances, and ultimately releases a spitfire coda, *presto con fuoco*.

Because of the lyrical, narrative, passionate nature of the music, many programme annotators have attempted to find stories in Chopin's ballades, using as an excuse the fact that Chopin was believed to have Mickiewicz's poetry in mind when he composed them. But if he did so, it was surely the spirit of the poetry he wished to convey, rather than the text, and the ingenious "explanations" compiled by some writers are best ignored. Here the young Russian pianist Vladimir Ashkenazy plays them in such a way that one thinks of them solely in terms of music. These are wonderfully sane, graceful, performances, which, though full of life, seem deliberately to avoid the histrionic approach that generations of virtuosi have brought to these pieces.

The three studies that complete the record were written some years after the larger and more famous sets, and are usually identified as the *trois nouvelles études*. Although intended as a contribution to a teaching manual by Moscheles entitled *The Method of Methods*, they are much less pedantic than this name implies.

CHOPIN: Fourteen waltzes. *Artur Rubinstein.* R.C.A. stereo SB 6600, mono RB 6600.

Chopin's waltzes show him at his most elegant and refined. Like the mazurkas, they are dances of the spirit rather than of the feet; but whereas the mazurkas are often intense and brooding, the waltzes for the most part are content to be charming. Some of them sparkle deliciously; others are slow and wistful. In comparison with the mazurkas, they are "minor" Chopin; but one would not be without them, especially when played with such complete feeling for their character as is revealed in this performance by one of the great Chopin pianists of our time.

CHOPIN: 24 preludes, Op. 28; Polonaise in A flat major, Op. 53. *Geza Anda.* D.G.G. stereo SLPM 138084, mono LPM 18604.

Chopin spread the composition of his mazurkas, nocturnes, and waltzes over most of his working life; but the 24 preludes were conceived as a single group of pieces, each of them in a different key, like Bach's *Well-tempered Clavier*. There is, therefore, justification for playing them all at one sitting; and indeed, their sharp, kaleidoscopic beauty can only be fully appreciated if this is done. Yet many of the pieces are world-famous out of context: the tiny, simple, mazurka-like A major prelude, which became an *idée fixe* of the ballet *Les Sylphides*, a posthumous potpourri of Chopin's music; the grim, funereal C minor prelude; the shadowy *Raindrop* prelude, and the yearning E minor and B minor ones. Although only a few of them were written there, it is hard to listen to this aching music without thinking of the wretched winter Chopin spent in Majorca, where tuberculosis made its first serious raid on his health. The polonaise included as an encore is the most fiery and majestic of a series of pieces in which Chopin's nationalistic inspiration worked in general at a slightly lower level than in the mazurkas. This record includes some of the most masculine music Chopin ever wrote—a quality Geza Anda brings out specially well in his strong but not over-driven performances.

CHOPIN: Ten nocturnes. *Stefan Askenase.* D.G.G. Heliodor mono 478037.

Other composers have written piano nocturnes, but it is Chopin who first comes to mind when the word is mentioned. These are the most meltingly lovely of his pieces—although sometimes, especially in their middle sections and closing bars, darker thoughts intrude on their tranquil atmosphere. Heard in bulk, they can make a rather enervating impression; and here perhaps a complete set is less desirable than in the case of the mazurkas. Stefan Askenase's tenderly played and well-compiled recital consists of half of them, including the most popular of the series, the hackneyed E flat major, which he turns into a miracle of simplicity, and the two haunting Op. 37 pieces, the G major being one of the superb stream of works he composed while staying at George Sand's country house at Nohant between 1839 and 1841. The complete nocturnes are available in numerical order in a good Decca recording by Peter Katin (mono LXT 5122 and LXT 5238).

CHOPIN: Piano sonata in B flat minor, Op. 35 (Funeral March); Piano sonata in B minor, Op. 58. *Artur Rubinstein.* R.C.A. stereo SB 2151, mono RB 16282.

These, the longest of Chopin's works for solo piano, prove that once in a while he could sustain a large design without losing grip of his material. Although each conforms to a traditional pattern of four movements, they are not "strict" sonatas. But one would not wish them otherwise, for they are constructed with a profound and satisfying logic of their own, and the flexibility of their shape gave Chopin elbow-room to work into them an abundance of his loveliest melodies, and to include some memorable strokes of imagination. The idea of the B flat minor sonata sprang from its funeral march, composed some time before the rest of the work and casting its shadow over all the other movements. In the first movement, Chopin's inspiration is at its most feverish; and the soft, rustling finale, which reminded Anton Rubinstein of "night winds sweeping over churchyard graves," is perhaps the most extraordinary piece he ever wrote—twentieth-century music composed, by chance, in 1839. The B minor sonata, which followed in 1845, is no less masterly. In it, the turbulent and lyrical aspects of Chopin's personality are mingled with confident ease, from the plunging opening of the first movement right through to the pounding, agitated vitality of the finale. In both works, Artur Rubinstein is at the top of his form, and his performances have a consummate brilliance and grace.

LISZT (1811-1886): Piano recital. *Gyorgy Cziffra.*
Philips stereo SAL 3465, mono AL 3465.

Liszt was born a year after Chopin, and, like the latter, was destined to become one of the most famous pianist-composers of his generation. But there was a considerable difference between them. Chopin preferred upright pianos to concert grands, because he considered their more intimate tone better suited to his music. Liszt, unquestionably, preferred concert grands, against which he pitted his strength with the most leonine valour and a keen eye for drama. In his enthralling book, *The Great Pianists,* Harold Schonberg quotes a British writer of the period who attended a Liszt recital in Paris and was fascinated by the composer's "agony of expression, mingled with radiant smiles of joy, which I never saw on any other human face except in the paintings of Our Saviour by some of the early masters." This commentator added that when Liszt's hands rushed over the keys, the floor shook like a wire. Then the composer "fainted in the arms of a friend who was turning over the pages for him, and we bore him out in a fit of hysterics. The effect of this scene was really dreadful. The whole room sat breathless with fear . . ."

Liszt lived 37 years longer than Chopin, and as a composer he developed much more slowly. Indeed it was not until he had given up his career as a virtuoso pianist that he got down seriously to composition. Even then, the theatricality of his character left its stamp on his music, though in some of his later works—the extraordinary *Nuages gris, La lugubre gondola,* and *Richard Wagner*—an almost Bartókian austerity and sombreness creep in. Gyorgy Cziffra's gorgeously performed recital concentrates on the more extrovert side of Liszt's nature; but the pieces are not to be sniffed at, for they accommodate some of the most

164

astonishing bravura writing ever produced. In *St. Francis of Paola walking on the waters,* the music surges with chromatic energy. In the concert study, *La leggierezza,* it is almost inconceivable that fingers can be made to move so fast. Happily, Cziffra does include a few pauses for reflection, and the presence of the beautiful Petrarch sonnet 123 is especially welcome.

Liszt's grandest work for solo piano, his B minor sonata, which he seems to have written in reply to Chopin's in the same key, forms the most substantial part of another fine Liszt recital, this time by the young British pianist, John Ogdon (H.M.V. stereo ASD 600, mono ALP 2051); and this work is also obtainable in a historic performance by Horowitz, successfully dubbed from 78 along with the grim *Funérailles* and four short pieces by Schumann (H.M.V. mono COLH 72).

SMETANA (1824-1884): String quartet No. 1 in E minor (From my life); String quartet No. 2 in D minor.
Smetana Quartet. Supraphon stereo SUA ST 50448, mono SUA 10448.

Chamber music is surely the most difficult method a composer could employ to tell his autobiography; but that is what Smetana did in the first of his two string quartets, in which, at the age of 54, he looks back on his youthful joy and energy, his fondness for dancing (the second movement is a lilting polka), his wooing of his wife, and the onslaught of the tragic deafness that suddenly overcame him in middle age. In a passage of stark pictorialism, unexpected in a string quartet, the whistling sound in the composer's stricken ear is reproduced towards the end of the finale by a high E from the first violin, after which the other strings shudder with forboding. The Smetana Quartet, named after the composer, is one of Czechoslovakia's leading string quartets; and here it gives a meticulously accented, vigorous performance, full of warmth and understanding. The D minor quartet, though it bears no written programme, sounds no less graphic and stirring than its predecessor; and it is equally well performed.

BRAHMS (1833-1897): String sextet in B flat major, Op. 18; Allegro from F-A-E sonata. *Yehudi Menuhin and Robert Masters* (*violins*), *Cecil Aronowitz and Ernest Wallfisch* (*violas*), *Maurice Gendron and Derek Simpson* (*cellos*). H.M.V. stereo ASD 587, mono ALP 2038.

Brahms often had second thoughts about his chamber music. He destroyed all but three of his twenty-odd string quartets because they did not meet his exacting standards; he rewrote his B major piano trio nearly forty years after he composed it (though both versions are still in print, and Tovey had a memorable story about a performance in which one player accidently used the early version and the others the revised edition, and it was some minutes before the horrible truth was discovered); and his F minor piano quintet saw service first as a string quintet and then as a sonata for two pianos before it emerged in its final form.

Brahms wrote so much chamber music, and took so much trouble over it, that we can assume he regarded it as a major portion of his output. Unfortunately, to all but the most devoted and uncritical Brahms-lover, much of his music in this form sounds laboured and unspontaneous. So often one's hopes are raised at the start of a work by a glorious, sailing, passionate theme; and so often they are shattered when one hears what Brahms, later in the movement, does with the theme in the interests of "development." Even in some of his greatest chamber pieces, the material sounds at times overworked and congested. Not so the early B flat major sextet, which, although digressive and leisurely, has a warmth of lyrical feeling that carries it safely over the hurdles on which some of his later, more ambitious works tripped. The addition of an extra viola and cello to the classic formation of the string quartet gives the music throughout a wonderful glow and geniality. The first movement is, for Brahms, welcomely relaxed and unemphatic; and although one should be generally opposed to the use of classical masterpieces as film background music, one remembers how beautifully the andante—a radiant, slow-climbing theme and variations—was used in Louis Malle's *Les Amants*.

The star-studded performance, by players closely associated with the Bath Festival, achieves a corporate spirit that performances of its kind cannot always be relied on to give us. The short filler is a scherzo which Brahms contributed to a composite composition written by him, Schumann, and a minor contemporary, Albert Dietrich, as a gift for the violinist Joachim. It is of no great moment, but is neatly played by Menuhin and his sister Hephzibah.

A second string sextet, composed five years later in tribute to a singer with whom Brahms was passingly in love, is similarly mellow, but slightly more urgent, in its feeling; and it receives a similarly tender performance from the same team of players (H.M.V. stereo ASD 643, mono ALP 2096), though the recording is not quite so well balanced.

BRAHMS: Variations on a theme by Handel, Op. 24; Variations on a theme by Paganini, Op. 35 (two books).
Julius Katchen.   Decca stereo SXL 6218, mono LXT 6218.

In September, 1853, Schumann jotted in his diary: "Brahms to see me (a genius)." By that time, Schumann, aged 43, was in the twilight of his career, with only a few months to go before he was sent to the madhouse; whereas Brahms, aged 20, was just beginning to show his strength with a succession of clumsy but full-blooded and richly promising keyboard works. The piano was Brahms's instrument, just as it was Schumann's. But Brahms was the more leonine pianist; and so his virtuosity is reflected in the masculine brilliance of much of his keyboard writing, in which he taxes the instrument—and the performer—to the utmost.

Like Schumann, Brahms was excessively aware of Beethoven's achievement in the earlier part of the nineteenth century; and, again like Schumann, he chose to wrestle, not always successfully, with what (to him) was the straitjacket of sonata-form. His shorter piano pieces and sets of variations, on the other hand, have a sharpness and shapeliness that often eluded him when he wrote in large forms. His most famous piano variations are those on themes of Handel and Paganini he composed when he was in his early thirties. Here we find him at his most succinct, shifting from mood to mood with a wealth of imagination, and at the same time employing the most dazzling array of technical devices, tonal contrasts and rhythms. The Handel variations are the more subtle of the two sets: 25 marvellously inventive variations followed by a ringing fugue. The two books of Paganini variations are based on the same theme—from one of Paganini's caprices for solo violin—as was used later by Rakhmaninov in his *Rhapsody on a Theme of Paganini*. The music is the most energetic Brahms ever wrote, and one can be sure that Paganini himself, that most acrobatic of composer-performers, would have delighted in it.

In recent years, Julius Katchen has been associating himself increasingly with Brahms's keyboard music; and the relationship, as can be heard from this record, is often a richly rewarding one. Technically, his performance has a masterly assurance; and interpretatively, he shows himself to be equally *au fait* with the style of both works.

BRAHMS: Piano quintet in F minor, Op. 34. *Rudolf Serkin/Budapest String Quartet.* C.B.S. stereo SBRG 72273, mono BRG 72273.

Written when he was 29, this work combines youthful passion with a sustained mastery of material that Brahms seldom managed to achieve in his later chamber music. Clara Schumann thought the first performance the greatest event of its kind since Schubert's great C major string quintet—a work the Brahms sometimes resembles. The first movement opens with a lithe, muscular theme whose sweep and power leave their stamp on the rest of the movement; the andante is a tender, richly melodious lullaby; the scherzo rattles along with a momentum rare in Brahms. Only in the finale does the inspiration seem a fraction less spontaneous, but even there the music has such vitality that the listener is swept along by the tide. Rudolf Serkin first recorded this work in the nineteen-thirties with the Busch Quartet; and although his 1966 performance lacks a little of the ardour of the original, it nevertheless has a spring and a warmth of feeling that are deeply satisfying; and the recording, of course is far more vivid.

BRAHMS: Cello sonata in E minor, Op. 38; Cello sonata in F major, Op. 99. *Janos Starker/Abba Bogin.* Saga mono XID 5164.

Of Brahms's two sonatas for cello and piano, the first is a powerful but rather grumpy work, composed when he was in his early thirties and not yet fully adept at handling this combination of instruments; the second, dating from twenty years later, is the magnificent outcome of the experience he gained in the E minor work. The first movement is in his broadest, most lyrical vein; the adagio is a profound meditation, with the cello ruminating, pizzicato, down in the depths; the scherzo and finale abound in noble, singing themes. Janos Starker and Abba Bogin present the music in its full mellow glory, sustaining the flow and beauty of the big melodies, and revealing a sure grasp of each movement. The bargain-price recording is outstandingly clear and smooth.

BRAHMS: Violin sonata No. 2 in A major, Op. 100; Violin sonata No. 3 in D minor, Op. 108. *Henryk Szeryng (violin)/Artur Rubinstein (piano).* R.C.A. stereo SB 6520, mono RB 6520.

Of Brahms's three violin sonatas, the second (sometimes called the *Meistersinger* because it opens rather like the *Prize Song*) is a genial work, full of warm melodies that are allowed to speak for themselves without being subjected to too much in the way of knotty Brahmsian "development." The third sonata is more assertive and masculine, with a restless opening movement and a vigorous, questing finale. Between these powerful movements, however, come one of Brahms's loveliest slow movements, based on the most luscious of themes, and a delicate, rueful scherzo. Often in performances of these works the pianist is wrongly relegated to the role of accompanist; in this performance the players are equal partners, with Rubinstein delighting in the beauty of the music just as much as Szeryng.

An equally outstanding recording of the first sonata, in which the intimacy of the A major work is blended with the fire of the D minor, has been made by the same artists (R.C.A. stereo SB 6513, mono RB 6513). It is coupled with an impeccable account of Beethoven's G major sonata, Op. 30, No. 3.

BRAHMS: Clarinet quintet in B minor, Op. 115.
MOZART: Duo for violin and viola in G major, K.423.
Vladimir Riha/Smetana Quartet. Supraphon stereo SUA ST 50677, mono SUA 10677.

In his last years, Brahms was inspired by the clarinettist Richard Muhlfield, a member of the Meiningen orchestra, to compose a series of masterpieces at least one of which—the B minor quintet—is comparable to the works which Mozart, in his last years, wrote for Anton Stadler. Indeed, there is ground for considering the quintet to be Brahms's most profound, as well as his most sheerly lovely, piece of chamber music. Anyone who listens to it, and finds himself out of sympathy with what it has to say, need proceed no farther with his study of Brahms. But only a heart of stone could fail to respond to it. The writing has none of the heaving fortissimi, and little of the muddiness, that so often disfigure Brahms's domestic works. Instead the texture is delicate, with the clarinet gleaming gently through the string tone; and the beauty has a subdued, valedictory quality that is very touching. The Czech performance is a sober, serious one, concentrating more on the inward qualities of the music than on tonal allure. The Melos Ensemble's rival performance on H.M.V. is more poised; but it costs more than twice as much, and its filler (a piece by Reger) cannot match the lithe, masterly, rarely-heard duo which Mozart ghost-wrote for Michael Haydn, and which is here captivatingly played by members of the Smetana Quartet.

BRAHMS: Three intermezzos, Op. 117; Six piano pieces, Op. 118; Four piano pieces, Op. 119. *Wilhelm Kempff.* D.G.G. stereo SLPM 138903, mono LPM 18903.

Towards the end of his life, with all his large-scale works behind him, Brahms produced several collections of short, intensely personal piano pieces, wonderful late crystallisations of all he had learnt as a pianist-composer. Here is a succinct beauty of a kind one wishes he had exploited more frequently, an autumnal pensiveness, a lyrical imagination and sense of adventure that put these pieces in a class with Chopin's mazurkas. "Even one listener is too many," Brahms said of them; and indeed, so confidential do the quieter pieces sound that one feels oneself to be eaves-dropping.

The first of the Op. 117 intermezzos uses an old Scottish ballade as the inspiration of an idyllic study in tone and harmony; the third is one of the few really light-hearted and delicate pieces Brahms ever wrote. Others are robust and ringing, in a more traditional Brahmsian way, yet with a new, clear-cut quality about them; others are poignant and brooding, and exactly suggest the composer's description of them as the cradle-song of his sufferings.

No pianist is better suited to this music than Wilhelm Kempff, whose probing, perceptive playing goes straight to the heart of each piece. A companion record of the three piano pieces, Op. 76, the two rhapsodies, Op. 79, and the seven fantasias, Op. 116, contains a similar poetic under-standing, though the veteran pianist sounds not fully up to the bravura of the big G minor rhapsody (D.G.G. stereo SLPM 138902, mono LPM 18902).

DVORAK (1841-1904): String quartet in D minor, Op. 34; String quartet in F major, Op. 96 (American). *Janacek String Quartet.* Decca stereo SXL 6103, mono LXT 6103.

Although they form a large and important part of his output, Dvorak's string quartets are not nearly so well known as his symphonies—which is a pity, for it would be fair to say that those who do not know his chamber music do not know Dvorak. The quartets—fifteen in all, spanning nearly the whole of his working life—include some of his most personal, thoughtful utterances. The D minor, written within eleven days at the age of 37, at the end of a year that had seen the deaths of his son and one of his daughters, is perhaps the most deeply moving of his early quartets. The F major dates from fifteen years later, and like the *New World* symphony, was a product of his famous visit to America—to which it owes the nicknames (originally *Nigger;* now, more tactfully, *American*) by which it has become known. In fact the music is thoroughly and endearingly Czech in spirit, a quality expressively caught in the wonderfully warm and idiomatic playing of the Janáček Quartet.

Admirable recordings of two of Dvorak's other quartets—the glowing C major, Op. 61, and the fine, late G major,

Op. 106, which reflects the composer's pleasure at returning home from America—are available at bargain price from the Czech company, Supraphon. The first (mono SUA 10197) is played by the Novak Quartet; the second (mono SUA 10172) by the Vlach Quartet.

DVORAK: Piano quintet in A major, Op. 81.
SCHUBERT: Quartettsatz in C minor, D. 703. *Clifford Curzon/Vienna Philharmonic String Quartet.* Decca stereo SXL 6043, mono LXT 6043.

Written shortly before his trip to America, the piano quintet is one of Dvorak's most radiant chamber works, prodigal in its themes and ideas, powerfully nationalistic in its feeling, with the most exquisite contrasts in colour and texture obtained by the addition of a piano to the traditional line-up of the string quartet. Several good recordings of it exist, but none catches as sensitively as Curzon's the touches of melancholy that sometimes pierce the high-spirits of the music; nor are the others quite so realistically recorded. The inclusion of Schubert's C minor *Quartettsatz*, intended as the first movement of a quartet he failed to complete, makes this record even more treasurable, for—although no more than a fragment—it is Schubert at his best and most intense, and it occupies the same place among his string quartets as the *Unfinished* among his symphonies.

DEBUSSY (1862-1918): String quartet. RAVEL (1875-1937): String quartet. *Vlach Quartet.* Supraphon stereo SUA ST 50040, mono SUA 10063.

Debussy composed just one string quartet. So, ten years later, did Ravel. And along with the quartets of Franck and Fauré (each of whom also wrote just one quartet) these constitute France's main contribution to the form during the nineteenth and early twentieth centuries. Ravel's quartet (1903) is perhaps the pick of the bunch—a youthful work of typical polish and suppleness, but with warmth of feeling as well, and a delight in the possibilities of sound which the four instruments offered him. The Debussy, too, is an early work, dating from the same year as *L'après-midi d'un faune*, and making interesting use of cyclic form. But for most listeners, it is not so much the construction as the atmospheric beauty of the writing that has made the music so popular. The Vlach Quartet, on one of Supraphon's bargain-price records, reveals a happy understanding of the idiom, and gives each work a clean, suave, alert performance.

DEBUSSY: Préludes, book one. *Walter Gieseking.* Columbia mono 33CX 1098.

Debussy's piano music has its roots in Chopin and Liszt; and he continued, with the utmost artistic refinement and sense of keyboard colour, the experiments they had begun. Perhaps the most characteristic and imaginative of his pieces are found among his *préludes*—delicate sketches, beautifully suggestive of the titles he chose for them. Of the two books he produced, each containing twelve pieces, the first (1910) includes some of the most famous—*La cathédrale engloutie, La fille aux cheveux de lin,* and *Minstrels,* as well as the lesser-known but equally evocative *Le vent dans la plaine* and *Les sons et les parfums tournent dans l'air du soir.* Walter Gieseking was the greatest of Debussy pianists, and what was intended to be a comprehensive survey of the piano music was cut short by his death in 1956, at the age of 61. Another record, containing the three *Estampes,* the two sets of *Images,* and the early suite, *Pour le piano,* is also available (Columbia mono 33CX 1137).

DEBUSSY: Cello sonata. BRITTEN (born 1913): Cello sonata. *Mstislav Rostropovich/Benjamin Britten.* Decca stereo SWL 8503, mono BR 8503.

The literature of music for cello and piano is less rich than that for violin and piano (which, in turn, is less rich than that for piano solo), but the present century has produced at least the two masterpieces coupled on this record. The Debussy (1917) dates from the twilight of his career, and was intended as part of an uncompleted series of six sonatas for different combinations of instruments. Because it shows his style pruned down to its essentials, this bare, austere music has always seemed to some ears to reveal a dwindling

173

in its composer's inspiration; but to others, it achieves the uncluttered, rather oblique beauty of expression that is also found in some of Sibelius's later works. Rostropovich and Britten make powerful advocates for the latter assessment, and provide an equally stimulating coupling in Britten's own cello sonata, composed in 1961 for performance by Rostropovich at the Aldeburgh Festival. A strong, rather nervy work in five movements, it is written with tremendous verve and an imagination characteristic of the composer. The performances, here coupled on a ten-inch bargain-price record, are also obtainable on a more expensive twelve-inch one, along with Schumann's delicate but perhaps less captivating *Fünf Stücke im Volkston.*

JANACEK (1854-1928): String quartet No. 1; String quartet No. 2. *Janacek Quartet.* Supraphon stereo SUA ST 50556, mono SUA 10556.

In Czechoslovakia, the fashion set by Smetana for composing descriptive chamber music was followed half a century later by Janáček, whose two string quartets relate a number of deep personal experiences. The first, written when he was 69, is principally devoted to his impressions of Tolstoy's *Kreutzer Sonata*, a novel whose basic theme—marital fidelity and tragedy—also inspired some of his other works. In addition, and more personally, the quartet is devoted to his love for Kamila Stosslova, a married woman nearly forty years younger than himself. "Wherever there is warmth of pure sentiment, sincerity, truth, and ardent love in my compositions," he wrote to her, "you are the source of it." The second quartet, dating from five years later, is his most ecstatic confession of this love. It was the last work he wrote. A few months later, while searching for Kamila's eleven-year-old son, who had got lost in the forest of Hukvaldy, he caught a cold which developed into fatal pneumonia.

The mood of the music is predominantly joyful, and the writing has a vividness and an idyllic radiance quite remarkable for a man of his years. The four compact movements of each work are quite as Czechoslovakian in character as Smetana's and Dvorak's quartets; but instead of the broad and easily flowing melodies of those earlier works,

174

the music is built from shorter, more pungent phrases, full of
two-bar repetitions typical of Czech folk-music, and full,
too, of abrupt contrasts and changes of pace and key,
which give the listener who is not yet accustomed to
Janáček's idiom the impression that the music is forever
stopping and starting. Yet the overall effect, on closer acquaintance, is extraordinarily eloquent. The instruments,
much of the time, seem almost to be speaking to each other
(in fact Janáček had a lifelong interest in speech intonations
which he reproduced in music, and there is a famous story
of how, while staying in a London hotel, he jotted down the
notes shouted by a page-boy who was searching for a
missing guest). The constant interchange of these pithy,
highly-charged speech patterns is intensely invigorating.

The Janáček Quartet plays with all the authority one
would expect of an ensemble that has chosen to name itself
after the composer. The immense technical and stylistic
difficulties of the music are fully mastered, and each work
emerges with a rapt intensity that is extremely compelling,
especially in so clear and smooth a recording—welcomely
issued at bargain price.

BARTOK (1881-1945): Six string quartets. *Fine Arts
Quartet.* Saga stereo STXID 5203-5, mono XID 5203-5.

Bartók's output of string quartets was smaller than Beethoven's, and smaller still than Haydn's. Yet the six masterpieces he wrote in this form occupy a place in the development of twentieth-century music quite as important as
Beethoven's seventeen in the nineteenth century and Haydn's
eighty-odd in the eighteenth. Like Haydn's and Beethoven's,
they span most of his career as a composer; like Haydn's
and Beethoven's, they are receptacles for many of his most
experimental thoughts, and have changed the face of
chamber music.

Bartók completed his first quartet (not counting an early
student essay) in 1908, when his music was still under the
influence of late nineteenth-century romanticism; the sixth
came 31 years later, when he was 58 years old and had
worked through a period of intense musical abrasiveness
and complexity to reach his "final" period, when his style
became simpler and his manner less aggressive. Even at their

175

most lyrical, however, Bartók's quartets can seem something of an aural assault course to anyone not yet attuned to his idiom; and this, as usual, is where a gramophone record is invaluable in helping us to get to grips with the music. It is eminently worth getting to grips with, no matter how daunting some of it may seem. Even at first hearing, one should be able to recognise the urgency of the composer's voice, the fierce power of his imagination and intellect, although one may be only dimly aware of what exactly is going on and of the logic behind it. The first, second, and sixth are often thought to be the most approachable of the works. Yet there is something to be said for jumping in at the deep end with No. 3 (1927), which dates from the height of his middle period and is usually thought to be the toughest, harshest and most uncompromising of the series. Yet the ferocious concentration of the music (it is by far the shortest of the quartets), its rhythmic intensity and the strange world of sonorities it opens up, make it a profound and exhilarating experience.

This quartet, coupled with the more lyrical fourth, will be found on (ST)XID 5204. But there is much to be said for buying all three records, for the Fine Arts Quartet's strong, idiomatic, well-recorded performances are among the finest bargains in the catalogue, costing only a quarter of the price of most other available recordings and being of a calibre that would make them highly competitive even at full price.

BRITTEN: String quartets Nos. 1 and 2. *Fidelio Quartet.* Pye Golden Guinea stereo GSGC 14025, mono GGC 4025.

The early maturing of Britten's inspiration is finely illustrated in these two works. The first, written in America at the age of 28, is an admirable piece of craftsmanship, strong and well argued; the second, dating from a few years later, is altogether deeper—a stirring tribute to Purcell, ending in a long chaconne of impressive power and feeling. The performance of the Fidelio Quartet, although lacking something in beauty of tone, has plenty of sinew and understanding. The recording is a little fierce, but sells at bargain price.

SHOSTAKOVICH (born 1906): Six preludes and fugues.
Sviatoslav Richter. Philips stereo SAL 3458, mono AL
3458.

The idea of writing 24 keyboard preludes and fugues is said
to have come to Shostakovich during a visit to Leipzig in
1950 for the 200th anniversary of Bach's death. The result,
completed the following year, is a series of pieces of extraordinary richness and imagination, which together form a
twentieth-century masterpiece that is far too little known in
the West. Far from being dryly contrapuntal, the music
explores a wide range of feeling, from the gentle-hearted,
songlike A flat major prelude and fugue to the solemn,
tolling grandeur of the passacaglia that serves as the G
sharp minor prelude. Since the composer has stated that
he does not regard the collection as a single, unified structure but as a series of pieces of similar character, there can
be no objection to Sviatoslav Richter's decision to select
six of them (Nos. 4, 12, 14, 15, 17, and 23)—though one
hopes that, in time, he will decide to complete the set.
Although the recording is rather rough in places, his performances are searching and technically quite breathtaking,
presenting the music with all the clarity of line and rhythm
it deserves.

PALESTRINA (c. 1525-1594): Stabat Mater and other choral works. *Choir of King's College, Cambridge, conducted by David Willcocks.* Argo stereo ZRG 5398, mono RG 398.

Liturgical music of the sixteenth century and earlier is usually thought a specialised field; but the person who listens once to a good performance of a mass by Palestrina or Victoria can become an enthusiast for life. Tovey has described Palestrina as a "God-intoxicated man"—an apt phrase, though it was an intoxication that produced music of the utmost purity and clarity of thought. None of his works is more serenely beautiful than the little *Stabat Mater* he wrote towards the end of his life for the Papal Choir in Rome, and none forms a better introduction to the cool nobility of his style. The rest of the record includes two more of his 500 motets and two rich works for double choir, a *Magnificat* and one of his six litanies addressed to the Blessed Virgin, all sung with unhurried, gentle beauty by a choir that is completely at home in' music of this period.

Readers eager to explore farther into the field of pre-1600 polyphony are recommended to another Argo record, containing the *Responsories for tenebrae* by Victoria, th: Spanish priest whose works have the same liturgical devotion as Palestrina's, plus a dramatic sombreness that is usually put down to his Spanish origin (stereo ZRG 5149, mono RG 149).

BYRD (1543-1623): Mass in three parts; Mass in four parts. *Choir of King's College, Cambridge, conducted by David Willcocks.* Argo stereo ZRG 5362, mono RG 362.

Although not, as is sometimes said, the father of British music, William Byrd is nevertheless one of the earliest and greatest figures in our musical history. In his early life he was organist of Lincoln cathedral; later he moved to London to join his mentor, Thomas Tallis, as an organist of Queen Elizabeth's Chapel Royal, and it was while there that he composed the bulk of what, in the present century, we have come to recognise as some of the most sublime examples of vocal polyphony ever produced. Anyone to whom Tudor music is still a closed book is urged to sample the two masses on this record. The music, far from being dustily historical, is vividly beautiful and alive, with just as much feeling to communicate as the choral masterpieces of more recent centuries. The mass in three parts, for altos, tenors, and basses, is a work of tranquil simplicity; the mass in four parts, which adds treble voices to the above, is more elaborately written, but no less direct and telling in its effect. The Cambridge performances, recorded, like the Palestrina, in King's College Chapel, have all the atmosphere and purity of tone one could hope for; and listeners who find themselves enthralled by the changing intensities and colours of this wonderfully luminous music may well wish to buy a companion record, containing the third of Byrd's three masses (this time in five parts) along with some of his other choral works (Argo stereo ZRG 5226, mono RG 226).

MONTEVERDI (1567-1643): Vespers. *Soloists/London Singers/Oiseau-Lyre Ensemble conducted by Anthony Lewis.* Oiseau-Lyre mono OL 50021-2.

Early in the seventeenth century, the unaccompanied vocal polyphony of composers like Palestrina, Victoria, and Byrd gave way to a more florid, vigorous, and declamatory mode of expression, with instrumental accompaniment. This found its leading exponent in Claudio Monteverdi, one of the most exciting of all musical innovators, known sometimes (and not without reason) as "the creator of modern music," who divided his prodigious energies mainly between church and opera house. In his early days he devoted himself to the compostion of madrigals, of extraordinary rhythmic subtlety and beauty; his appointment as choirmaster at St. Mark's in Venice led to the performance, in 1610, of his marvellous *Vespers*, a work which, for startling variety and vivacity, was to have no equal until Bach's Brandenburg concertos; and then, with the opening of the world's first true opera house, in the same city in 1637, he turned his attention (though he was by now seventy years old) increasingly and with new energy to this fascinating young art form.

No work gives a better impression of Monteverdi's versatility than the *Vespers*, in which various combinations of voices sing through an orchestral accompaniment that is full of joyous love of experiment. Among the pieces that comprise this long work arc spirited psalms, ravishing settings of texts from the *Song of Solomon*, and a final *Magnificat* every note of which glows with life. It is a work packed with surprises; one of the enthralling features of Monteverdi is that one never knows which way he will jump. The spirited swing and snap of his rhythms, his coruscating, convoluted vocal lines, are exhilarating in their effect. There are passages of noble grandeur, of sweet and touching simplicity (such as the delicate echo effects for oboe in the course of the *Magnificat*) and of almost amorous loveliness.

Professor Lewis obtains a masterly performance which is admirably scholarly and yet bursting with life. The soloists —Margaret Ritchie and Elsie Morison (sopranos), William Herbert and Richard Lewis (tenors), and Bruce Boyce (baritone)—sing their elaborate lines with obvious relish, and the chamber choir and orchestra produce throughout the most magical sounds. The recording, dating back to 1954, is a model of clarity. One can think of few records that are so refreshing to possess.

SCHUTZ (1585-1672): Christmas Oratorio. *Georg Jelden/ Edith Mathis/Claus Ocker/Windsbach Boys Choir and Instrumental Ensemble conducted by Hans Thamm.* Columbia stereo SAX 2584, mono 33CX 1945.

Born about half a century after Palestrina and exactly a century before Bach, Heinrich Schütz was one of the most important composers of his period, whose genius is heard at its most inspired and meditative in the tireless stream of choral works he produced when he was in his late seventies. In this setting of the Christmas story, one of his last works, the narrative of the Evangelist, sung by a tenor, alternates with solos by a soprano, representing the angel of glad tidings, and a bass, representing King Herod. The whole work is framed by choruses of great tranquillity, full of glowing textures that wonderfully convey their composer's inventive mastery. The performance, lucidly recorded in the Gothic cathedral at Heilsbronn, near Nurnberg, is sung with entrancing freshness, and the delicate instrumental accompaniment is of magical sweetness.

**BUXTEHUDE (1637-1707): Cantatas—Alles, was ihr tut;
Was mich auf dieser Welt betrubt. Missa Brevis;
Magnificat in D.** *Soloists/Cantata singers of New York
and String Ensemble conducted by Alfred Mann.* Saga
mono XID 5140.

Buxtehude is one of those composers whose name is better
known than his music. So often has he been dismissed as an
inferior forerunner of Bach that most people tend to accept
this assessment of him without trying to find out for themselves. In fact his music has much to offer; and this bargain
record makes an attractive sampler of its sturdy, melodious
beauty. In listening to it, one can see why Bach walked 200
miles from Arnstadt to Lübeck to hear Buxtehude's music.
It is a pity that no room has been found on the record for
some of his organ works, for he was one of the fathers of
organ playing; but the vocal items have been well chosen,
and the first cantata, *And whatever you do*, is a winner, with
parts for soprano, counter-tenor, tenor, and bass soloists,
and choral movements of great charm. The second cantata,
for soprano solo, two violins, and continuo, is much shorter
and has a gentleness of style typical of its composer.
Performance and recording could be better focused, but
are very adequate. Those who find the music to their taste
are recommended to progress to a full-price Archive disc
(mono APM 14088) in which Dietrich Fischer-Dieskau,
Helmut Krebs, and others sing five more cantatas, all of
high quality.

PURCELL (1658-1695): Music for the Chapel Royal.
*Soloists/Choir of St John's College, Cambridge/Academy of
St Martin-in-the-Fields conducted by George Guest.*
Argo stereo ZRG 5444, mono RG 444.

The circumstances of his life compelled Purcell to pour out
an immense amount of "occasional" music—works for royal
birthdays, funerals, and so on—but his genius was such that
it triumphed over even the most mundane commissions (and
the most mundane texts) to produce music of rich and
imaginative beauty, full of striking colours and audacious
effects, revealing a constant joy in the art of composition, and
providing a constant sense of surprise. Today we may regret

184

that he used his gift for dramatic music on a series of masques, odes, and incidental pieces for long-forgotten plays, instead of devoting it to opera. Yet he has left us an immense amount to be thankful for: his masterly, concentrated trio sonatas and string fantasias (a selection of which are sensitively but rather soberly performed by Yehudi Menuhin and others on an H.M.V. record, stereo ASD 635, mono ALP 2088); his solitary opera, *Dido and Aeneas*; his songs; and such choral works as are included on this record, in which he blew fresh air into English church music after its period of dormancy under the Puritans. In *My Beloved Spake*, one of the six anthems included in this varied and delightful concert, he found a text fully worthy of him—some lines from the Song of Solomon. And in *They that go down to the sea in ships*, he was inspired by John Gostling, a virtuoso singer of the period (whose range was said to extend through more than two octaves, from low C to top D), to provide a pyrotechnical bass part, here splendidly put over by Inia Te Wiata.

BACH: St. Matthew Passion. *Soloists/Munich Bach Choir, Boy's Choir, and Orchestra conducted by Karl Richter.* D.G.G. Archive stereo SAPM 198009-12, mono APM 14125-8.

Just as the non-Catholic listener should be able to appreciate the beauties of Palestrina, Victoria, and Byrd, so the non-Protestant should be equally moved by the vast narrative sweep and grandeur of Bach's greatest masterpiece of religious feeling. First heard in 1729 in the Thomaskirche in Leipzig, where Bach had been cantor for six years, its vivid portrayal of the Passion of Christ was evidently too much for its early listeners and the music went into abeyance for exactly a century until Mendelssohn revived it in 1829. Today our attitude to it has gone rather to the other extreme, and we have turned it, like Handel's *Messiah*, into an annual ritual—which is no way to treat a masterpiece. Still, in no matter what circumstances we have come to know it, a good performance always has the power to stir us and involve us in the sombre unfolding of its story. Karl Richter's is a very good performance, intimately scaled, admirable in style, with Ernst Häfliger as the Evangelist and Dietrich

185

Fischer-Dieskau as Jesus. The choral singing and orchestral playing are of a high standard, the woodwind tone is sweet and pure, and the alternating simplicity and intensity of the music is movingly caught.

Equally recommended is a performance by the same team of the great B minor Mass, a work less unified but no less moving and enthralling, which Bach composed in the years following the St. Matthew Passion (D.G.G. Archive stereo SAPM 198190-2, mono APM 14190-2).

BACH: Cantata No. 56—Ich will den Kreuzstab gerne tragen: Cantata No. 82—Ich habe genug. *Dietrich Fischer-Dieskau/Berlin Motet Choir and Chamber Orchestra conducted by Karl Ristenpart.* D.G.G. Archive mono APM 14004.

These are two of the most beautiful and intimate of Bach's many solo cantatas. The first, popularly known as the *Cross* cantata, was composed for the nineteenth Sunday after Trinity and describes Christ's journey over the sea and the healing of the man with palsy. The music radiates hope and compassion; and in a passage of sublime simplicity, the voyage is depicted by gently lapping cello figures which end abruptly when Christ steps on to dry land. The other work, *I have enough*, was composed for the festival of the purification of Mary and tells of contempt for life and longing for death. Its long introductory aria, with a text from St. Luke, is grave and eloquent. The slumber song that follows is one of Bach's most serenely lovely inspirations. Both works find in Dietrich Fischer-Dieskau an ideal interpreter, alert to their meaning and their style; and they receive from Karl Ristenpart an accompaniment which conveys the "inner" feeling of the music with memorable intensity.

HANDEL (1685-1759): Coronation Anthems. *Choir of King's College, Cambridge/English Chamber Orchestra conducted by David Willcocks.* Argo stereo ZRG 5369, mono RG 369.

To the foreigner, Britain's *Messiah* cult—like our Gilbert and Sullivan cult and to some extent our Sir Thomas

Beecham cult—sometimes seems a puzzling eccentricity. At best it is regarded as harmless, at worst as proof of our supposed unmusicality. In other countries, *Messiah* is not treated as Handel's solitary masterpiece, but, rightly, as one of many masterpieces. Whether such a broad-minded state of affairs will ever exist in Britain is hard to predict, but it would be a salutary change. Too many people are still too willing to lend their ears, and lungs, to *Messiah*, while keeping them tight shut against all other Handel and indeed all other music. *Messiah*, they claim in explanation of their laziness, is uplifting. Which of course it is. But so are the four magnificent anthems Handel composed for the coronation of George II in 1727, though one doubts if they are known to more than a tiny fraction of the people who turn out for every available performance of *Messiah*, no matter how styleless. Here, the Cambridge choir states a persuasive case for the music. The performance, an all-male one, is as stylish and impressive as one would expect, rising finely to the solemn grandeur of *Zadok the Priest* and peacefully conveying the gentler beauties of *Let thy hand be strengthened*.

HANDEL: Messiah. *Soloists/London Symphony Chorus and Orchestra conducted by Sir Adrian Boult*. Decca stereo SET 218-20, mono MET 218-20.

Messiah is a work we all imagine we have known since childhood. In fact, what most of us have known is a travesty of this noblest of oratorios. Even today, when scholarship is being brought to bear on so much of Handel's music, *Messiah* still tends to slip through the net and we continue to be treated to big bow-wow performances that turn the work into a vast, heavy, pompous, ill-decorated Victorian mausoleum, when in fact it should sound as light and springy as most of Handel's other masterpieces. None of the available recordings fulfils those requirements. And until Charles Mackerras is invited by some enterprising company to record the stylish new Basil Lam edition of the work, which he broadcast at New Year, 1966, Sir Adrian Boult's handsome and well-sung performance is recommended as the nearest—though it is not very near—approach to Handel's original intentions. Choir and orchestra are carefully balanced and are not inflated to Crystal Palace proportions; and at least one of the soloists, Joan Sutherland, shows awareness that the vocal line needs to be embellished in order to yield its full beauty. Postscript—A Mackerras recording of "Messiah" is in preparation as these pages go to press, and an "eighteenth century" performance is also due from Colin Davis.

HAYDN (1732-1809): Theresa Mass. *Soloists/Choir of St. John's College, Cambridge, and the Academy of St. Martin-in-the-Fields conducted by George Guest.* Argo stereo ZRG 5500, mono RG 500.

Towards the end of his life, Haydn composed six masses for the wife of his patron, Nicolaus II Esterhazy. All of them have their great moments, but none is more radiantly beautiful than the so-called Theresa Mass, with its vigorous choral writing and its soaring solo soprano line, gloriously sung here by the Dutch singer Erna Spoorenburg. The other soloists (Bernadette Greevey, John Mitchinson, Tom Krause) are also very much at home in the delightfully operatic parts that Haydn has written for them; the chorus sings with buoyant relish of the contrapuntal splendour of the *Et vitam venturi* fugue; the conductor, George Guest, clearly understands Haydn and is able to convey his joy in the music; and the recording lives up to the rest of the enterprise by being superbly vivid and well-balanced.

MOZART (1756-1791): Motet—Exsultate, jubilate, K.165. *Maria Stader/Berlin Radio Symphony Orchestra conducted by Ferenc Fricsay.* D.G.G. mono EPL 30595.

Mozart wrote this little motet when he was sixteen for the male soprano Venazio Rauzzini, who had sung the lead in his opera *Lucio Silla* a few weeks earlier. It is a charming piece, really a miniature three-movement concerto for voice and orchestra, ending with the sparkling *Alleluia* that is often performed out of context. The music, expressive of Christmas rejoicing, sounds innocent and easy; but in fact its florid passages, its unusually wide intervals, and its high notes (with a compass extending up to top C) make it hard to put over with the purity and relaxation it demands.

188

Rauzzini must have been a remarkable artist. Today the piece is a favourite among female sopranos, not all of whom make a success of it. Recordings of it have had a high casualty rate; but Maria Stader, apart from one or two moments when fluency falters, handles it delightfully, and her performance is neatly contained on a 45 r.p.m. disc.

MOZART: Mass in C minor, K.427. *Soloists/South German Madrigal Choir/Southwest German Chamber Orchestra conducted by Wolfgang Gonnenwein.* Columbia stereo SAX 2544, mono 33CX 1894.

Mozart's unfinished C minor mass has been called the only significant choral work composed between Bach's B minor mass and Beethoven's D major. To say this is to underestimate Mozart's other unfinished masterpiece, the D minor requiem, and the best of the sublime stream of masses that Haydn produced towards the end of his life. All the same, the C minor mass is a work of particularly touching beauty, in which choruses, some of them dark-toned and solemn, other forthright and vigorous, mingle with solo arias of ornate, operatic radiance. Composed as a thanksgiving for the recovery of his fiancée, Konstanze, from a serious illness, it occupies a special, personal place in Mozart's output; and tradition has it that the first performance was given in the lovely Peterskirche in Salzburg a year after they were married, with Konstanze herself as one of the four soloists. How she coped with the florid lines of the music is anybody's guess, but our knowledge of her abilities suggests that she would have been no match for either Edith Mathis or Helen Erwin, the two serene sopranos on this record. Beethoven's great Missa Solemnis, a summing-up of all he had learnt as a composer and human being, and delivered "from the heart, to the heart," has now been recorded with noble authority by Klemperer and the New Philharmonia Chorus and Orchestra, and issued just in time for inclusion in these pages (H.M.V. Angel stereo SAN 165-6, mono AN 165-6).

ROSSINI (1792-1868): Stabat Mater. *Soloists/Choir of St. Hedwig's Cathedral, Berlin/Berlin Symphony Orchestra conducted by Karl Forster.* H.M.V. stereo ASD 588, mono ALP 2039.

This was Rossini's last masterpiece, and we owe its existence to a Madrid banker friend who asked him to provide a work for performance in a local monastery. Surprisingly, the composer consented—surprisingly, because his self-imposed inactivity had already begun, and he had written nothing of consequence for three years. Not that the composition of the *Stabat Mater* flowed entirely smoothly: an attack of lumbago caused him to abandon it after the first six numbers, the work never received the performance for which it was commissioned (although, in payment, Rossini had been given a gold snuff-box encrusted with eight large diamonds), and it was not until a financial wrangle ten years later over the publishing rights that he drove himself to produce another four numbers.

Like Verdi's requiem of thirty years later, the *Stabat Mater* was an immediate hit—except among dour protestant listeners, who, using Bach as their norm, found its sweeping red-blooded melodies and jaunty rhythms too frivolous for their taste. In Britain, Sir Henry Hadow went so far as to call it "immoral." Today, anyone who cannot respond to its exuberance has no sunshine in his soul. In this excellent German performance, it is sung with all the relish it needs; the soloists, especially Pilar Lorengar (soprano) and Josef Traxel (tenor), pour out their arias and ensembles with lyrical fervour, culminating in a splendidly dramatic account of the powerful *Inflammatus*, so Verdian in character that one wonders what operas Rossini might have composed in his later years had he stirred himself to do so.

SCHUBERT (1797-1828): Twelve songs. *Elisabeth Schwarzkopf/Edwin Fischer.* Columbia mono 33CX 1040.

"The loveliest melody has just come into my head. If only I had some music paper with me!" The story of how *Hark, hark, the lark* came to be scribbled on the back of a menu in a beer garden is one of the many that are told about this most melodious and poetic of song writers. As Arthur

Hutchings has remarked in his book on the composer, "Had Schubert written for nothing but the human voice and its accompanying pianoforte, both musicians and musical historians would have still regarded him as a major composer." His sense of whether a poem would suit his purposes seems to have been completely instinctive: among his 600 songs are settings of some of Goethe's noblest lines side by side with settings of sentimental doggerel—but all are equalised by being transformed into music of supreme inspiration.

This recital by Elisabeth Schwarzkopf and Edwin Fischer was one of the first Schubert programmes to appear on LP, and it remains one of the best-loved records ever issued. The choice of songs is superbly compiled and balanced to give an idea of the range of the composer's genius. Here, all performed with the utmost artistry, are *Gretchen am Spinnrade* (Gretchen at the spinning-wheel), the first of his seventy-odd Goethe settings and perhaps the first real revelation of his powers, composed at the age of eighteen; *Im Frühling* (In springtime), *Ganymed*, and *Nachtviolen* (Night violets), three of his most enchanting and fragrant outdoor settings; the tender *An die Musik* (To music); the gloriously undulating *Auf der Wasser zu singen* (To be sung on the water) and the tempestuous *Die junge Nonne* (The young nun), which Beethoven pored over during his last illness.

SCHUBERT: Die schöne Müllerin, D.795. *Gérard Souzay/Dalton Baldwin.* Philips stereo SAL 3501, mono AL 3501.

Towards the end of his short life, Schubert wrote two song cycles based on verses by a minor German poet, Wilhelm Müller. The first of these, *The Beautiful Maid of the Mill* (1823), describes how a young miller falls in love with his master's daughter, confides his daydreams to the passing brook, and ultimately throws himself into the waters when he discovers that she loves someone else. The words may be mawkish, but the music rivets the imagination with its profound responsiveness to every detail of the story, its mingling of hope and impatience, its flowing water-melodies, its subtle sense of harmony, its changing attitudes

191

to the word "green"—the green ribbon the singer sends to his beloved, the green woods from which the hated hunter emerges, the green turf on the grave. But in spite of the death-wish of the later songs, this is essentially a lyrical and youthful cycle, and it needs to be sung with lightness. To choose a performance by a French singer when the songs have been twice recorded by that prince of lieder, Dietrich Fischer-Dieskau, may seem eccentric. But in fact Gérard Souzay, too, is a lieder singer of rare sensitivity, and his approach, crisper and more delicately intimate than Fischer-Dieskau's, is ideally suited to these songs. Dalton Baldwin's sparkling accompaniments, beautifully geared to the voice of the singer, enter the imaginative world of each song with great perceptiveness.

SCHUBERT: Die Winterreise, D.911. SCHUMANN (1810-1856): Dichterliebe, Op. 48. *Peter Pears/Benjamin Britten.* Decca stereo SET 270-1, mono MET 270-1.

Four years after composing the twenty songs of *The Beautiful Maid of the Mill*, Schubert turned again to Müller and set the 24 that form *The Winter Journey*. Whereas the first cycle opens by being airy and romantic, the second is stark and tragic from start to finish. The hero is again a thwarted lover; but this time, instead of drowning himself, he sets off through the bleak winter countryside, seeing everything he passes as a projection of his despair—the weather vane spinning on his sweetheart's house, the postman who brings no letters, the frost that whitens his hair as he walks, the snarling dogs, the "inn" that is really a graveyard, the staggering, barefooted hurdy-gurdyman with whom, at the end, he strikes a numbed contact. The black, frozen intensity that Peter Pears and Benjamin Britten bring to this music is one of the most powerful and disturbing experiences the gramophone has to offer. This is not merely a "performance", but a profound note-by-note illumination of Schubert's hauntingly poetic world. At the end, the childlike intonation that Pears brings to the music of the organ-grinder has the same moving effect as the simpleton's song at the close of *Boris Godunov*.

The two-record set is completed by an almost equally masterly account of another great song cycle, Schumann's *Dichterliebe* (A poet's love), sixteen settings of poems by

Heine in which, once again, the hero expresses his feelings on being thwarted in love.

SCHUBERT: Schwanengesang, D.957. *Dietrich Fischer-Dieskau/Gerald Moore.* H.M.V. stereo ASD 544, mono ALP 1993.

Swansong was the title thought up by a publisher, after Schubert's death, for a wonderful late crop of fourteen songs to poems by Heine and Rellstab. This time, as Schubert did not conceive them as a cycle, there is no continuous narrative, but their unity of inspiration makes them a profoundly satisfying group. Among them are the powerful, declamatory *Die Stadt* (The town), in which the singer surveys the distant, misty image of the turreted town in which he lost his love; the spine-chilling *Der Doppelgänger* (The double), in which he gazes at a deserted house, wringing his hands with grief at the sight of himself in former days; and the mellifluous, open-hearted *Die Taubenpost* (Pigeon post), whose dancing rhythm is made all the more touching by our knowledge that this was the last song this fecund composer was ever to write. Dietrich Fischer-Dieskau sings the more strongly emotional songs with marvellous control and insight, and brings to *Standchen* (Serenade) and *Das Fischermädchen* (The fisher girl) a gentleness that stirs the heart. In Gerald Moore he finds, throughout, an ideal partner. The same singer and pianist are featured in two beautifully-compiled recitals, the first entitled "Popular Schubert Songs," but containing some rarities (H.M.V. stereo ASD 2263, mono ALP 2263), the second entitled "A Schubert Recital" (stereo ASD 2273, mono ALP 2273).

SCHUBERT: 43 songs. *Elisabeth Schumann.* H.M.V. mono COLH 130-1.

Elisabeth Schumann was one of the greatest of Schubert singers, and anyone with a taste for lieder should have at least one souvenir of her in his collection. In 1963, H.M.V. gathered many Schubert recordings she had made between 1927 and 1949 and issued them on two LPs in the *Great*

Recordings of the Century series. Inevitably, these occasionally overlap some of the records mentioned earlier in these pages, but her performances are so full of character that no one should object to an alternative version of *Nachtviolen* and *Wohin*.

Each disc contains several of Schubert's greatest songs—on the first the evergreen *Heidenröslein* (Meadow rose), *Du bist die Ruh* (You are rest and peace), *Die Forelle* (The trout), *Horch, Horch, die Lerch'* (Hark, hark, the lark), and *Ave Maria*, and on the second the sparkling *Seligkeit* (Happiness), the gloriously sustained *Nach und Träume* (Night and dreams), and the sombre *Der Jungling und der Tod* (The youth and death). "She had a beautifully controlled high soprano of delicate, ringing timbre and of crystalline purity, and a charming stage presence, especially in demure, mischievous parts." Thus Grove's Dictionary appraises the art of Elisabeth Schumann. These records live up to the appraisal.

BERLIOZ (1803-1869): Nuits d'été.   RAVEL (1875-1937): Shéhérazade.   *Regine Crespin/Orchestre de la Suisse Romande conducted by Ernest Ansermet*.   Decca stereo SXL 6081, mono LXT 6081.

Perhaps the most tender of all Berlioz's music appears in two of his vocal works—the delicate, youthful song-cycle, to words by Théophile Gautier, which he entitled *Summer Nights*, and the sacred trilogy *The Childhood of Christ*. Nowhere is the melancholy ruefulness of his nature more succinctly conveyed than in these six settings, full of rapt, private feelings, and exquisite, trembling imagery. It is music one wishes to listen to while completely alone; no work is better suited to the gramophone. The most famous of the songs, *The spectre of the rose*, is based on the poem that inspired the ballet of the same title. It is a beautifully imagined song, far more subtle in its atmosphere than the Weber waltz used as the basis of the ballet. Equally haunting are *Villanelle* and *Absence*, the first a flowing and intensely Berliozian picture of a springtime walk through the woods, the second a radiantly declamatory lament for an absent love.

194

Although the wide range of the vocal line makes some of these songs extremely hard to sing with consistent beauty of tone, one would never think so from Régine Crespin's wonderfully poised, fine-spun phrasing, her full, lustrous top notes and her equal assurance in the lower register, her light and shade, her ability to surrender herself completely to the music. In the lusher atmosphere of Ravel's three Klingsor settings she sounds just as much at ease, catching the Oriental scenes and colours with magical sensitivity.

BERLIOZ: The Childhood of Christ. *Soloists/St. Anthony Singers/Goldsborough Orchestra conducted by Colin Davis.* Oiseau-Lyre stereo SOL 60032-3, mono OL 50201-2.

The grandeur of Berlioz's Requiem, Te Deum, and *The Damnation of Faust* finds its antithesis in *The Childhood of Christ*, the "sacred trilogy" in which he cultivated a more subdued and idyllic manner in order to tell the story of Herod's search for the Holy Family in Jerusalem, the flight into Egypt, and the hospitality provided by the household of Ishmaelites. The atmosphere is beautifully set by the soft, stealthy, uneasy march that suggests the Roman soldiers patrolling the streets at night. Later, the flight into Egypt is described in some of Berlioz's most gently pastoral music, with a graceful shepherds' chorus that has become well known out of context. And in the final section, the music moves from one inspiration to another; the Holy Family's panting, distraught search for shelter in the unknown city, the ravishing trio for two flutes and harp played by the young Ishmaelites, the strange and fascinating sounds of the epilogue, in which one can take delight, no matter how often one hears it, at the extraordinary originality of Berlioz's thought. For all the restraint of the writing, none of his scores is more vivid than this. Scene after scene is brought strikingly and movingly to life. Colours, rhythms, phrases, melodies consistently enchant the ear.

Colin Davis responds to the music with an unfailingly perceptive sense of line and rhythm. It is a performance of great purity, with Peter Pears an eloquent narrator, and choral and orchestra tone that is marvellously fresh and expressive. Although more recent concert performances by Davis of *The Childhood of Christ* suggest that his interpretation has deepened still farther since these discs were released in 1961, the Oiseau-Lyre recording will nevertheless be one to prize for many years to come.

Berlioz's other big choral works have so far evaded ideal recording; but readers who, understandably, are keen to add them to their collections are recommended to Charles Münch's account of the magnificent Requiem with the New England Conservatory Chorus and Boston Symphony Orchestra (R.C.A. stereo SB 2096-7, mono RB 16224-5) and to Igor Markevitch's of *The Damnation of Faust* with the Elisabeth Brasseur Choir, the Lamoureux Orchestra, and an uneven team of soloists (D.G.G. stereo SLPM 138099-100, mono LPM 18599-600).

SCHUMANN (1810-1856): Liederkreis, Op. 39, and other Eichendorff songs.   *Dietrich Fischer-Dieskau/Gerald Moore.*   H.M.V. stereo ASD 650, mono ALP 2103.

"I should like to die singing, like a nightingale," wrote Schumann when he was thirty—the year he married Clara Wieck and poured out, in one of his greatest bursts of lyrical inspiration, the bulk of his music for voice and piano. Among the 132 songs dating from that time were the sixteen Eichendorff settings included here, with their magical evocation of breezes and forests, birds and streams, waving corn and the quietness of snow. Unlike *Dichterliebe*, the *Liederkreis* cycle does not tell a continuous story—which is perhaps why it is featured less often in recital programmes. But it does contain unity of romantic feeling; and one song, the gentle *Mondnacht*, is arguably the most magical depiction of moonlight ever written, as well as one of the hardest of all songs to sustain with soft beauty of tone. Dietrich Fischer-Dieskau delivers its exquisite floating phrases with a rapt intimacy, and with all the insight and control we have come to expect of him—qualities he brings also to the rest of the record, in which Gerald Moore's tender accompaniments contribute equally to one's pleasure.

SCHUMANN: Frauenliebe und Leben. RICHARD STRAUSS (1864-1949): Seven songs. *Lisa della Casa/ Sebastian Peschko.* H.M.V. stereo ASD 593, mono ALP 2044.

Schumann, like Schubert before him, could be erratic in taste when it came to choosing poems for his songs, and seemed just as happy with the naive banality of Chamisso as with the grandeur of Goethe. The main thing was that he usually chose words which managed to spark his imagination—which was better than possessing exemplary literary taste (as some composers of the present century have done) without the inspiration to match it. The cycle of eight songs, *Women's Love and Life*, dates from the same *annus mirabilis* as *Liederkreis*, and weds mawkish thoughts on love, marriage, motherhood, and death with music of the utmost lyrical beauty. Lisa della Casa's heartfelt performance has many original and convincing touches, and at times an impulsiveness that is delightfully in keeping with the moods of the music.

Richard Strauss, seven of whose songs are included on the reverse, was perhaps the last of the great lieder composers. Again one finds an erratic taste in words—and at times, too, an erratic taste in setting them! Here, Lisa della Casa's choice includes the idyllic *Morgen*, the deliciously witty *Mein Vater hat gesagt*, and the scrumptious *Schlechtes Wetter*, that sharp little picture of a greedy girl anticipating the baking of a cake. From this record, readers are strongly recommended to progress to a Strauss recital Lisa della Casa has recorded for R.C.A. (stereo SB 6590, mono RB 6590). This time there are no fewer than seventeen songs with no duplicates) arguably even more entrancingly sung and accompanied (by Arpad Sandor), including the shimmering *Ständchen*, the cynical *Für Fünfzehn Pfennige*, the serene *Ruhe, meine Seele*, and a number of rarities that are scarcely less enchanting.

VERDI (1813-1901): Requiem Mass. *Elisabeth Schwarz-kopf/Christa Ludwig/Nicolai Gedda/Nicolai Ghiaurov/ Philharmonia Chorus and Orchestra conducted by Carlo Maria Giulini.* H.M.V. Angel stereo SAN 133-4, mono AN 133-4.

Much ink has been wasted through the years on appraising the operatic elements in Verdi's Requiem, and on deciding whether they add to or detract from the religious conception of the text. What matters is that Verdi's sure sense of drama, as well as his grief at the death of Manzoni ("I would have knelt before him," he wrote, "if men worshipped men"), spurred him, at the age of 60, to compose one of the most thrilling of all settings of the Latin words.

Although very difficult to perform—like *Trovatore* it needs the four best singers in the world—Verdi's Requiem has been lucky in its recordings. The most famous is Toscanini's, an overwhelming experience still to be had by courtesy of R.C.A. (mono RB 16131-2), though somewhat harshly recorded and (for some tastes) too brutally conducted. A more recent and quite different interpretation is Giulini's, whose performance of it in London and elsewhere have come to be regarded, with good reason, as the most outstanding of our day. Giulini combines an integrity as fanatical as Toscanini's with an approach to the music that is gentler and more sensuous. Yet the effect is never tame, and from the very opening bars—shaped with memorable eloquence by the cellos—this H.M.V. recording catches the Giulini interpretation in full bloom. The solo quartet is not perhaps the best in the world; but it is at least as good as those in the other available recordings, and the Philharmonia Chorus sings with incomparable warmth and beauty.

BRAHMS (1833-1897): Fifteen songs. *Dietrich Fischer-Dieskau/Jörg Demus.* D.G.G. stereo SLPM 138011, mono LPM 18504.

Schubert and Schumann, in their songs, usually turned voice and piano into an equal partnership. Brahms, although a superb pianist, tended to give priority to the voice, and his accompaniments seldom have quite the poetic insight and intensity that stamped the work of his two great predeces-
198

sors in the art of lieder. Wolf and Nietzche were both scathing in their judgment of Brahms's vocal music. Yet among his 200 songs are some pearls one would not care to be without. In this recital, Dietrich Fischer-Dieskau has chosen some of the most serious and poignant, including the haunting "Mit vierzig Jahren," which describes the sadness of lost youth and which made its first singer, Julius Stockhausen, break down with emotion when he performed it to the composer's accompaniment.

FAURÉ (1845-1924): Requiem. *Soloists/Elisabeth Brasseur Choir/Paris Conservatoire Orchestra conducted by André Cluytens.* H.M.V. Angel stereo SAN 107, mono AN 107.

"Whereas his master, Saint-Saëns, employed an admirable technique to conceal a void, Fauré developed a similarly finished idiom to express the genial perceptions of a sensuous and energetic personality." At a time when musical reputations have been rising and falling with bewildering speed, the *Record Guide's* neat appraisal, delivered in 1953, still seems comfortingly valid today. Fauré was one of the least demonstrative figures of French music. Although he has always been something of a specialised taste, one would think that—nearly half a century after his death—his virtues would now shine vividly for all to hear. Yet he is now no better represented in the record catalogues than when the *Record Guide* was published. Nor can we yet rely on finding him regularly in concert programmes. It may be that for the casual listener, Fauré's world is too refined, too flowing, too uneventful. He was never greatly attracted to the symphony orchestra as a means of expression. He destroyed his only symphony; he never completed his violin concerto; and his music drama, *Promethée*, is unlikely to reach the stage of Covent Garden. The essence of his delicate style is to be found in his chamber and intrumental works; in his songs, which are as lucid as those of Debussy; and in his serenely lovely Requiem, one of his few large works, but one whose atmosphere is very different from the requiems of Berlioz and Verdi.

Composed in 1887 in memory of his father, who had just died, the music is scored with great gentleness for soprano

199

and baritone soloists, chorus, and orchestra. Originally, the soprano part was intended for a choirboy. But the H.M.V. recording, with Victoria de los Angeles and Dietrich Fischer-Dieskau as soloists, is so beautifully sung that one does not regret the change.

FAURÉ: La Bonne Chanson (song cycle) and other songs. *Gérard Souzay/Dalton Baldwin.* Philips mono ABL 3371.

Fauré wrote several song cycles, of which *La Bonne Chanson* (1892) is the most famous and the most delicately lyrical. The nine songs, settings of poems by Verlaine, describe the happy thoughts of a bridegroom as he prepares for marriage. Rather surprisingly, Fauré dedicated the cycle to a woman, and women singers have ever since regarded it as part of their repertoire; but the songs are more logically characterised by a man, and Gérard Souzay here makes a most eloquent case for giving them to a baritone voice. The accompaniment, exquisitely interwoven with the vocal line, is handled with similar mastery by Dalton Baldwin. The eleven other songs on the record include *Soir* and *Le parfum impérissable*, two of Fauré's most meditative inspirations, and *Aurore*, a magical evocation of the dawn after a night of love.

ELGAR (1857-1934): The Dream of Gerontius. *Soloists/ Hallé Choir and Sheffield Philharmonic Chorus/Ambrosian Singers/Hallé Orchestra conducted by Sir John Barbirolli.* H.M.V. stereo ASD 648-9, mono ALP 2101-2.

Composed in 1900, a sort of choral equivalent of Strauss's *Death and Transfiguration*, this setting of Cardinal Newman's long dramatic poem has been called the last of the great English oratorios. Although, in its sentiments and style, it now sounds more obviously "dated" than Elgar's other major works, and has never caught on abroad, it none the less clings stubbornly to the repertoire in Britain—mainly because of its many passages of quiet, but intense, beauty, and the poignancy that can be achieved when singers and conductor are in full rapport with each other and with the music. Sir John Barbirolli has long been identified with this work, and here his conception of it is captured at something close to full radiance. Of the soloists, Richard Lewis sings carefully and devotedly as Gerontius, but it is the wonderful tenderness of Janet Baker's portrayal of the Angel that leaves the most moving impression.

DEBUSSY (1862-1918): Song recital. *Maggie Teyte/ Alfred Cortot/Gerald Moore.* H.M.V. mono COLH 134.

Although inevitably overshadowed by the German Lied, the French chanson has its own particular flavour and beauty—and nowhere more so than in the delicate songs of Debussy, of which H.M.V. here provides a ravishing selection. Here are the cool *Chansons de Bilitis*, the airy settings of Verlaine's *Fêtes galantes*, the powerful *Ballades de François Villon*, all incomparably performed by one of the greatest exponents of the chanson, accompanied by one or other of two famous pianists. The performances, originally issued on 78 in the nineteen-thirties, have retained much of their bloom; and indeed this is among the smoothest of H.M.V.'s *Great Recordings of the Century.*

Two other records of French chansons are specially recommended, one of them devoted to songs by Duparc (a composer of frugal but high-quality output), the other to a delightful mixed bag of items by Gounod, Chabrier, Bizet, Ravel, Roussel, Poulenc, and others, both artistically sung by Gérard Souzay, and both issued by Philips (the first on stereo SAL 3434, mono AL 3434; the second on stereo SAL 3480, mono AL 3480).

WOLF (1860-1903): 17 songs from the romantic poets. *Elisabeth Schwarzkopf/Gerald Moore.* Columbia mono 33CX 1946.

Not even Schumann in his *annus mirabilis* composed lieder with such fierce intensity and speed as Hugo Wolf. In a few years around 1890 he poured out the bulk of his best songs —the forty-odd Mörike settings, the fifty Goethe, the twenty Eichendorff, the 44 of the *Spanisches Liederbuch*—devoting all his energies to one poet before passing on to the next. By 1896 he had completed the 46 songs of the *Italie-nisches Liederbuch;* then the three dark, magnificent Michel-angelo sonnets; then, as with Schumann, came madness and early death. Sometimes, in a frantic burst of industry, he would compose several songs a day; at other times, inspira-tion hung fire for weeks. Of all the great lieder of the nine-teenth century, Wolf's are the sharpest and most succinct. His literary sense was more highly developed than that of his predecessors, and most of the time he had the musical inspiration to do justice to the words he chose. Some of his songs, not unexpectedly when one considers his tragic background, have a wry, nervy, bitter edge to them. But he could also write with great lyrical beauty, as in the earlier songs of Elisabeth Schwarzkopf's unusual and delightfully compiled recital—songs like the almost Schubertian *Morgentau* (Morning dew), the lovely *Wiegenlied in Sommer* (Summer lullaby), and the swaggering *Tretet ein, hoher Krieger* (Come in, lofty warrior). Only one Mörike setting is included, but it is a delicious one—*Mausfallen-Sprüchlein* (Spell for a mousetrap), sung with great charm and wit. Later comes a Byron setting, *Sonne der Schlummerlosen* (Sun of the sleepless), and four of Goethe. Throughout, singer and pianist form the most penetrating and artistic team: one listens in delight to their every word and note.

WOLF: 19 lieder. *Elena Gerhardt/Coenraad van Bos.* H.M.V. mono COLH 142.

One of the great achievements of the gramophone was the founding, in 1931, of the Hugo Wolf Society. Six volumes of songs were issued, each consisting of six records; but, reprehensibly, the first volume quickly went out of circu-lation, depriving us of nineteen of the finest songs, per-formed by one of the most subtle of all interpreters of his music, the German soprano Elena Gerhardt. Happily, this milestone in lieder recording is now safely back in the cata-logue, transferred to a single LP in H.M.V.'s *Great Record-ings of the Century* series. Not all old vocal records take kindly to transfer; this one comes over well, with much of the surface noise cleaned away, and the sparkle left in the voice. And the singing is all one remembered it as being— ~vellously poised, sensitive and intelligent, with a sharp ~ning of intensity in *Gesang Weylas* (Weyla's song), one of the group of Mörike settings, and an exquisite composure in the tender songs selected from the Spanish and Italian songbooks. Postscript—As this book goes to press, H.M.V. have announced the deletion of this great recording of the century—so we are back to where we started. But the disc is worth tracking down in second-hand shops.

MAHLER (1860-1911): Des Knaben Wunderhorn.
Lorna Sydney/Alfred Poell/Vienna State Opera Orchestra conducted by Felix Prohaska.   Philips mono GL 5684.

Mahler, a great opera conductor, composed no operas himself—or at least none he ever completed. But the human voice was never far from his mind and played a central part in his output, appearing even in a number of his symphonies. No composer has combined voice and orchestra more masterfully, or made the orchestral song so much his own. One of his main sources of inspiration was the collection of German folk-poetry called *Youth's Magic Horn*, from which he drew material for the finale of his fourth symphony, his *Songs of a Wayfarer*, and the set of fourteen songs actually entitled *Youth's Magic Horn*. These, although fairly early Mahler, nevertheless contain many of the most typical elements of his character and style: hints of military marches, pastoral touches, wistfulness, regret, a sense of wonder. In one song, a drummer boy is awaiting execution; in another, a guard thinks nostalgically of home during the long hours of the night watch. Alfred Poell sings these with great perception, and it is a pity that the American mezzo-soprano, Lorna Sydney, with whom he shares the record, lacks something of his artistry and refinement of phrasing. All the same, this bargain-price disc is strongly recommended. Felix Prohaska draws pure, lyrical, wonderfully touching sounds from the orchestra which Mahler himself once conducted; and by a feat of compression, involving no loss of quality, all but one of the songs have been contained on a single record (when this performance was first issued, at full price, it spread over four sides).

MAHLER: Das Lied von der Erde. *Kathleen Ferrier/ Julius Patzak/Vienna Philharmonic Orchestra conducted by Bruno Walter.* Decca mono LXT 5576.

Whether one calls it a cantata or a symphony, this setting, in German, of six Chinese poems is one of Mahler's greatest achievements—indeed, for many people, his masterpiece. Composed in 1907-8, it is contemporary with his eighth symphony. Ernest Newman called it the swansong of nineteenth-century romanticism; and the last of its six movements, the famous *Abschied*, is the most poignant of all Mahler's expressions of farewell: tender, grief-stricken, haunted by thoughts of death, but finally radiant and consoling, with the knowledge that beauty is immortal. "For ever," sings the contralto, with a wistfulness that melts the heart, "this lovely earth will flower and turn green in the springtime. For ever and everywhere will the horizons shine blue." The other songs are varied in subject, but generally elegiac in feeling, The first, sung by the tenor, is a pungent "Drinking song of earth's sorrow." In the second, the contralto sings of autumn loneliness, her words reflected in an orchestral accompaniment of sad but ravishing beauty, ending with the oboe and clarinet conversing plaintively against a cool, gently rustling breeze from the violins—the whole effect as exquisite and clear as a Chinese painting. Then, before the long *Abschied*, come three shorter, more robust songs, one of them exclaiming the joys of drinking and the beauty of spring.

The Decca *Song of the Earth*, dating from 1952, is one of the most famous recordings ever made. Its history goes back to the first Edinburgh Festival in 1947, when Kathleen Ferrier and Bruno Walter first came together to perform it in the aftermath of the Second World War. Walter had been closely associated with the music ever since he conducted its premiere, in 1911, shortly after the composer's death; Kathleen Ferrier had never sung it before, but, with Walter's guidance, brought to the music a profound and shining artistry, audible in every note of this recording, made within a year of her own death.

SCHONBERG (1874-1951): Pierrot Lunaire. *Alice Howland/Instrumental Ensemble conducted by Herbert Zipper*. STRAVINSKY (born 1882): Dumbarton Oaks Concerto. *Haydn Orchestra conducted by Harry Newstone*. Saga mono XID 5212.

Still believed by some people to be a terrifying revolutionary and by others to be a mere musical mathematician, Arnold Schönberg is nevertheless beginning to be recognised as a more accessible and human figure than was at one time thought. And nowhere is his warmth of feeling more evident than in *Pierrot Lunaire*, his "melodrama" based on German translations of 21 poems by Albert Giraud. This work, written in 1912 before he had formulated his ideas into the twelve-note system, has considerable claim to be his masterpiece; and what Cecil Gray wrote about it in 1924 still seems as valid today. Since Gray is now so often accused of having championed Sibelius at the expense of the Schönbergian school, perhaps his vivid description of *Pierrot Lunaire* deserves to be quoted: "Out of the unpromising material afforded by these highly artificial, precious, and decadent little poems, Schönberg has created a whole world of strange fascination and enchantment, of nameless horrors and terrible imaginings, of perverse and poisonous beauty and bitter-sweet fragrance, of a searing and withering mockery and malicious, elfish humour, which the poet most assuredly never contemplated . . . If Schönberg had written nothing else, this work alone would be sufficient to assure him a place apart in musical history."

The music is set for solo voice and a small instrumental ensemble, used with fantastic variety and imagination. The composer directed that the voice part was to be neither sung nor spoken, though the exact mean between the two has subsequently proved practically impossible to achieve. The vocalist on this record, Alice Howland, leans somewhat towards a singing style; but she is a considerable artist, and the result is a distinct success. No less successful is the atmospheric playing of the five American instrumentalists. And as a generous filler, this record (which costs, like the Bartók quartets issued by the same company, only a few shillings) includes Stravinsky's light-heartedly Bachian *Dumbarton Oaks Concerto*. As a continuation course in Schönberg, readers are recommended to Volume Three of the comprehensive C.B.S. survey, directed by Robert Craft,

of *The Music of Arnold Schönberg,* including his two important chamber symphonies, his five orchestral pieces, Op. 16,
some of his vocal music, plus a 54-page guide (stereo SBRG
72358-9, mono BRG 72358-9).

STRAVINSKY: The Soldier's Tale.   *Soloists/Instrumental
ensemble conducted by John Pritchard.*   H.M.V. mono
HQM 1008.

Realising that the orchestral ferocity of *The Rite of Spring*
marked the end of a line, Stravinsky in 1914 turned his
attention to the human voice and to a barer, more subdued
idiom. *The Soldier's Tale* (1918), like many of his youthful
works, has its origin in a Russian fable—that of a violin-
playing soldier who loses his soul, and his violin, to the
devil. A grotesque mixture of speech, mime, and dance, with
jazz influences, it is very much a child of its time; but that
it has worn remarkably well, and indeed gained in impact
with the years, was proved by the 1954 Edinburgh Festival
production, upon which this superbly lucid bargain-price
recording—with Robert Helpmann, Terence Longdon, and
Anthony Nicholls in the roles of devil, soldier, and narrator
—is based.

**STRAVINSKY: Symphony of Psalms; Symphony in C
major.**   *Festival Singers of Toronto/C.B.C. Symphony
Orchestra conducted by Igor Stravinsky.*   C.B.S. stereo
SBRG 72181, mono BRG 72181.

"Composed for the glory of God and dedicated to the
Boston Symphony Orchestra on the occasion of the fiftieth
anniversary of its existence." Although the words on the
title-page have something of the sublime pathos of a poem
206

by McGonagall, the *Symphony of Psalms* is one of Stravinsky's noblest inspirations—a setting, in Latin, of parts of Psalms 38 and 39 and the whole of Psalm 150. "In this remarkable composition," writes Rollo Myers, "he reveals his full stature, and attains heights of emotional intensity and genuine religious ecstasy which are without a parallel in any of his previous works." In the first movement, *Here my prayer*, the chorus sing in broad, exultant lines over a hypnotically chugging rhythm from the orchestra. The second movement, *Waiting for the Lord*, is described by the composer as "an upside-down pyramid of fugues," and has a wonderfully cool, lucid introduction from the woodwind. The final hymn of praise incorporates a striking vision of Elijah's chariot climbing the heavens, and the ending, with the female voices slowly singing *Allelujah* and the males responding with a bell-like *Laudate* is one of the loveliest passages in modern music (though it is rivalled by the close of the Symphony in C, also included on this record, and by that of the *Apollo* ballet music). Writing of the word *allelujah*, Stravinsky has said that it always reminds him of a Hebrew galosh-merchant who lived in the apartment below his in St. Petersburg, and who on High Holy Days used to erect a prayer tent in his living-room. "The hammering sounds as he built this tent and the idea of a cosmopolitan merchant in a St. Petersburg apartment simulating the prayers of his forefathers in the desert impressed my imagination almost as profoundly as any direct religious experience of my own."

Anecdotes like this lend humanity to the work of a composer who always claims to pride himself on his ability to write "non-expressive" music. But the best refutation of this claim is to be found in the music itself—not only the *Symphony of Psalms*, but also the Symphony in C, composed ten years later for the fiftieth anniversary of another orchestra, the Chicago Symphony. Written at a time of intense personal unhappiness (his wife and one of his daughters died while he was working on it), it pours out its troubles in an idiom as polished, elegant, and luminous as that of a Mozart symphony.

The performances—Stravinsky was 82 when he recorded them—have a few little imprecisions. But the general incisiveness, the feeling for line and rhythm, would be hard to surpass. This is a great record. As a "chaser," a collection of some of Stravinsky's shorter choral works, from the rich,

early cantata *Le roi des étoiles*, through his radiant variations on Bach's *Vom Himmel hoch*, up to the more austere
A Sermon, a Narrative, and a Prayer of 1961, is also warmly
recommended. These are performed by the same forces,
again conducted, inimitably, by the composer himself
(C.B.S. stereo SBRG 72272, mono BRG 72272).

**BRITTEN (born 1913): Nocturne for tenor, seven obbligato
instruments and strings.** *Peter Pears/London Symphony
Orchestra conducted by Benjamin Britten.* Decca stereo
SWL 8025, mono BR 3079.

Britten's *Nocturne*, composed for the 1958 Leeds Festival,
is a kind of follow-up to the famous *Serenade* he wrote for
Peter Pears fifteen years earlier, and it begins more or less
where that work left off. The *Serenade* was scored for tenor,
horn, and strings; the *Nocturne* extends that ensemble to
include flute, cor anglais, clarinet, bassoon, harp, and
drums. The *Serenade* ended with the most exquisitely
drowsy setting of Keats's sonnet on sleep; the *Nocturne*
begins with a magical evocation of the sound of sleep itself:
a soft breathing suggested by a simple, in-an-out motive
from the muted strings. The rest of the work consists of
eight settings of poems concerned with various aspects of
sleep or dreams, linked by brief instrumental interludes of
great subtlety, giving the impression of one dream leading
gently into another. Thus, at the end of the Shelley setting
that opens the cycle, the bassoon steals in mysteriously and
introduces Tennyson's sea monster, the Kraken, "far
beneath in the abysmal sea."
   Each song has a different group of instruments to accom-
pany it. Flute and clarinet give a gossamer texture to Keats's
Sleep and Poetry; the cor anglais anticipates the *War
Requiem* in a setting of some touching lines by Wilfred
Owen; drums conjure up the French Revolution in a passage
from Wordsworth's *Prelude;* and in Middleton's *Night
Song*, the horn is required to imitate in quick succession the
sound of a bell, a howling dog, a nightingale, an owl, a
raven, a cricket, a mouse, and a cat. In the hands of a lesser
composer, the effect would no doubt seem merely clever
and superficial. But with Britten, it takes its place in the
music with perfect naturalness. On this record, which neatly

accommodates the music on two ten-inch sides (though the need to turn over during such a sublime stream of unconsciousness seems a pity), the difficult horn part is played by Barry Tuckwell with the necessary blend of virtuosity and poetry—the qualities for which the whole performance is remarkable, and nowhere more present than in the rapt, entrancing singing of Peter Pears.

BRITTEN: War Requiem. *Galina Vishnevskaya/Peter Pears/Dietrich Fischer-Dieskau/Bach Choir/Highgate School Boys' Choir/Melos Ensemble/London Symphony Orchestra conducted by Benjamin Britten.* Decca stereo SET 252-3, mono MET 252-3.

No present-day composer has written more naturally or effectively for the voice than Benjamin Britten, and none of his music shows his genius working at greater intensity than the *War Requiem* he composed in 1962 for the opening of the new Coventry Cathedral. The basic idea of the work —that of juxtaposing the words of the Latin Mass with some of Wilfred Owen's most bitter war poems—has the kind of inspired simplicity that has occurred to Britten in writing so many of his masterpieces, but never more movingly than here.

Since its message is of concern to all, and its idiom so direct, the *War Requiem* has rapidly become the most popular large-scale work of our time. It is performed in halls and cathedrals all over the world. The recording is a best-seller. And the music deserves its success—though one hopes the British public will not demean it by insisting on making an annual ritual of it, as they have done with *Messiah*, the *St. Matthew Passion*, the *Christmas Oratorio*, *Elijah*, and *The Dream of Gerontius*. The *War Requiem* is a very special work; and we should keep it special. Its directness of utterance, like Mozart's, is of a kind which has grown from the composer's operatic as well as concert-hall experience, and which, for all its seeming straightforwardness, contains layer upon layer of beauty and subtlety.

The music reveals new wonders every time one hears it. The big moments are ever overwhelming—the conjunction of the soprano's *Lacrimosa* and the tenor's *Move him into the sun*, which is the heart of the work; the grim ending of the *Abraham and Isaac* setting; the shimmering *Sanctus*; the stillness of the two enemies meeting in death; the final feeling of release, with the words *Let us sleep now*, and the gradual, tender, welling up of the voices (a passage which has a parallel in the equally humane, radiant ending of Ravel's *L'Enfant et les Sortilèges*). Other passages make their effect more gradually—the hushed, desolate opening pages, with the sinister muttering of the word "requiem" by the chorus and the softly tolling bells; the tenor solo, *One ever hangs where shelled roads part*, which, placed beween the *Sanctus* and the intense outburst of the *Libera Me*, tends to pass before one has fully realised its beauty.

Not until the 1964 Holland Festival did the three singers for whom Britten conceived the music come together in public to sing it. By that time, the recording of their voices had already been available for more than a year. Perhaps it does not "add" anything to the musical worth of the *War Requiem* to have the *Lacrimosa* sung by a Russian, and to hear a German sing to a Briton the line *I am the enemy you killed, my friend*; but it undoubtedly adds to the humanity, dignity, and pathos of this great performance, one of the supreme achievements in the history of the gramophone.

BRITTEN: Cantata Misericordium; Sinfonia da Requiem.
Peter Pears/Dietrich Fischer-Dieskau/London Symphony Chorus and Orchestra/New Philharmonia Orchestra conducted by Benjamin Britten. Decca stereo SXL 6175, mono LXT 6175.

Britten composed his *Cantata Misericordium* in 1963 for the centenary of the International Red Cross. It is a setting, in Latin, of the parable of the Good Samaritan, with the solo baritone representing the wounded traveller and the solo tenor the Samaritan. The scene is set, the action unfolded, with that vividness and conciseness of which Britten is now completely the master. "Music for me is clarification," he once said in an interview. "I try to clarify, to refine, to sensitise." In the clean, beautiful lines of this work, one sees how far he has succeeded. Few other composers today could convey the sudden attack on the traveller with such economy and clarity; no other could so movingly capture the wounded man's desolation as the two strangers pass by, and his relief when the Samaritan stops to help; no other could fill a composition with such funds of pity and sympathy and hope. It is a heartfelt and lovely work, and here it has a heartfelt and lovely performance from the two soloists and the London Symphony Chorus and Orchestra. The record is supplied with a sheet containing the Latin words and translation.

The coupling draws welcome attention to one of Britten's earlier works, the *Sinfonia da Requiem* he composed at the age of 25 in memory of his parents. At one time admired chiefly for the brilliant assurance of its writing, it now seems —in the light of more recent compositions such as the cantata—to contain far more compassion than one had imagined. The composer obtains from the New Philharmonia Orchestra a strong, supple performance, of great intensity.

TRISTAN AND ISOLDA
PRELUDE

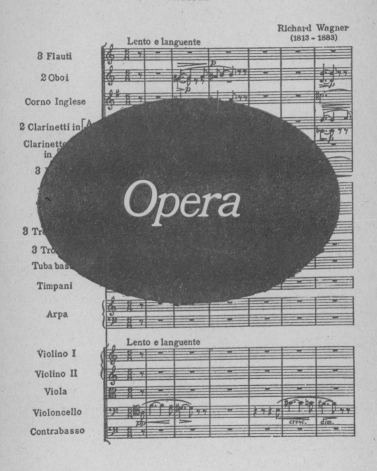

213

MONTEVERDI (1567-1643): L'Incoronazione di Poppea.
Glyndebourne Festival Opera conducted by John Pritchard.
H.M.V. Angel stereo SAN 126-7, mono AN 126-7.

The Coronation of Poppea is one of the foundation stones of opera. Its composer was 75 years old when he wrote it, in 1642; and the glowing youthfulness of the music found a parallel, in later centuries, in Verdi's *Falstaff* (written at the age of 79) and in the works of Janacek's old age. The story, as clear and hard as a diamond, tells how Nero dispatches his wife, Ottavia, and replaces her with his beautiful and ambitious mistress, Poppea. The ending, a musical (and at Glyndebourne a visual) flood of gold, is Poppea's coronation. Upon this cool, classical story, Monteverdi hung music of rich and fascinating diversity and freedom, whose highlights include a sombrely memorable scene in which the philosopher, Seneca, prepares for death; Ottavia's highly charged lament on leaving Rome for ever; an airy little love duet for two servants, the great-grandparents of Papageno and Papagena; a rousingly tongue-twisting duet for Nero and his friend Lucano (treated at Glyndebourne, rather controversially, as a show-stopping drunken scene—as if it were something Cole Porter had written as a pastiche of Monteverdi); and a radiant closing scene for Nero and Poppea. "No more strife," they sing, "no more death, o my love, o my treasure." The story does not reveal that Poppea died soon after, through Nero's brutality.

Although Monteverdi's music has long fascinated scholars, it is only fairly recently that the public have realised that an opera composed in 1642 can be as vibrantly alive as a work by Verdi. *Poppea* has been a "hit" at Glyndebourne since 1962. This recording shows why. Although the music has regrettably been cut so as to fit on to two records, the performance is gorgeously sung by Magda Laslo (Poppea), Richard Lewis (Nero), Carlo Cava (Seneca), and Frances Bible (Ottavia); and Raymond Leppard's trim arrangement of the score, with its shimmeringly lovely accompaniment of harpsichords, chamber organs, cellos, and an array of plucked instruments, is sensitively conducted by John Pritchard.

PURCELL (1865-1695): Dido and Aeneas. *Janet Baker/*
Patricia Clark/Raimund Herincx/St. Anthony Singers/
English Chamber Orchestra conducted by Anthony Lewis.
Oiseau-Lyre stereo SOL 60047, mono OL 50216.

Purcell composed his one real opera towards the end of his
life for the pupils of a girls' school in Chelsea. Deliberately,
he made it a work of modest length and scored it for modest
forces. But that is not to say it is a "children's" opera. The
part of Dido needs a soprano of considerable presence,with
a voice grand enough to convey the tragic intensity of the
final lament, *When I am laid in earth.* Consequently, most
performances tend to fall between two stools. A performance by young, amateur voices may catch the freshness of
the music, but miss its power; a performance with Dido
sung by someone like Kirsten Flagstad is usually too fruity
(as her recording of it proves). Although we can wish that
this great composer had left an opera that posed fewer
problems, we should be thankful that he did leave one
sample, tantalising though it is, of what he might have
achieved if he had found a few more b̲r̲e̲a̲t̲h̲i̲n̲g spaces
between his "official" compositions. The Oiseau-Lyre
recording, predictably enough, is not quite ideal. But in
Janet Baker it has a youthful, yet full-toned, Dido; and
Anthony Lewis draws stylish, spirited playing from his
nicely-balanced forces.

HANDEL (1685-1759): Giulio Cesare (excerpts). *Joan*
Sutherland/Margreta Elkins/New Symphony Orchestra of
London conducted by Richard Bonynge. Decca stereo
SXL 6116, mono LXT 6116.

The person who knows only Handel's oratorios and instrumental works has yet to discover the cream of his music.
This lies in his operas, which, happily, are at last beginning
to be rediscovered by the British public, for whom so many
of them were written (in Germany the revival started sooner,
with the result that Handel is now a standard figure in the
repertoire—which he is not yet in Britain, despite the efforts
of the Handel Opera Society). *Julius Caesar* (1724) is usually
said to hold an important place in his output, because it is
dramatically more "effective" than the works he had written

earlier, and marked the start of a richer phase in his career. But we should be wary of accepting handed-down beliefs about the weaknesses of Handel's early operas. In 1965, a revival of his youthful *Agrippina* (1709) in London and at the Ledlanet Festival in Scotland proved it to be an entrancing piece, fresh and melodious and alive. More discoveries surely lie ahead; and one hopes that the record companies, whose attention to Handel's operas has so far been erratic, will keep up with developments.

The freedom of Monteverdi's operas had narrowed, by Handel's time, into conventions. How Handel enlivened those conventions can be heard in *Julius Caesar*, *Semele*, *Xerxes*, and other works that have been revived in recent years. It is typical of our traditional misconception of him that the famous *Largo* from *Xerxes*, which has long been treated as a religious melody, is in fact nothing of the kind. Anyone who decides to explore these works will discover all kinds of new facets of Handel's personality—and discover, too, that his melodic invention was even richer than is generally supposed. Among the meagre supply of records, this batch of extracts from *Caesar* is outstanding, not only for the sustained beauty of the music, but also for the style with which it is performed. Cleopatra's seduction aria, for which Handel provided a truly seductive melody and an accompaniment for two orchestras, is luxuriously sung by Joan Sutherland. The part of Caesar is taken by a mezzo-soprano, which is a happier solution than transposing this castrato role downwards so that it can be sung by a man. The vocal line is lavishly decorated throughout, and Richard Bonynge obtains crisp, unhurried playing from the orchestra.

More expensive, but again strongly recommended, is a complete recording of *Alcina* (1735), another work full of florid and dramatic, tender and passionate music, in which Joan Sutherland as the sorceress heroine is joined by Teresa Berganza, Monica Sinclair, and Graziella Sciutti (Decca stereo SET 232-4, mono MET 232-4; excellently-chosen excerpts on stereo SXL 6080, mono LXT 6080). A complete *Semele* (the one that includes *Wher'er you walk*), with Jennifer Vyvyan in the title role, is well performed under Anthony Lewis but only moderately well recorded (Oiseau-Lyre mono OL 50098-100). On the other hand, the little pastoral opera *Acis and Galatea* (1720) is sheer delight in every way, beautifully recorded, with Joan Sutherland and

Peter Pears in elegant voice, a rollicking account of *O ruddier than the cherry* from Owen Brannigan, and the lightest of accompaniments from the Philomusica of London under Sir Adrian Boult (Oiseau-Lyre stereo SOL 60011-2, mono OL 50179-80).

OPERATIC RECITAL: Arias by Gluck, Cherubini, Pergolesi, Handel, and Paisiello. *Teresa Berganza/Royal Opera House Orchestra conducted by Alexander Gibson.* Decca stereo SXL 2251, mono LXT 5611.

This recital, apart from being a striking example of the singing of the delightful Spanish mezzo-soprano Teresa Berganza, usefully fills several gaps among the records chosen for this section. Gluck helped to lift opera out of the rut into which it was threatening to sink during the eighteenth century; but his works, though of great historical importance and often of sublime beauty, have never been favourites of the record companies. The absence of a recommendable version of *Orpheus*—and the absence altogether of *Iphigenie en Tauride*—is particularly regrettable. Of the two *Orpheus* airs chosen by Berganza, *Che faro* is Orpheus's famous lament, whose long, pure lines were said by Einstein to transcend all expression. She also sings the great renunciation aria from the first act of *Alceste*, and Paris's lovely *O del mio dolce ardor*, with its exquisite oboe obbligato, from the first act of *Paride ed Elena*. Handel, unfortunately, is represented by Cleopatra's lament that is also included in the *Julius Caesar* disc described earlier in this section; but both performances of this noble aria are so fine that comparison becomes a pleasure. Among the other items, the extract from Pergolesi's enchanting little comic opera, *La Serva Padrona*, is especially welcome; and the whole recital is sung with the precision and grace, and the warm fullness of tone from top to bottom of the register, which we have come to expect of this admirable artist.

MOZART (1756-1791): Le Nozze di Figaro, K.492. *Vienna State Opera conducted by Erich Kleiber.* Decca stereo SXL 2087-90, mono LXT 5088-91.

Mozart composed operas throughout his career. His first,
218

La finta semplice, was written at the age of thirteen; his last, *The Magic Flute*, was completed three months before his death. He was the greatest of all opera composers, and his four mature masterpieces—*The Marriage of Figaro*, *Don Giovanni*, *Cosi fan tutte*, and *The Magic Flute*—are surely not only the greatest of all operas but also the greatest works in musical history. Listening to the Count singing *Contessa perdono*, to Fiordiligi's *Per pieta*, to the little duet between Papageno and Papagena, one brims over with love for the characters and for the genius who brought them to life for us. As time passes, we can only go on adding to our love and knowledge of him, and go on wondering, misty-eyed, at the profound and instinctive rightness of his music, his ceaseless ability to produce a phrase, a chord, that will turn the heart over, his sense of drama and beauty, and the sheer scale of his achievement.

But we have not always felt so strongly as this. In the nineteenth century, the famous British composer-historian, Sir Hubert Parry, was able to write that Mozart "represents the type of man who is contented with the average progress of things and finds no necessity to aim at anything more novel than the doing of what comes to him to be done in the very best manner he can." In the eighteen-nineties, Bernard Shaw, to his eternal credit, protested vigorously about the disgraceful neglect of Mozart in London. But the present century, whatever its faults, has witnessed the discovery of Mozart's full greatness, and surely few would dispute Brigid Brophy's claim that, as an artist and dramatist, he stands "on the very pinnacle of Parnassus." The book in which she writes this, *Mozart the Dramatist*, is sometimes wrong-headed; but its heart is in the right place, and all who are fascinated by Mozart's operas should read it.

Several recordings are available of each of the main works; and naturally, since each opera is the most penetrating of character studies and contains a whole world of musical feeling, none of these recordings can be called "definitive." Furthermore, fashions in Mozart performance change. In the present century, it has been customary for many years to adhere scrupulously to the printed score—with the ironic result that what we hear is not at all what Mozart intended, because in the eighteenth century various points of musical syntax were implied and not written. In Britain at present a revolution is on the move to restore to the vocal line of Mozart's operas the appoggiaturas and

219

some of the vocal embellishments which were taken for granted in his own day, but which a later tradition has chosen to ignore. To the layman, the question whether Mozart should be sung with or without appoggiaturas may seem a minor academic nicety which a number of scholars and critics have been inflating out of all proportion to its actual worth. Can it really make much difference to a performance? The answer is to be found in Charles Mackerras's reconstruction of *The Marriage of Figaro* for Sadler's Wells, and nowhere more clearly than in Susanna's aria, *Deh vieni, non tardar*, in the last act. Here, instead of letting many of the phrases end with a pair of identical notes (as written in the score) Mackerras has replaced these "blunt" endings with the graceful curve and the little harmonic stab of an appoggiatura. The aria, thus restored to its true shape, flows with a sweet serenity that breaks the heart.

None of the current Mozart recordings pays more than token courtesy, if as much as that, to appoggiaturas. But this is not to say that these performances should therefore be written off. We can now see that they would sound better if they had the benefit of appoggiaturas; but it would be ungrateful and foolish to deny that, in spite of their illiteracies, they contain singing of memorable beauty and feeling. Many fine Mozart conductors—Giulini among them—still persist in a plain, undecorated approach. It remains standard practice in many countries; and as long as "international" performances of Mozart are put on, it will be difficult to eradicate. But the Sadler's Wells *Figaro* is surely an important signpost to the future, and the day will surely come when Mackerras's corrections reach the gramophone.

Meanwhile the warm humanity of Erich Kleiber's Vienna recording of *Figaro*, dating back to 1955 but sounding as delicious as ever, makes this the most affecting of recorded performances of one of the most affecting of all operas. *Figaro* is the first of three masterpieces Mozart wrote in collaboration with the librettist Da Ponte; and so completely did they make the Beaumarchais characters their own that the original play gained a new dimension. As Victor Gollancz has put it in one of his books of musical memoirs: "Beaumarchais' *Figaro* is intrigue on earth: Mozart's *Figaro* . . . is intrigue near the outskirts of Heaven." And for proof of these words, one has only to turn to the last pages of the opera, where the Count asks the Countess's forgiveness, the Countess gives her tender reply, and the orchestra for a few moments holds us in the heights before gently bringing us back to earth for the final happy chorus. After all the musical miracles of the previous three hours, this passage is the greatest miracle of all. Has more sublime music ever been written? Can anyone listen to it without turning to jelly? In the Kleiber recording, Lisa Della Casa, her voice in full bloom, is an entrancing, youthful Countess; Hilde Gueden, blunt endings and all, is the most lovable Susanna; and Cesare Siepi makes a lithe, witty, intelligent Figaro. The ensembles, so important to the success of this opera, are full of life, and the whole work moves at a sparkling but unhurried pace.

A good cheap edition, lacking only the last ounce of magic, is available from Philips (mono GL 5777-9), with Sena Jurinac as the Countess, Rita Streich as Susanna, Walter Berry as Figaro, and Paul Schöffler as Almaviva, with the Vienna Symphony Orchestra under Karl Böhm, another conductor who recognises that Mozart should not be hustled, and that the woodwind, like the singers, perform their best when given time to breathe. Anyone who cannot afford to pay nearly three times the price for the Kleiber set should be very happy with this one.

MOZART: Don Giovanni, K.527. *Eberhard Wächter/ Joan Sutherland/Elisabeth Schwarzkopf/Graziella Sciutti/ Philharmonia Orchestra conducted by Carlo Maria Giulini.* Columbia stereo SAX 2369-72, mono 33CX 1717-20 (excerpts on stereo SAX 2559, mono 33CX1918).

The Marriage of Figaro ends with a night scene. *Don Giovanni*, composed for Prague the following year, begins with one. Indeed, all its main events—the murder of the Commendatore, the party at Giovanni's palace, the mock serenading of Elvira, the visit to the cemetery, the hellfire finale—take place at night. The dark key of D minor dominates the score. The creeping scale passages are full of menace. Mozart called it a *dramma giocoso*; and the character of a performance depends on how much emphasis is given to the drama, and how much to the harsh humour of the piece. The part of the satanic hero can be played in many ways—from the foppish "student" Giovanni of Renato Capecchi at the 1965 Edinburgh Festival to the sleazy, balding, lecherous Giovanni of the same singer two months earlier at the Holland Festival. Leporello can be the traditional comic manservant, or he can, more convincingly if less likeably, be a sadistic thug, a Giovanni without the breeding. Masetto can be a baffled country bumpkin or a true eighteenth century lower-class revolutionary, behind whose singing one can imagine the distant rumble of the tumbrils. Perhaps because it can be approached from so many angles, *Giovanni* is often thought to be the most eternally fascinating of Mozart's operas. Certainly it is the most "romantic"—and one can understand why, in the nineteenth century, composers like Liszt and Alkan were so attracted to it that they wrote piano fantasies on themes from the opera. And themes the opera possesses in abundance: none of Mozart's other operas possesses quite such a profusion of varied and beautiful arias. This leads to the danger that, divorced from the stage action, a recording will tend to sound merely like a series of "highlights". To give the music coherence, it has to be performed with the utmost intensity; and this demand is met by Giulini in a performance which, right from its opening chords, is incisive and threatening—and at the same time extremely elegant. Eberhard Wächter, in common with other recorded Dons, does have a tendency to snarl his words rather than rely on seductive tone; but his portrayal comes over vividly, and in Joan Sutherland (Anna), Elisabeth Schwarzkopf (Elvira), and Graziella Sciutti (Zerlina) he has a superb trio of sopranos. The rest of the cast, including Giuseppe Taddei (Leporello) and Luigi Alva (Ottavio), are generally up to standard; and one of the special delights of the set is the purity of the Philharmonia's woodwind playing, every phrase of which is lovingly shaped. Again there is a goodish Philips cheap edition, conducted by Rudolf Moralt, with George London as Giovanni, Walter Berry as Leporello, and Hilde Zadek, Sena Jurinac, and Graziella Sciutti as the three sopranos (mono GL 5753-5).

MOZART: Cosi fan tutte, K.588. *Elisabeth Schwarzkopf/Christa Ludwig/Alfredo Kraus/Giuseppe Taddei/Hanny Steffek/Walter Berry/Philharmonia Orchestra conducted by Karl Böhm.* H.M.V. Angel stereo SANS 103/SAN 104-6, mono ANS 103/AN 104-6.

After the outstanding success of *Figaro* and *Giovanni*,

Mozart and Da Ponte collaborated in 1790 on *Cosi fan tutte*, whose supposedly superficial and immoral plot—based, it is said, on an actual incident in Vienna—for many years roused the hostility of audiences. Even now there are people who see in this opera nothing more than an icing-sugar charade, a viewpoint encouraged by all too many performances, in which the singers and orchestra merely skate over the sparkling surface of the music. But with Mozart a sparkling surface often means depths of feeling underneath, and *Cosi fan tutte* is no exception: it is best treated as a basically serious human comedy, light-hearted yet supercharged with emotional undercurrents and truth and compassion. Where many performers and listeners are no doubt led astray is in the knowledge that the story revolves round a practical joke. But it is a joke that gets badly out of hand; and although all seems to end happily enough, the lives of the main characters have surely been irreparably altered by what they have experienced.

Cosi fan tutte is usually said to be less rich in tunes than Mozart's other great operas; but this is because it is the most flawlessly constructed, the most unified and coherent of the series, and therefore contains fewer "highlights." None of Mozart's operas takes more happily to the gramophone than this. On records, the singers are freed from the sight-gags with which so many producers are determined to garnish the score, and can concentrate entirely on the beauty of the music. This is especially true of Karl Böhm's celestial, strongly-characterised performance, which treads, as it should, a tightrope between comedy and tragedy. His leisurely tempi have meant that the performance spreads over seven sides instead of the customary six, but the gain in beauty of tone and phrasing is enough to justify the expense. Once again, however, there is a recommended Philips bargain issue (mono GL 5703-5), with Teresa Stitch-Randall, Ira Malaniuk, Waldemar Kmentt, and Walter Berry as a very acceptable quartet of lovers, but marred by the rather distant sound of the Vienna Symphony Orchestra under Rudolf Moralt (and in *Cosi fan tutte* the orchestral writing is even more ravishing than in the other works). Still, at half the price of the H.M.V., this has much to commend it; and although Teresa Stitch-Randall cannot command quite the radiance of Elisabeth Schwarzkopf, she at least makes some amends by including more appoggiaturas.

MOZART: Die Zauberflöte, K.620. *Gundula Janowitz/*
Nicolai Gedda/Walter Berry/Lucia Popp/Philharmonia
Chorus and Orchestra conducted by Otto Klemperer.
H.M.V. Angel stereo SAN 137-9, mono AN 137-9.

From a series of Italian libretti Mozart turned for his last
opera to a German one. *The Magic Flute* is a "vernacular"
opera, based on an Oriental fairy-tale, with words by
Emanuel Schikaneder, a gifted actor-playwright, who added
a Masonic element to the story, played the part of Papageno
in the first production, and owned the Vienna suburban
theatre in which it was performed. Like *Cosi fan tutte*, *The
Magic Flute* has sometimes been accused of triviality. But
its trivialities are of the most sublime order. It is a marvellously varied score, ranging from the drooping G minor
lament of the heroine Pamina to the high-speed pyrotech-
nics of the Queen of the Night, from the cheerful jingles of
the comedian Papageno to the solemn choruses of Sarastro
and his priests. Yet the effect, as always in Mozart, is never
disjointed: each change of mood magically enhances the
next. But to strike the ideal balance in performance is by no
means easy. Some conductors and producers emphasise the
farcical elements, others the solemn ones. The best solution is
to treat the work as fundamentally serious, and let the
humour bubble out of this serious foundation. This, as one
would expect, is Klemperer's way. He gives the music a
noble breadth, but ensures that the rhythm has a spring that
keeps everything alive and not too heavy. The decision to
omit the spoken dialogue is controversial, but for home
listening the loss can scarcely be considered very important
—indeed the jokiness of many of the lines can become a
bore when divorced from the stage action. About the casting
there is no controversy at all: it is generally excellent, the
female roles particularly so, from Gundula Janowitz's
shining-voiced Pamina and Lucia Popp's mercurial Queen
of the Night down to the three ladies-in-waiting, sung by
Elisabeth Schwarzkopf, Christa Ludwig, and Marga Höffgen
(and how often can one hope to hear these smaller roles so
immaculately cast?). Nicolai Gedda is a poetic, stylish
Tamino, showing some awareness of the existence of
appoggiaturas, but Walter Berry sounds a little too in-
gratiating as Papageno—curiously, for he is an admirable
singer who never gives this impression in the flesh. The
Philharmonia Chorus and Orchestra perform throughout

224

with a wonderful warm purity of line, and though the atmosphere of the recording perhaps leans more to the concert hall than the opera house, the overall effect is enthralling and deeply moving.

BEETHOVEN (1770-1827): Fidelio. *Christa Ludwig/ Jon Vickers/Gottlob Frick/Walter Berry/Philharmonia Chorus and Orchestra conducted by Otto Klemperer.* Columbia stereo SAX 2451-3, mono 33CX 1804-6 (excerpts on stereo SAX 2547, mono 33CX 1907).

Beethoven's only opera cost him more effort than any of his other works. He was not a natural opera composer; he tinkered with *Fidelio* for nearly ten years, between 1805, when it had its unsuccessful premiere, and 1814, when it took the form in which we know it today; yet in this work he created one of the greatest of all operas, whose noble subject becomes all the more moving because it is made to grow (like that of *The Magic Flute*, said to be the only opera Beethoven really admired) out of the homely background of a German singspiel. *Fidelio* is the most heroic of "escape" operas, with a theme—the courage of a faithful wife who saves her husband from death in a Spanish jail— into which Beethoven was able to pour his heart and soul. Klemperer's famous recording reveals the music in all its glory. Predictably, it is a performance of the utmost breadth and steadiness of impulse. But it is never porridgy: every note is alive, whether it be the hushed announcement from the strings of the prisoners' emergence into the open air, or the final choral celebration of good over evil. The humanity of the story is conveyed with an intensity and a uniform excellence of singing and orchestral playing one seldom hopes to hear in the opera house. Christa Ludwig is a magnificent Leonora, brave, tender, at ease from top to bottom of her register; Jon Vickers, the finest Florestan of our time, is in his best form; and Walter Berry is a really musical villain, instead of being, as so often happens, a merely snarling one. Spoken dialogue is included; *Leonora No. 3* is rightly omitted (for this one must turn to Klemperer's recording of all four of the *Fidelio* overtures).

ROSSINI (1792-1868): L'Italiana in Algeri. *Teresa Berganza/Luigi Alva/Fernando Corena/Chorus and Orchestra of the Maggio Musicale Fiorentino conducted by Silvio Varviso.* Decca stereo SET 262-4, mono MET 262-4.

Rossini was one of the most precociously gifted and fecund of all opera composers. In a career of nineteen years, he poured out no fewer than 38 works. At least four of them are comic masterpieces of the highest order; a fifth, the serious opera *William Tell*, reveals a different but no less impressive side of his character, and it is sad that we are given so few opportunities to see it. *L'Italiana*, composed at the age of twenty, was his first big success. It is said that he wrote it in 27 days. Decca took rather longer to record it, in 1963, at the Teatro della Pergola in Florence; and evidence of loving care shines through every note of the performance. *L'Italiana* today holds third place in the Rossini hit parade. Still some way behind the *Barber*, it is catching up fast on *Cenerentola*. And rightly so, for it is as fleet and sparkling and lyrical, with particularly rich ensembles and a first act finale (*Confusi e stupide*) that is one of Rossini's most rollicking outpourings of pure buffo spirit.

Perhaps the Decca performance concentrates more on beauty of tone than on the full comic possibilities of the music. At times one longs for the extra drop of wit that Beecham, above all, could bring to Rossini. But over the radiance of sound there need be no cavil. In the role of Isabella, the Italian girl who rescues her lover from slavery in the palace of Mustapha (the plot is a little like *Seraglio* in reverse), Teresa Berganza is in delectable voice. Luigi Alva, as the lover, shapes his high intricate roulades with charm and ease; and, as the infatuated Bey of Algiers, Fernando Corena is a solid and dependable *basso profundo*. Silvio Varviso conducts an alert and elegant performance, vividly realised by the recording engineers.

ROSSINI: Il Barbiere di Siviglia. *Glyndebourne Festival Opera conducted by Vittorio Gui.* H.M.V. Angel stereo SAN 114-6, mono AN 114-6.

Rossini composed his opera thirty years after Mozart's

Figaro, but took up the Beaumarchais story at an earlier stage in its progress—here we see Count Almaviva's elaborate wooing of his future Countess, and learn how things were with Figaro before Susanna came into his life. Less tender, more energetic (in some productions far too energetic) than Mozart's treatment of the characters, the *Barber* represents the high-water mark of Rossini's comic invention. It was written, miraculously, in a fortnight—though a few numbers were lifted, in haste, from other works. Yet for all its sunny, straightforward high spirits, the *Barber* is not a work that has fared well on records, and until the Glyndebourne set was issued in 1963 no previous recording had caught the exact blend of wit and warmth, and the avoidance of gratuitous horseplay, that are necessary to make the opera a success. Here the veteran Italian conductor Vittorio Gui reveals in every bar a mature understanding of the music, and has assembled a cast who clearly agree with him how it should go. Victoria de los Angeles is in pure, delicate voice as the most lovably vivacious of all Rossini's coloratura mezzo heroines; and a special delight of her performance is that, instead of following the erroneous fashion of interpolating an aria in the act two lesson scene, she gives us the one Rossini himself wished to be sung here. The other members of the cast, all in good form, include Luigi Alva (Almaviva), Carlo Cava (Basilio), Sesto Bruscantini (Figaro), and Ian Wallace (Bartolo).

ROSSINI: La Cenerentola. *Marina de Gabarain/Juan Oncina/Sesto Bruscantini/Ian Wallace/Glyndebourne Festival Chorus and Orchestra conducted by Vittorio Gui.* H.M.V. mono HQM 1011-3.

If *The Barber of Seville* and *The Italian Girl in Algiers* are the most intoxicating of Rossini's operas, *Cenerentola* is his most human comedy. The magical elements of the fairy-tale —the pumpkin and mice and so on—are dispensed with, and the story treated more from a social standpoint, with the moral that a human heart is more important than the glamour of rank and wealth. Rossini was seldom a touching composer; but here, among some of his most sparkling arias and ensembles, are passages whose sighing beauty brings tears to the eyes. It is a lovely score. Although, for technical achievement, the 1953 Glyndebourne recording is no match for the 1964 Decca one, it is more elegantly performed, and catches more effectively both the wit of the music and the plaintiveness of the heroine's part (sung in introspective, clarinet-like tones by Marina de Gabarain). The records sell at bargain price.

BELLINI (1801-1835): Norma. *Maria Callas/Nicola Zaccaria/Franco Corelli/Chorus and Orchestra of La Scala, Milan, conducted by Tullio Serafin.* Columbia stereo SAX 2412-4, mono 33CX 1766-8.

Bellini and Donizetti are another of those pairs of musical twins who, for all their surface similarity, are really quite different when you get to know them. The Sicilian Bellini was a hypersensitive consumptive who died in his early thirties, and his music has a hothouse sweetness and a profusion of poignant, fine-spun melodies which greatly influenced another consumptive composer of the period, Frederic Chopin. His lyrical gifts are found at their most passionate and sustained in his Druid opera, *Norma* (1831), of which Maria Callas has twice recorded the part of the priestess heroine. In her 1954 recording, now withdrawn, her voice was in its prime, but she was let down by her supporting cast. In her 1961 recording she produces a spattering of ugly notes, but the dramatic intensity of her performance has increased with the years, and it would be a dull listener who failed to be gripped by her portrayal. The supporting cast is stronger than in the earlier performance; Tullio Serafin conducts a shapely accompaniment; and the recording, in stereo and mono, is generally fine.

Listeners who desire more than one Bellini opera for their collection are recommended also to the Callas version of *La Sonnambula*, in which this rustic romance, composed in the same year as *Norma*, is brought radiantly to life (Columbia mono 33CXS 1469/33CX 1470-1); and to a splendidly lively performance of *I Puritani* (1835), in which another great exponent of bel canto, Joan Sutherland, is heard at the top of her form (Decca stereo SET 259-61, mono MET 259-61).

DONIZETTI (1797-1848): L'Elisir d'Amore. *Hilde Gueden/Giuseppe di Stefano/Fernando Corena/Florence Festival Chorus and Orchestra conducted by Francesco Molinari-Pradelli.* Decca mono LXT 5155-7.

Donizetti was the most prodigal of opera composers. In a career of a quarter of a century, he poured out more than sixty works; the last act of *La Favorite* is said to have been written in a few hours; and on hearing that Rossini composed *The Barber of Seville* in a fortnight, he made a caustic remark about Rossini's laziness. Quantity, in Donizetti's case, did not invariably mean quality; and a number of his operas, despite such enticingly romantic names as *Emilia di Liverpool, Il Castello di Kenilworth, Otto Mesi in due ore* (Eight months in two hours), and *Il Diluvio universale* (The universal deluge), have fallen by the wayside. But the current enthusiasm for bel canto has brought about a successful revival of several Donizetti operas which, only a few years ago, were thought to be as dead as dodos. More, no doubt, will follow; but for most people, the "essential" Donizetti is to be found in three works, two of them comic (*Don Pasquale* and *L'Elisir d'Amore*) and one tragic (*Lucia di Lammermoor*), none of them so consistently beautiful as Bellini, but each with its own character and attraction. *Don Pasquale* (1843), one of the last works he wrote before insanity cut short his career, is widely considered to be his masterpiece; but it has never fared well on LP, and neither the Decca nor the D.G.G. recording catches the lightness and fun of this sparkling score. On the other hand, the Decca recording of his earlier buffo opera, *L'Elisir d'Amore* (1832), is beautifully done, with Hilde Gueden in capital voice as the heroine Adina, Giuseppe di Stefano scarcely less good as her bashful swain, and Fernando Corena superbly fruity as the quack who purveys the patent "love potion."

A good recording of *Lucia di Lammermoor* (1835), with its famous sextet, has Joan Sutherland as the ill-fated Lucy (Decca stereo SET 212-4, mono MET 212-4).

VERDI (1813-1901): Rigoletto. *Dietrich Fischer-Dieskau/*
Renata Scotto/Carlo Bergonzi/Chorus and Orchestra of
La Scala, Milan, conducted by Rafael Kubelik. D.G.G.
stereo SLPM 138931-3, mono LPM 18931-3.

Had he died as young as Bellini, Verdi would hold a
somewhat different position on the musical Parnassus from
the one we have now allotted him. *Attila* and *Macbeth* would
be regarded as his mature masterpieces instead of fairly early
intimations of his genius; *Rigoletto, Il Travatore*, and *La
Traviata*, and the great subsequent chain of operas right up
to *Otello* and *Falstaff*, would never have been written. It is
still fashionable, in some quarters, to sneer at early Verdi
for being nothing more than crude barrel-organ music.
Certainly, the music does have its crudenesses; so has the
dramatic development; but Verdi, even in his least significant works, had a gift for melody and a red-bloodedness
that swept the music along. One after another, those works
have been revived in recent years and found to be still full
of life. Not many of them have so far been recorded; but
anyone wishing to explore those pre-*Rigoletto* works is
recommended, in particular, to the Decca *Macbeth*,
conducted by Thomas Schippers, with Birgit Nilsson as
Lady Macbeth (stereo SET 282-4, mono MET 282-4), and
Nabucco, with Tito Gobbi in the title role, and Elena Suliotis
a full-blooded Abigail (stereo SET 298-300, mono MET 298-
300).

The first of Verdi's key works is *Rigoletto*, which he wrote
at the age of 38 and in which his inspiration seemed to gain
a powerful new assurance that has made this work a firm
favourite in opera houses all over the world. The drama
unfolds at white heat (the opening scene, a mere twenty
minutes long, is one of the most concentrated and stirring
passages in any opera); the melodies, and especially the
duets, have a new richness and passion; and the whole work
reeks of atmosphere. More recordings exist of *Rigoletto*
than of any other opera, and the D.G.G. issue, since it
occupies three records instead of the usual two, is one of
the most expensive. But it is worth the extra cost for the
sake of Dietrich Fischer-Dieskau's intense, probing
portrayal of the crippled jester—surely one of the most
introspective, finely characterised, and least ostentatious
performances of the part ever sung. Renata Scotto is a
deeply musical Gilda, and her important duets with
230

Fischer-Dieskau have the utmost feeling and beauty of tone. Carlo Bergonzi makes a stylish Duke, the smaller parts are adequately filled, and Rafael Kubelik gives the music space to breathe without loss of emotional heat—though the orchestra, as so often in D.G.G. recordings, sounds rather distant.

Admirers of *Rigoletto* will no doubt also wish to possess *Trovatore* and *Traviata*, but here there is no such strongly recommendable recording. The most musical version of *Trovatore* is still perhaps the old American one conducted by Renato Cellini, with Zinka Milanov and Jussi Björling in the cast (H.M.V. mono ALP 1832-3), though stereo addicts may prefer the lustier and more recent version conducted by Schippers (H.M.V. Angel stereo SAN 151-3, mono AN 151-3). *La Traviata*, recorded in Florence with Joan Sutherland in the lead and John Pritchard as conductor, is very adequate without being outstanding (Decca stereo SET 249-51, mono MET 249-51).

VERDI: Otello. *Renata Tebaldi/Mario del Monaco/ Aldo Protti/Vienna State Opera Chorus and Vienna Philharmonic Orchestra conducted by Herbert von Karajan.* Decca stereo SET 209-11, mono MET 209-11 (excerpts on stereo SXL 2314, mono LXT 5683).

After *Aida* (of which the three-disc Karajan recording, on Decca, is recommended) Verdi waited sixteen years before writing another opera. But just when people had begun to fear his career might be over, he was shown a draft, by Boito, of a libretto based on Shakespeare's *Othello*. Soon the ageing composer's imagination was once again aflame; and when *Otello* appeared in 1887, in his 74th year, critics and public united in acclaiming it a masterpiece. Originally, the opera was to be called *Iago*—and it could well have justified such a title, since the role of the villain is one of the greatest Verdi composed for the baritone voice. But Othello and Desdemona, too, are portrayed in depth, and with remarkable intensity. No one would claim that in *Otello* Verdi surpassed Shakespeare. But he gave us an opera quite as great as the play—and who could ask for more?

To a listener reared on early Verdi, the music of *Otello*

231

may at first seem short-winded. Instead of flowing, clear-cut arias, the characters are given material that is compressed and often violently dramatic. Yet there is tenderness, too; and the final scene, in which Desdemona's delicate *Willow Song* and *Ave Maria* are followed by Othello's subdued monologue, is Verdi at his most subtly inspired. Although anyone who possesses the old Toscanini recording on R.C.A. will wish no other performance, the newer and warmer-toned Karajan one has much in its favour—including strong portrayals of the leading parts, superb orchestral playing, and an admirable overall grasp of the score.

VERDI: Falstaff. *Giuseppe Valdengo/Herra Nelli/ Teresa Stich-Randall/Robert Shaw Chorale/N.B.C. Symphony Orchestra conducted by Arturo Toscanini.* R.C.A. mono RB 16163-5.

Verdi's first comic opera, *Un Giorno di Regno* (King for a Day), was a youthful failure; his second, composed more than half a century later, was a supreme masterpiece. A comic opera was on Verdi's mind from the moment *Otello* had its premiere. First he considered basing it on *Don Quixote;* then he and Boito turned once again to Shakespeare, producing a conflation of *The Merry Wives of Windsor* and *Henry IV* (Part One) which is one of the raciest operas ever written, yet which possesses those sudden moments of poignancy, those changes of mood and pace, which always differentiate a true comic opera from a mere farce. Again and again, one marvels at the freshness and nimbleness of the octogenarian composer's mind. The eight-part fugue with which the opera ends is no stuffy academic exercise, but counterpoint at its most joyfully and wittily inventive. The scene setting—the musical picture of Windsor Forest at night—is wonderfully sensitive. The characterisation is profound. In none of Verdi's previous scores are voices and orchestra, solos and ensembles, quite so subtly blended. Although he lived another eight years after composing it, *Falstaff* was his last opera and the mellow crown of his achievement. To listen to it at home inevitably makes one long for the high spirits of the stage action. Yet a recording does provide an opportunity to savour at leisure a work which, in the opera house, speeds past all too quickly. The Toscanini performance, exuberant yet tender, is a milestone in gramophone history; never has the evergreen beauty of the music been more glowingly caught.

WAGNER (1813-1883): Tristan und Isolde.   *Kirsten Flagstad/Ludwig Suthaus/Philharmonia Orchestra conducted by Wilhelm Furtwängler*.   H.M.V. mono HQM 1001-5.

Although Hanslick's vindictive attitude to Wagner is usually cited as a classic example of a critic being wildly wrong, there are in fact many people today who are just as opposed to his music as ever Hanslick was. Indeed, no other great composer arouses quite such violent feelings, both for and against. Yet it is foolish to try to deny Wagner's greatness. You may not like all his music; but if you do not like any of it, the loss is yours. It is sometimes said of Wagner that he is an "all or nothing" composer, but this is not entirely true. Certainly he is a composer who requires nothing less than one's full attention in performance—he cannot be used as background music. And certainly the complete Wagnerite tends to devote himself to the Master's works with a fanatical single-mindedness approaching that of the complete Gilbert-and-Sullivan enthusiast. But even the non-Wagnerian is usually willing to make exceptions for two works—*Tristan and Isolde* and *The Mastersingers*, the one noble and heroic, the other warm and humane, and both of them brimming with compassion for the characters they contain. However egotistic some of Wagner's theories may seem, however irritated one may be by his belief that he and he alone could save the art of opera from decay, there is no doubt that his music in many ways vindicated what he said. He desired change, and had the inspiration and knowhow to carry it out; he was an extremely industrious composer, who also wrote his own excellent librettos; and his precise knowledge of what he wanted brought about the building, to his own specifications, of the Bayreuth theatre—today still the leading centre in which to hear his music, even although Wieland Wagner, who is now in charge of the *Festspielhaus*, is proving just as controversial a producer as his father was a composer.

Nowhere is the invention of the LP record more welcome than in listening to a Wagner opera. What once took twenty to thirty records now takes five. Excellent recordings have been made of most of Wagner's main operas. The early *Flying Dutchman* (1843) and *Tannhauser* (1845) can be had in well-engineered "live" recordings made by Philips at Bayreuth, the first conducted by Wolfgang Sawallisch, with Franz Crass in the title-role and Anja Silja as Senta (stereo SABL 218-20, mono ABL 3412-4), the second again conducted by Sawallisch, with Wolfgang Windgassen, Anja Silja, and Grace Bumbry (stereo SAL 3445-7, mono AL 3445-7). Georg Solti's *Ring* recordings for Decca, especially *The Twilight of the Gods* (stereo SET 292-7, mono MET 292-7), are landmarks in the history of recording, in which the gramophone becomes not just a means of reproduction but (thanks to the producer, John Culshaw) a musical medium in its own right.

As the basis of a Wagner collection, however, it is not perhaps to these recordings—wonderful though they are—that the buyer should turn first, but to the H.M.V. *Tristan*. Recorded in 1953, reissued at bargain price in 1965 (with considerable improvement in sound), it is the most valuable souvenir we have of perhaps the greatest of all Wagner conductors. The forces he had at his command—the Philharmonia Orchestra, Ludwig Suthaus and Kirsten Flagstad in the title roles, Dietrich Fischer-Dieskau as Kurwenal and Josef Greindl as King Mark—were all inspired by the occasion to perform with the utmost grandeur; and it is hard to think of any recording worthier of a place in one's collection, that more overwhelmingly conveys the restless beauty of the music (composed in 1865 and said by Wagner to be the perfect flowering of his theories), or is better able to repay, as a sublime experience, the money spent on it.

WAGNER: Die Meistersinger von Nurnberg. *Ferdinand Frantz/Gottlob Frick/ Rudolf Schock/Elisabeth Grummer/ Berlin Opera Chorus and St. Hedwig's Cathedral Choir/ Berlin Philharmonic Orchestra conducted by Rudolf Kempe.* H.M.V. mono ALP 1506-10 (excerpts on mono ALP 2253).

Comedy was no more Wagner's forte than Verdi's. Yet, like Verdi, he produced a comic opera that is not only one of the greatest works of its kind but one of the greatest and most warm-hearted of all operas. This was *The Mastersingers* (1867), a work as glowingly German as *Falstaff* is glowingly Italian. Its humanity, geniality, and flashes of wit make one wish Wagner had "stooped" more than once to music such as this. Its characters are real: the ordinary townsfolk of Nuremberg in the sixteenth century, caught in the act of deciding who sould win the local song contest. Ordinary? Well, Hans Sachs, the cobbler who is the pivot of the opera, is rather more than that, but at least he is a *person*, not a god or a superhuman. The story, with its wealth of characterisation—the philosophical Sachs, the crabbedly academic Beckmesser (a caricature of the Viennese critic, Hanslick), the ten other mastersingers, the young lovers, the apprentices—drew from Wagner a fine-spun web of melodic counterpoint, full of vitality and with a classical clarity of texture. *The Mastersingers* has been called a Haydnesque score—and the comparison is by no means as ridiculous as it might seem, though to call it Handelian might at times be equally apt. Rudolf Kempe stresses the classical nature of the music in a performance of golden-toned spruceness that never becomes heavy of line. The excellent cast is headed by Ferdinand Frantz as a wonderfully mellow-voiced Sachs. Gottlob Frick, as Pogner the goldsmith, is today in a class of his own, and Rudolf Schock and Elisabeth Grummer are an accomplished Walther and Eva. The Berlin Philharmonic revels in the flow of beautiful invention that Wagner bestowed on the orchestral part, and the well-balanced recording takes even the weightiest choral passages in its stride.

BIZET (1838-1875): Carmen. *Maria Callas/Nicolai Gedda/Andrea Guiot/Robert Massard/Rene Duclos Chorus and Paris Opera Orchestra conducted by Georges Pretre.* H.M.V. Angel stereo SAN 140-2, mono AN 140-2.

With *Carmen*, the French tradition of *opéra comique* reached its high noon. It took Bizet almost the whole of his short life to find a story (by Mérimée) and a libretto (by Meilhac and Halevy) that fully suited his particular lyrical and dramatic genius. Within a few weeks of its first, moderately unsuccessful, performance, he was dead. Usually it is said that it was his disappointment over *Carmen* that killed him. Yet this cannot have been entirely true, for on the night of his death the opera was receiving its 23rd performance in Paris—not a bad innings for a new work— and was reasonably well launched on its road to success. Today it is among the most popular operas in the world— and is one of the hardest to perform well. Its title-role requires a singer of burning intensity with a voice of a particularly dusky and seductive timbre, a singer who must look good and sound even better. The hero, Don Jose, is a bit of a weakling, always a difficult kind of character to portray on the opera stage. But the American tenor, Jon Vickers, has proved that a Jose need not be merely wooden. Similarly with Micaela, the "good" girl who can seem all too pallid, but who, in the hands of a Sutherland, becomes a fully-rounded character. And then there is the orchestral playing, which needs the kind of spring which Beecham, above all, could give it.

Unfortunately, no single recording of *Carmen* has provided us with all these commodities. Beecham (H.M.V.) shapes the score with all the allure one would expect of him, but his Carmen (Victoria de los Angeles) is a trifle sedate. Sutherland is teamed with a famous Carmen (Regina Resnik), but the Jose (Mario del Monaco) bawls his role in pidgin French. Karajan's Carmen (Leontyne Price) commands beauty of tone but sounds a little immature. And so we come to Callas. In one of the biggest pre-publicity campaigns ever given a recording, E.M.I. proclaimed "Callas IS Carmen." And although her voice reveals all its familiar drawbacks, she gives a performance of extraordinary finesse, conviction, and seductiveness. Nicolai Gedda is a warm-voiced, generally tasteful Jose, who, like Callas, sounds at ease singing in French. Andrea Guiot is a sweet Micaela, with a voice of welcome fullness and colour. The smaller parts are mainly stock casting, but satisfactory enough, and Georges Pretre obtains a lively account of the score. A completely ideal *Carmen* seems to be impossible to find. This performance, though one would not claim it to be altogether superior to Karajan's or Beecham's, has the special fascination of the greatest dramatic soprano of our time applying her keen intelligence to a role Bizet might have written for her.

TCHAIKOVSKY (1840-1893): Eugene Onegin. *Belgrade National Opera Company conducted by Oscar Danon.* Decca mono LXT 5159-61.

Although we think of him primarily as an orchestral composer, Tchaikovsky was very much a man of the theatre. We have always neglected his operas in Britain. Of the ten works, some no doubt deserve their neglect; but both *Eugene Onegin* and *Pique Dame* should be seen far more often than they are. *Onegin* (1879) is the earlier of the two, and was considered by the composer—and in recent times by many other good people—to be his masterpiece. The story, based on Pushkin's "novel in verse", is perhaps a little sketchy. But it provided him with the material for some of his finest scenes—that in which Tatyana writes a letter to Onegin, declaring her love for him; the ballroom scenes with all their undertones; the early morning duel between Onegin and Lensky, the orchestra setting the atmosphere with icy beauty. The liveliest passages, the waltz and polonaise, are festive and effec ive; but otherwise the mood of the music is mainly ele , in Tchaikovsky's most piercing vein.

The Belgrade performance, sun n Russian, is not the last word in subtlety, but it has t feel of the music. The part of the brooding Byronic hero is played by Dushan Popovich, whose voice, despite a characteristic Eastern European wobble, has a dark richness well suited to the role. The Tatyana and Lensky are Valeria Heybalova and Drago Startz, both appealing singers. A more authentic Bolshoi performance, with Vishnevskaya as Tatyana, has been released under the M.K. label in an evil-smelling box. It is worth tracking down.

MUSSORGSKY (1839-1881): Boris Godunov (excerpts). *Boris Christoff/Evelyn Lear/Sofia National Opera Chorus/Paris Conservatoire Orchestra conducted by André Cluytens.* H.M.V. stereo ASD 2257, mono ALP 2257.

For many people, this is the greatest of all Russian operas—a work of sombre realism in which the rise and fall of a Tsar is enacted against a background of powerful crowd scenes, depicting the Russian people in moods of despair, frenzy, and rebellion. Based on Pushkin, it is the only opera Mussorgsky managed to complete in person (a life of wretched drunkenness made him the most erratic of composers); but the number of changes he made in it between 1869, when he finished it, and 1874, when it was published in an abbreviated version, have provided performers with a pretty problem, especially as other revisions of the score have been made by, among others, Rimsky-Korsakov and Shostakovich. The de luxe Rimsky edition—which places excessive emphasis on the star part, adds glitter to the orchestration, and "corrects" the harmony—has long been favoured by international opera houses. A production built around a great bass, with lots of pomp and colour, is obviously easier to "sell." But, as Scottish Opera showed us in 1965, the original Mussorgsky can be a far more intense experience. We have learnt that the darker, more subdued colours of Mussorgsky's orchestration, and the harsh edge of the "ungrammatical" harmonies that Rimsky well-meaningly altered, give the work a pungency it loses when it is upholstered in Rimsky's rich velvet.

Unfortunately, no recording has yet been made of Mussorgsky's own version. It seems a pity that Boris Christoff, the most famous Godunov of our time, has settled for Rimsky on both occasions he has recorded the work. We must hope that when Covent Garden come round to recording *Godunov*, the original version will be used—though so far Covent Garden's attitude to this masterpiece has been curiously ambivalent. In 1958 they earned our gratitude by performing the original version, but in 1965 inexplicably reverted to the Rimsky. For the moment, rather than lash out on the expensive four-disc H.M.V. Angel recording of the Rimskification (stereo SAN 110-3, mono AN 110-3) listeners may prefer to make do either with a well-chosen batch of excerpts from this issue, or with a similar batch from an earlier performance, when Christoff's voice was in slightly better fettle, though not so well recorded (mono ALP 1323).

PUCCINI (1858-1924): La Bohème. *Victoria de los Angeles/Jussi Björling/Robert Merrill/R.C.A. Victor Chorus and Orchestra conducted by Sir Thomas Beecham.* H.M.V. mono ALP 1409-10.

La Bohème holds the same position in Puccini's output as

238

Rigoletto in Verdi's. Each was written when its composer was 38 years old; and each was his first really popular masterpiece. Puccini's inspiration, of course, did not run so deep as Verdi's, but it had certain of the same qualities: it was direct, it was strongly theatrical, and it was richly melodious. Only a curmudgeon could fail to be stirred by a good performance of *Bohème*. Its story of student life in Paris in the nineteenth century is the most delightfully youthful of any opera: light-hearted, truthful, packed with charming incident, tender and touching. The characters are sharply drawn, the music bursts with life.

The premiere of *Bohème*, in Turin in 1896, was conducted by a 29-year-old maestro called Arturo Toscanini, who, more than half a century later, recorded the work in America (now deleted, this is a collectors' item that can sometimes be found in second-hand shops). Of current recordings, the one which is the most beautifully performed, and which best catches the atmosphere of the opera, is Sir Thomas Beecham's. This, too, was made in America— almost by chance, one gathers, because it happened that a famous Mimi (Victoria de los Angeles), a famous Rodolfo (Jussi Björling), and the great conductor were all in New York at the same time. Each was in superb form, and the whole occasion took fire excitingly. Quite apart from the sensitive beauty of the singing—reason enough to buy the set—Sir Thomas shapes the score with love and reveals all sorts of subtleties in the ensembles and the orchestral layout of which, previously, one was scarcely aware.

PUCCINI: Tosca. *Maria Callas/Carlo Bergonzi/Tito Gobbi/Paris Opera Chorus and Paris Conservatoire Orchestra conducted by Georges Pretre.* H.M.V. Angel stereo SAN 149-150, mono AN 149-150.

From the exuberant Paris scenes of *La Bohème*, Puccini turned four years later to Sardou's "cheap shocker" of a play about political and sexual violence in Rome in 1800, turning it with relish into an opera of melodramatic intensity. A violent work, *Tosca* provokes more violent reactions than *Bohème*. Some listeners can never take to the gaudiness of its story and music, any more than they can take to the gaudiness of Strauss's *Salome* and *Elektra*, composed a few years later. But as a piece of theatre, *Tosca*

239

undoubtedly "works." For a star like Callas in the title role, audiences are willing to pay exorbitant prices; and even when there is no star, the sheer effectiveness of the music still carries the work along. Callas, the most famous Tosca of our time, has twice recorded the part. In her earlier (1953) recording, her voice is undoubtedly in better condition than in her 1965 one; and in the former she has an ideal conductor in Victor de Sabata. But the later issue, more vividly recorded both in mono and stereo, is the one that most listeners will prefer. Callas's voice may be more strained, and contain more impurities; but her interpretation has matured, and the force of her performance is overwhelming. Here is a great dramatic singer playing the role of a great dramatic singer. Between the other main characters there is little to choose. Tito Gobbi was a finely villainous Scarpia in 1953, and he still is. Giuseppe di Stefano was at his most velvety in 1953 as the hero tenor; so, too, Carlo Bergonzi in 1965.

PUCCINI: Madama Butterfly. *Victoria de los Angeles/ Jussi Björling/Miriam Pirazzini/Rome Opera Chorus and Orchestra conducted by Gabriele Santini.*
H.M.V. stereo ASD 373-5, mono ALP 1795-7.

Madama Butterfly (1904) is the third, and most entrancing, of Puccini's famous triptych of operas. Here the scene switches to Japan for an expansion of David Belasco's one-act play, whose theme—mixed marriage—has if anything grown in force through the years. The music reveals a new fluency, the melodic sweep is more sustained, the craftsmanship still more polished than in *Bohème* and *Tosca*. Although Puccini wrote other masterpieces after it (especially his comic opera, *Gianni Schicchi*, of which Tito Gobbi has recorded an excellent performance on H.M.V. stereo ASD 295, mono ALP 1726), *Madama Butterfly* remains for many people the crown of his achievement.

Collectors who want a *Butterfly* are faced with a galaxy of talent: Victoria de los Angeles, Maria Callas, and Renata Tebaldi have all recorded it in recent years. If the Spanish singer seems the most rewarding choice—and it is a near thing—it is because her conception of the part is the most fastidiously and convincingly imagined; and she sings beautifully, with delicate understanding of the music and the character. Furthermore, she has as her Pinkerton one of the greatest of Puccini tenors—Jussi Björling, who pours out his lines with an almost insolent ease that is fully in keeping with the role. The conductor, Gabriele Santini, does not quite match Karajan in the Callas set, but is always alert to the shape of a phrase and the disarming sweetness of the harmonies.

RICHARD STRAUSS (1864-1949): Der Rosenkavalier.
Maria Reining/Sena Jurinac/Hilde Gueden/Ludwig Weber/ Vienna State Opera Chorus and Vienna Philharmonic Orchestra conducted by Erich Kleiber. Decca mono LXT 2954-7.

Salome (1905) and *Elektra* (1909) were the ferocious operas on which Strauss built his reputation. A superb recording of the former, with Birgit Nilsson and the Vienna Philharmonic under Georg Solti (Decca stereo SET 228-9, mono MET 228-9), and a goodish one of the latter, with Inge Borkh and the Dresden State Opera under Karl Böhm (D.G.G. stereo SLPM 138690-1, mono LPM 18690-1), have been issued; but many collectors will prefer to head straight for *Der Rosenkavalier* (1911), which Strauss described as his "Mozart opera," and which remains the richest, most human and delectable manifestation of his genius. The plot, set in period Vienna, could perhaps be called much ado about nothing. Certainly, the opera takes a long time to unfold a brief chapter in the life of a countess who, at the age of 32, is in the process of losing one in a series of youthful lovers and who fears herself to be growing old. But Strauss has adorned Hofmannsthal's polished text, and its varied gallery of portraits, with music of such ravishing sweetness that one delights in the whole work. True, there are passages—such as the noisy joke played on Baron Ochs during the inn scene—where even the most ardent Strauss-lover must admit that the work is a little protracted. But when, later in the act, Strauss eases us into the great final trio, and the three sopranos sweep us to the heights, we quickly forgive him the more loquacious moments of the opera.

    Der Rosenkavalier has been fortunate in its recordings. Apart from the historic recording by Lotte Lehmann, Maria Olszewska, Elisabeth Schumann, and Richard Mayr of a substantial part of the work—a highly desirable issue dating from 1933 and now available, in good pressings, in H.M.V.'s *Great Recordings of the Century* series (mono COLH 110-1)—two excellent full-length performances have been issued with modern casts. Some listeners will favour the Karajan performance (Columbia stereo SAX 2269-72, mono 33CX 1492-5) because it is extremely exciting, has Elisabeth Schwarzkopf as the Countess, and is available in stereo; but the slightly older Kleiber issue is more genuinely Viennese and tender, is equally well cast (Sena Jurinac's Octavian and Ludwig Weber's Ochs being particularly outstanding), is a model of teamwork, and has a stronger atmosphere of the opera house.

RICHARD STRAUSS: Capriccio (closing scene); **Four last songs.** *Lisa Della Casa/Vienna Philharmonic Orchestra conducted by Heinrich Hollreiser and Karl Böhm.* Decca mono BR 3100.

Strauss's last opera, *Capriccio* (1941), is an entrancing conversation-piece about whether words or music are the more important contribution to an opera. The scene is a castle outside Paris in 1775. Madeleine, the countess heroine, is loved by a young composer and a young poet; and so the relationship between words and music is pursued on two levels, the human and the abstract. Strauss, in this rather Anouilh-like piece, naturally loaded the argument in favour of music; and, in Britain, Glyndebourne have loaded the argument further by singing it in German—thus depriving the bulk of their audience of full understanding of the elegant repartee which Clemens Krauss provided as libretto. It is a work of great intimacy, and nowhere more so than in its closing pages, when, the guests having departed and the lights been dimmed, the countess drifts into the room for her final monologue. As she ponders on which lover she will choose, in music of soaring, tender loveliness, the orchestra meltingly provides the answer.

No composer has written a more eloquent farewell to the opera stage than this; nor has any composer written a more eloquent farewell to the soprano voice than the *Four last songs* which Strauss finished in 1948, just before his death. The marvellously-wrought orchestral accompaniments glow with autumn tints, through which Lisa Della Casa's voice floats with a calm, sublime purity. A more pensive account of the songs, by Elisabeth Schwarzkopf, has the merit of a cleaner, more modern recording. Here the coupling is a group of Strauss's earlier songs, expressively accompanied by the Berlin Radio Orchestra under George Szell (Columbia stereo SAX 5258, mono 33CX 5258).

RAVEL (1875-1937): L'Enfant et les Sortilèges.
Soloists/Chorus and Orchestra of the R.T.F. conducted by
Lorin Maazel. D.G.G. stereo SLPM 138675, mono LPM 18675.

Of Ravel's two short operas, *L'Heure Espagnole* is witty and heartless; *L'Enfant et les Sortilèges*, on the other hand, has considerable claim to be his most humane and beautiful work, in which a characteristic radiance of sound is matched by an unexpected tenderness of feeling. The delicate and imaginative libretto, by Colette, tells of a naughty child who teases the household animals and vents his temper on the furniture until it comes to life and rebels against him. The armchair refuses to let him sit down; the flames in the hearth threaten him; the shepherd and shepherdess on the torn wallpaper march out of the house in dudgeon; the walls of the room disappear and the child finds himself out in the garden where, moved by the plight of a wounded squirrel, he bandages its paw. This act of kindness restores things to normal. By the end of the opera, the child has discovered what it is like to feel fear and loneliness, sorrow and love; and the music wonderfully reflects his feelings, creating a magical sound-world for the events of the story, and in the end pouring out a genuine, not a simulated, compassion that melts the heart. If Ravel had not written *L'Enfant et les Sortilèges*, only Britten, among subsequent composers, could have given us music as refined and apt and touching.

Lorin Maazel obtains a breathtakingly lovely performance from his Paris forces, drawing from the R.T.F. orchestra a gleaming warmth of tone and from his soloists the most enchanting of characterisations.

243

JANACEK (1854-1928): The Cunning Little Vixen.
*Soloists/Children's Chorus/Chorus and Orchestra of the
Prague National Theatre conducted by Vaclav Neumann.*
Supraphon mono LPV 453-4.

Janacek, like Bartók, was a naturalist as well as a composer;
and *The Cunning Little Vixen* is his most vivacious and
imaginative musical tribute to nature. Before composing it,
he visited the Tatra mountains and wrote: "I would like to
sing the majesty of these mountains, the soft tepid rain,
the frozen ice, the flowers in the meadows, the snow fields.
The bright peaks touching the sky and the gruesome
darkness of the forests, the love-song of the birds and the
shrieks of the animals of prey. The dreamy silence of noon
and the humming tremolo of a thousand midges." Something of this atmosphere found its way into his woodland
opera, which he composed in a cottage situated in a game-
reserve. While working on it, he went out with gamekeepers
at night to watch and listen to foxes and other animals;
and what he heard he poured into his music, transforming
the sounds of the forest into orchestral and vocal sonorities
of shimmering beauty.

Many of the characters of the opera are animals. At the
start, a badger peers out of his lair, smoking a long meer-
schaum pipe, while midges and a dragon-fly dance around
him. A cricket and grasshopper enter with a tiny street
organ. The music glistens softly. It is one of the most
delectable opening scenes in all opera. The main characters
are the vixen and the gamekeeper who is intent on capturing
her. The story may smack a little of Walt Disney, but cuts
much deeper. Disney, after all, was never lucky enough to
have Janacek as his composer. If the operatic life of Britain
were not so narrow-mindedly arranged, *The Cunning Little
Vixen* would by now be a standard repertoire piece, loved
by adults and children alike, and as popular as *Hansel and
Gretel*. The Czech recording shows us what we have been
missing. It is conducted with great sympathy by Vaclav
Neumann, who conducted the premiere in 1924. The
records, with libretto, have been issued in Britain in a
limited edition, but are well worth searching for.

JANACEK: From the House of the Dead—excerpts.
Soloists and Chorus of the Janacek Opera, Brno/Brno State
Philharmonic Orchestra conducted by Bretislav Bakala
and Jaroslav Vogel. Supraphon mono SUA 10095.

"Misfortune, suffering, insanity, misery, pain, injustice,
violence, privation—this is what fills the major part of
human life. This is also a clear indication of what should
fill the major part of the works of these artists who want to
be truthful and sincere." With this quotation from Stassov,
Jaroslav Vogel opens his study of *From the House of the
Dead* in his splendid book on Janacek, and there are few
who would disagree with him as to its aptness. Within two
hours, the opera runs the gamut of these miseries, but it
also includes some qualities Stassov does not mention:
optimism and compassion and the warmth of feeling brought
about by comradeship, even if it is only the comradeship of
a Siberian prison camp in the middle of the last century.

The story of *From the House of the Dead*, Janacek's last
opera, is based on Dostoevsky's autobiographical novel,
which the composer transformed with extraordinary skill
into a series of stark vignettes of prison life. Skill is a tame
word to use when the result is a masterpiece, and perhaps
genius would be more appropriate. Janacek was 74 when
he composed it, and was just preparing the finishing touches
when he died. It shows his unique talents—for compression,
for building a powerful score from short-breathed phrases
of piercing beauty—working with an intensity of expression
that belied his age. It is a very remarkable work, a great
work; and the excerpts on this record are performed with
complete understanding by the resident opera company of
the town where Janacek spent most of his life (a company
which, like the string quartet of the same name, has called
itself after the composer).

The five excerpts include two of the most touching and
beautiful passages of the score: the haunting scene in the
prison hospital where Shiskov, one of the prisoners, gives a
detailed description of how he murdered his wife for being
unfaithful to him, without realising that his wife's lover is a
fellow-prisoner, lying dying only yards away; and the scene
on the river bank, where the prisoners perform amateur
theatricals on an improvised stage—first a Don Juan story,
then a Russian tale about a miller's wife. The latter scene,
which culminates in a warm-hearted chorus, flooding the
245

theatre with sound, is especially characteristic of a composer who seemed capable of treating even the grimmest situation with radiant humanity.

BRITTEN (born 1913): Peter Grimes. *Peter Pears/ Claire Watson/Covent Garden Chorus and Orchestra conducted by Benjamin Britten* Decca stereo SXL 2150-2, mono LXT 5521-3.

No British opera holds a more deserved place in the international repertoire than *Peter Grimes*. Apart from his youthful *Paul Bunyan*, later withdrawn, this was Britten's first attempt at an opera; and in it, at the age of 32, he proved himself to be a composer of unquestionable dramatic power, with an almost Puccini-like gift for making simple but overwhelming effects. Like *Wozzeck*, *Peter Grimes* is an intense psychological study. The fisherman hero is a complicated, persecuted outsider, who is accused by his fellow villagers—not without reason—of being cruel to his boy apprentices. But such is the compassion of the music, we gradually grow to understand Grimes and even to sympathise with him. The idea of an opera based on Crabbe's poem came to Britten during his period in America; and it was this, more than anything, that made him decide to return home. The music is redolent with his love for Aldeburgh and the part of the Suffolk coast where he now lives, and where the action is set. Among other composers, only Debussy has managed to portray the sea so atmospherically. Not surprisingly, the four sea interludes and passacaglia from *Peter Grimes* have achieved a separate existence as a striking concert suite; but it is in the context of the opera that they make their strongest effect.

The recording made under the composer's directorship in 1959 is all one could hope for, and has rightly been hailed as a milestone in the history of the gramophone. Peter Pears, for whom the role was written and who has always been its most impressive interpreter, is in vital voice. The American soprano, Claire Watson, may seem an unexpected choice for the part of Ellen Orford, the schoolmistress who is the only character to understand Grimes, but this turns out to be an inspired piece of casting. And all the minor but vivid characters of the village are sharply portrayed, Owen

246

Brannigan as the lawyer Swallow and David Kelly as the carrier Hobson (one of Britten's most endearing musical portraits) being especially convincing. The performance, as we have grown to expect when this composer is at the helm, is immaculately conducted, with a sure sense of pace and atmosphere.

BERG (1885-1935): Wozzeck. *Dietrich Fischer-Dieskau/ Evelyn Lear/Karl Christian Kohn/Berlin Opera Chorus and Orchestra conducted by Karl Böhm.* D.G.G. stereo SLPM 138991-2, mono LPM 18991-2.

Although it is not impossible to write an atonal comic opera—such works have been written—there is no doubt that the breakdown of tonality has so far lent itself more effectively to tragic and morbid subjects. In this respect, *Wozzeck* might be thought an atonal opera *par excellence*. The hero is a downtrodden wretch of a soldier who lacks, to a lamentable degree, the ability of the good soldier Schweik to extricate himself from awkward situations. Wozzeck seems doomed from the moment when, in the opening scene, we see him shaving his commanding officer's face and being made the butt of the streak of sadism that characterises several of the protagonists in the drama. Wozzeck, we quickly realise, is loose in the head; but so, it turns out, are most of the other characters, with the principal exception of Wozzeck's mistress, Marie, who is merely loose in her body. Surely no other opera brings us so face to face with insanity. The doctor who analyses Wozzeck's madness is madder than Wozzeck himself—as indeed is the commanding officer. And one of the most hair-raising scenes in this hair-raising opera is when the captain and the doctor meet in the street and hold a weird conversation about the state of the captain's health.

Not unexpectedly (although based on a play, by Buchner, written a century earlier) *Wozzeck* met considerable opposition when first performed; and Willi Reich, in his biography of the composer, quotes a Berlin critic of the period who described Berg as "A master criminal—a musical impostor and a treacherously dangerous composer. Yes, one seriously has to consider the question whether and to what extent activity in music can be criminal. *Wozzeck* is a matter of a capital crime in the field of music." But that was in 1925. For many years now, the German critics and public have fully accepted *Wozzeck* as the masterpiece it is. It is in the repertoire of the main German opera houses, is regularly performed, and was seen on television in 1966 by millions of viewers. In Britain, this state of affairs still seems to be a long way off. *Wozzeck* did not reach us until 1952— 27 years after its German premier. And even now, opportunities to see it remain few and far between. And so a recording as good as the D.G.G. one is especially useful in enabling us to become fully acquainted with one of the key operas of the century. As expected, Dietrich Fischer-Dieskau gives a carefully studied portrayal of the title role, and has sunk his personality completely into the part; Evelyn Lear, one of the best of the American sopranos working in Europe, is a memorable Marie; and Karl Christian Kohn sings with ferocious relish as the doctor. Karl Böhm conducts with admirably nervy intensity, and with complete understanding of this tautest of operas.

STRAVINSKY (born 1882): The Rake's Progress.
Alexander Young/Judith Raskin/John Reardon/Sadler's Wells Chorus/Royal Philharmonic Orchestra conducted by Igor Stravinsky. C.B.S. stereo SBRG 72278-80, mono BRG 72278-80.

In his *Memories and Commentaries*, Stravinsky traces his interest in *The Rake's Progress* back to a chance glimpse of the Hogarth pictures in the Chicago Art Institute in 1947. The opera which he completed four years later, to a libretto by W. H. Auden and Chester Kallman, is as sharp and precise as the pictures that inspired it. Criticised at first for being too much of a classical pastiche—with borrowings from Bach, Handel, and Mozart—it is now recognised as inimitably Stravinskian in the way it treats its eighteenth-century trappings, in the exuberant vivacity and snap of its rhythms, and the piquancy of its melodies and harmonies. It is a rich and enthralling score, and one of the few post-war operas one would claim wholeheartedly to be a masterpiece. Here it receives an ideally springy performance under the veteran composer's alert direction, with Alexander Young and John Reardon in clear, incisive voice as Tom Rakewell and his devilish servant Nick Shadow.

INDEX

250

251

"Remarkable, mind-spinning, rave of a novel. Uniquely funny." KENNETH ALLSOP, *Daily Mail*

"Comic, macabre, knockabout, nightmarish, ironic, bawdy, illogical, formless, Shavian." *Books and Bookmen*

"Blessedly, monstrously, bloatedly, cynically, funnily, and fantastically unique. *No one has ever written a book like this.*" *Financial Times*

... AND NO ONE MAY EVER WRITE A BOOK LIKE THIS AGAIN ... So read it now, while you're still young enough to enjoy ...

CATCH-22 by Joseph Heller (FN1500 U.K. price 5/-)

A SELECTION OF FINE READING
AVAILABLE IN CORGI BOOKS

Novels

☐ GN	7409	FAUSTO'S KEYHOLE	*Jean Arnaldi* 3/6
☐ GN	7335	THE SNOW BALL	*Brigid Brophy* 3/6
☐ GN	7440	JEALOUS WOMAN	*James M. Cain* 3/6
☐ FN	7317	THE CHINESE ROOM	*Vivian Connell* 5/–
☐ FN	7387	THE DEEP FREEZE GIRLS	*Eva Defago* 5/–
☐ XN	7473	VONDA ROSEGOOD	*Richard Dohrman* 6/–
☐ FN	1278	THE GINGER MAN	*J. P. Donleavy* 5/–
☐ FN	1500	CATCH-22	*Joseph Heller* 5/–
☐ EN	7371	TOWN WITHOUT HONOUR	*Jack Hoffenberg* 7/6
☐ EN	7193	MOTHERS AND DAUGHTERS	*Evan Hunter* 7/6
☐ EN	7334	SPEAK NOT EVIL	*Edwin Lanham* 7/6
☐ FN	7460	EVA	*Meyer Levin* 5/–
☐ GN	7474	THE BRITTLE GLASS	*Norah Lofts* 3/6
☐ FN	7301	WEEP NOT, MY WANTON	*Nan Maynard* 5/–
☐ DN	7456	A BANNER WITH A STRANGE DEVICE	*Arona McHugh* 10/6
☐ XN	7351	CARAVANS	*James A. Michener* 6/–
☐ GN	7472	THE JILKINGTON DRAMA	*Edgar Mittelholzer* 3/6
☐ FN	1066	LOLITA	*Vladimir Nabokov* 5/–
☐ FN	7203	APPOINTMENT IN SAMARRA	*John O'Hara* 5/–
☐ XN	7251	ELIZABETH APPLETON	*John O'Hara* 6/–
☐ EN	7438	THE HORSE KNOWS THE WAY	*John O'Hara* 7/6
☐ EN	7370	THE HAT ON THE BED	*John O'Hara* 7/6
☐ EN	7457	THE LIMITS OF LOVE	*Frederic Raphael* 7/6
☐ FN	1162	A STONE FOR DANNY FISHER	*Harold Robbins* 5/–
☐ FN	1187	79 PARK AVENUE	*Harold Robbins* 5/–
☐ SN	1204	NEVER LEAVE ME	*Harold Robbins* 2/6
☐ FN	7459	THE RED BAIZE DOOR	*Ellen Ryder* 5/–
☐ EN	7219	JUSTINE	*The Marquis de Sade* 7/6
☐ XN	7389	SUCH AS WE	*Pierre Sichel* 6/–
☐ FN	7458	MATADOR	*Marguerite Steen* 5/–
☐ FN	1133	THE CARETAKERS	*Dariel Telfer* 5/–
☐ EN	7352	EXODUS	*Leon Uris* 7/6
☐ EN	7300	ARMAGEDDON	*Leon Uris* 7/6
☐ FN	7405	THE CONSPIRACY	*R. H. Ward* 5/–
☐ FN	7116	FOREVER AMBER Vol. I	*Kathleen Winsor* 5/–
☐ FN	7117	FOREVER AMBER Vol. II	*Kathleen Winsor* 5/–
☐ FN	7118	THE LOVERS	*Kathleen Winsor* 5/–
☐ FN	7222	STAR MONEY	*Kathleen Winsor* 5/–

War

☐ FB	7256	THE JUNGLE IS NEUTRAL	*F. Spencer Chapman* 5/–
☐ GB	7340	FLAMES IN THE SKY	*Pierre Clostermann, DFC* 3/6
☐ FB	7119	THE BIG SHOW (illustrated)	*Pierre Clostermann, DFC* 5/–

☐ GG	7314	WRESTLING (illustrated)	*David Marchbanks* 3/6
☐ FG	7277	THE CORGI SPORTS ALMANAC	*Compiled by Tom Owen* 5/–
☐ FG	7349	THE SAFFRON ROBE	*T. Lobsang Rampa* 5/–

Westerns

☐ GW	7481	SUDDEN STRIKES BACK	*Frederick H. Christian* 3/6
☐ GW	7397	THE NIGHT OF THE TIGER	*Al Dewlen* 3/6
☐ GW	7414	30,000 ON THE HOOF	*Zane Grey* 3/6
☐ GW	7380	THE HASH KNIFE OUTFIT	*Zane Grey* 3/6
☐ GW	7419	KID RODELO	*Louis L'Amour* 3/6
☐ GW	7467	MUSTANG MAN	*Louis L'Amour* 3/6
☐ GW	7447	HOPALONG CASSIDY RETURNS	*Clarence E. Mulford* 3/6
☐ GW	7448	HOPALONG CASSIDY'S PROTEGE	*Clarence E. Mulford* 3/6
☐ GW	7449	HOPALONG CASSIDY AND THE EAGLE'S BROOD	
			Clarence E. Mulford 3/6
☐ GW	7274	SHANE	*Jack Schaefer* 3/6
☐ FW	7482	MONTE WALSH	*Jack Schaefer* 5/–
☐ GW	7466	SPAWN OF EVIL	*Paul I. Wellman* 3/6

Crime

☐ GC	7412	POLE REACTION	*Jean Bruce* 3/6
☐ GC	7464	DEEP FREEZE	*Jean Bruce* 3/6
☐ GC	7478	A BRANCH FOR THE BARON	*John Creasey* 3/6
☐ GC	7465	MISSING OR DEAD	*John Creasey* 3/6
☐ GC	7445	A ROPE FOR THE BARON	*John Creasey* 3/6
☐ GC	7396	ALIAS THE BARON	*John Creasey* 3/6
☐ GC	7377	LAM TO THE SLAUGHTER	*A. A. Fair (Erle Stanley Gardner)* 3/6
☐ GC	7479	TURN ON THE HEAT	*A. A. Fair* 3/6
☐ GC	7224	THE LIQUIDATOR	*John Gardner* 3/6
☐ GC	7463	UNDERSTRIKE	*John Gardner* 3/6
☐ GC	7444	TRAP FOR CINDERELLA	*Sebastian Japrisot* 3/6
☐ GC	7341	THE MAN WHO SOLD DEATH	*James Munro* 3/6
☐ GC	7411	DAY OF THE GUNS	*Mickey Spillane* 3/6
☐ GC	7307	THE SNAKE	*Mickey Spillane* 3/6
☐ GC	7480	DEADLIER THAN THE MALE	*Ellery Queen* 3/6

All these great books are available at your local bookshop or newsagent; or can be ordered direct from the publisher. Just tick the titles you want and fill in the form below.

CORGI BOOKS, Cash Sales Department, Bashley Road, London, N.W.10.
Please send cheque or postal order. No currency, PLEASE. Allow 6d. per book to cover the cost of postage on orders of less than 6 books.

NAME ....

ADDRESS ....

(SEP 66) ....